Moral Geography

RELIGION AND AMERICAN CULTURE

The Religion and American Culture series explores the interaction between religion and culture throughout American history. Titles examine such issues as how religion functions in particular urban contexts, how it interacts with popular culture, its role in social and political conflicts, and its impact on regional identity. Series Editor Randall Balmer is the Ann Whitney Olin Professor of American Religion and former chair of the Department of Religion at Barnard College, Columbia University.

MICHAEL E. STAUB
Torn at the Roots: The Crisis of Jewish Liberalism in Postwar America

CLYDE R. FORSBERG, JR.
Equal Rites: The Book of Mormon, Masonry, Gender, and American Culture

Moral Geography

MAPS, MISSIONARIES, AND THE
AMERICAN FRONTIER

Amy DeRogatis

Columbia University Press, New York

Columbia University Press

Publishers Since 1893

New York   Chichester, West Sussex

Copyright © 2003 Columbia University Press

All rights reserved

Library of Congress Cataloging-in-Publication Data

DeRogatis, Amy.

Moral geography : maps, missionaries, and the American frontier / Amy De Rogatis.

p.cm. — (Religion and American culture)

Includes bibliographical references and index.

ISBN 978-0-231-12788-2 (alk. paper) — ISBN 978-0-231-12789-9 (pbk. : alk. paper)

1. Western Reserve (Ohio)—Church history—19th century.

2. Missions—Ohio—Western Reserve—History—19th century.

3. Christianity and geography—Ohio—Western Reserve—History—19th century.4. Congregational churches—Connecticut—Missions—Ohio—Western Reserve— History—19th century.

5. Presbyterian Church—Connecticut—Missions—Ohio—Western Reserve— History— 19th century.

6. Missionary Society of Connectucit—History—19th century.

I. Title. II. Religion and American Culture (New York, N.Y.)

BV2803.03 D47   2002

277.71'3081—dc21   2002031338

∞

Columbia University Press books are printed on permanent and durable acid-free paper.

Printed in the United States of America

To Chris and Emma

Contents

List of Illustrations ix

Acknowledgments xi

Introduction 1

1. The Benevolent Design: Mapping the Landscape 15

    Mappers and Missionaries 15
    The Connecticut Land Company: Mapping 21
    "In regard to the Heathen on our borders": Erasing the Natives 32
    The Connecticut Missionary Society: Missionizing 35
    "Sprightly towns" and "numerous churches which gem the
        whole landscape": Spatial Nostalgia 41
    "The most benevolent designs": Missionary Publications 47

2. Models of Piety: Protestant Missionaries on the Frontier 61

    "I find I can preach, if I can ride": Missionary Letters 66
    "Difficulties inseparable to a family": Age, Marital
        Status, and Missions 74
    "I have no prospect of being popular": Social Status
        and Missionary Labor 77
    "Book knowledge is not all": The Heart, Not the Head 81
    "Born and raised in the woods": Homegrown Missionaries 84

3. The Moral Garden of the Western World: Bodies, Towns, and Families 90

    "Nurseries of piety": Body, Town, and Family 93
    "A considerable phalanx of infidelity":
        Religious Rivalry and the Body 101
    "Scattered promiscuously over the face of the
        country": Town Planning and Moral Order 111
    "One great step towards a state of barbarism": Family and Home Order 120

4. Geography Made Easy: Geographies and Travel Literature   127
   Geography Made Easy: Mapping and Moralizing   130
   Domestic Travel Narratives   135
   Fairy-Tale Reports: Western Reserve Travel Literature   142
   A Correct View: New Connecticut as the Promised Land   152

5. A Beacon in the Wilderness: Moral Inscriptions on the Landscape   157
   The Oberlin Colony and Institute   159
   Building Up Society: Missionary Institutions   166
   Ecclesiastical Outlaws   174
   Moral and Spatial Order   178

Conclusion: Moral Geography   181

Notes   185
Bibliography   217
Index   235

Illustrations

1. "New Lands," advertisement in *Connecticut Courant* (January 4, 1820) 13
2. Amos Spafford's map of Cleveland (1796) 23
3. Seth Pease's "A Map of the Connecticut Western Reserve, from Actual Survey" (1797) 25
4. "An Exact Mapp of New England and New York"; engraving in Cotton Mather's *Magnalia Christi Americana* (1702) 27
5. "Heckewelder Map" (1796) 31
6. James Wadsworth's "A Plan of the Town of New Haven" (1748) 43
7. Map of county seat, Huron, Ohio 46
8. Title page of *Connecticut Evangelical Magazine* 1 (July 1800–June 1801) 49
9. *Connecticut Evangelical Magazine* 1 (March 1801): 358 51
10. Engraving of Thomas Robbins 68
11. Engraving of Joseph Badger 69
12. Front page of *An Address to the Emigrants from Connecticut, and from New England Generally, in the New Settlements in the United States* (1817) 99
13. "A Scheme in which you have, at once, a view of my missionary Preaching"; letter from Jonathan Lesslie to Connecticut Missionary Society Trustees (March 7, 1808) 102
14. "Map of Chardon in the County of Geauga, Ohio" 114
15. Title page of Jedidiah Morse's *Geography Made Easy* (1816) 131
16. Western Reserve portion of map of Ohio in John Melish, *Travels in the United States* (1812) 141

17. "Western Emigration" broadside (1810s?); also front page of H. Trumbull, *Western Emigration. Journal of Doctor Jeremiah Smipleton's* [sic] *Tour to Ohio* (1819)   151

18. "A plan of Oberlin Colony, 1835"   165

19. "Map of the Western Reserve, including the Fire Lands in Ohio" (September 1826)   180

Acknowledgments

Many friends and colleagues have helped me to write this book, and it is a great pleasure to thank them. As a graduate student at the University of North Carolina at Chapel Hill, I had the good fortune of working with a group of insightful and generous scholars at Chapel Hill and Duke University. Among these many teachers and friends, I especially want to thank my writing group—Erin Lang Bonin, David Weaver-Zercher, Hilary Wyss, and Keith Zahniser—for helping me to shape my fledgling ideas into dissertation chapters and keeping me laughing in the process. The Duke-UNC Colloquium in American religious history provided a lively arena for presenting my work. Much of my thinking has been influenced by conversations with students and faculty in that group. I am particularly grateful for the encouragement and incisive criticisms offered by my dissertation committee at the University of North Carolina at Chapel Hill. Laurie Maffly-Kipp, my dissertation director, Thomas A. Tweed, Donald G. Mathews, Philip F. Gura, and Peter I. Kaufman generously gave their time and support. Many others read drafts of chapters or listened patiently. My thanks go to Philip Goff, David Hackett, Lisa Blansett, David Chidester, Georgia Frank, Patrick Rivers, Jim Wetzel, Belden Lane, Martha Finch, Sarah McFarland Taylor, the anonymous reviewer for Columbia University Press, and my colleagues at Michigan State University.

I delivered a number of conference papers as I worked on this book, and a good many of the questions and suggestions that I received from both official and unofficial respondents are answered—at least in part—in its pages. Though I don't know all of your names, I thank you for your help. I want to recognize the participants in the Seventeenth International Conference on the History of Cartography (Lisbon, 1998), especially Matthew Edney and David Woodward, who provided me with a wealth of information and encouragement at a crucial moment.

This project was supported financially by four institutions. For that assistance, I thank the Pew Fellowship in Religion and American History at Yale University, the Morgan Fellowship for research at the Western Reserve Historical Society, as well as the Frederick B. Artz Fellowship for research in the Oberlin Archives at Oberlin College. Michigan State provided a junior research leave and awarded me an Internal Research Grant that relieved me of teaching responsibilities to conduct further research and complete the revisions for this book. A version of chapter 2 appeared as "Models of Piety: Plan of Union Missionaries on the Western Reserve, 1800–1806," in *Journal of Presbyterian History: Studies in Reformed History and Culture* 79, no. 4 (Winter 2001): 257–275. I acknowledge the Presbyterian Historical Society for granting me permission to reprint it.

The librarians and staff at the Connecticut Historical Society, the Archives of the Connecticut Conference, United Church of Christ, the Beinecke Rare Book and Manuscript Library, the Map Library at Yale University, the Andover-Harvard Theological Library, the Presbyterian Historical Society, the Newberry Library, and Special Collections at Michigan State University all provided aid and insight to the materials housed in their collections. I am indebted especially to Ann Sindelar of the Western Reserve Historical Society and Roland Baumann of the Oberlin College Archives for their cheerful assistance and prompt responses to my endless questions.

I owe a great debt to Randall Balmer for his enthusiastic support of this book and to Wendy Lochner of Columbia University Press, who has shepherded this project. I greatly appreciated copyeditor Jan McInroy's careful reading of the text.

A number of other people have helped me along the way and also deserve to be mentioned: Maria Hey Dahl, Catherine A. McLean, Carolyn P. Bess, Richard and Carolyn Morgan, Elizabeth J. H. Toman, Faith Merrill, Anthony and Judith Frilingos, Hope DeRogatis, Joy and John Robbins, Paul and Lucille DeRogatis, and Peter and Katheryn DeRogatis. To my parents, David and Eunice DeRogatis, there will never be enough words to express my thanks.

My greatest debt is to Chris Frilingos. He has shared the intellectual and emotional challenges of writing this book, rereading chapters, sharpening my arguments, and discussing details of nineteenth-century missionaries that are far beyond the scope of his own interests in antiquity. I could not have finished this book without his help, nor would I have wanted to: life would be hopelessly dull without him. I am deeply grateful to our daughter, Emma, who was born in the middle of this project and who fills my life with joy. It is to them that I dedicate this book.

Moral Geography

Introduction

In 1817 the Connecticut Missionary Society realized that the moment had arrived to caution the public about the "moral dangers" of the American frontier.[1] In a nineteen-page pamphlet signed by its chairman, Yale president Timothy Dwight, the home missionary society outlined the perils for settlers "planted down in the wilderness" without the proper social and moral restraints. Writing to Connecticut's sons and daughters now living in frontier settlements where missionaries had labored for nearly fifteen years, Dwight urged settlers to "guard with peculiar vigilance" and "restrain sinful inclinations." He reminded them that "moral habits," above all else, combat "moral dangers." Comparing the frontier inhabitants' wilderness plight to those of the Israelites and the Pilgrims, Dwight outlined the steps to the creation of a moral society. This was neither the first time that American Protestants would conflate the physical and the moral landscapes, nor would it be the last. But for Dwight the moment was extraordinary because the frontier settlers were, in his words, "peculiarly acting for posterity." Their smallest decisions regarding the material and spiritual contours of the landscape would affect future generations. The symbolic and literal meanings of physical space combined fluidly in his urgent plea that settlers adopt moral habits as building blocks for a moral society. "The early habits of a people," Dwight explained, "are like the first roads in a new country, which it is extremely inconvenient to alter, after the inhabitants have long been accustomed to them, and have built their houses and shaped their farms by them."[2]

Dwight's spatial metaphor reveals his assumed link between spatial and moral order. At first glance, his statement is unexceptional, because it typifies a New England Congregationalist's conception of the "moral dangers" present on the post–Revolutionary War frontier. From Dwight's spatial and moral perspective, the frontier emigrants were surrounded by dangerous influences, none more worrisome than the wilderness itself. By the time Dwight signed this cautionary pamphlet, missionary letters and travelers' accounts painted colorful portraits of the rugged characters and desolate landscapes of remote parts of western New York and Ohio. Dwight knew that settlers, living so far beyond the gaze of the watchful "public eye," could easily "violate the Sabbath," "swear profanely," "cheat," and "drink to excess." His call to refrain from immoral habits in the wilderness was, of course, a familiar warning to New England Protestants. It is not surprising that Dwight likens the nineteenth-century frontier settlers to the Israelites and the Puritans, who eventually overcame their own physical and spiritual struggles in the wilderness. The Puritans serve as the most relevant example for Dwight, for they sought to "improve" landscape as they hoped to improve their souls. For the first generation of Puritans, cultivating the physical landscape through "planting" towns and organizing churches went hand in hand with the cultivation and regeneration of souls. Dwight forges a link between himself and the frontier inhabitants by claiming a shared lineage that extends back in biblical history to the Israelites and in recent national history to the Puritans. Tying the frontier settlers' destinies to those of the Israelites and the Puritans demonstrates that they are important actors in sacred history that is unfolding on American soil. Dwight brushed off and reissued the wilderness metaphor, which always held in tension both promise and peril for American Protestants. In doing so, he reminds nineteenth-century frontier settlers of the sacred and historical link between spatial and moral order.

Dwight's strategy of harking back to the Puritans carried enormous cultural weight. His allusions to Puritan texts such as John Winthrop's Arbella speech reminded western settlers that they, like the Puritans, had the unique opportunity to create a moral community in the wilderness for the rest of the world to emulate.[3] It is crucial to notice this because it highlights the importance of space in the Puritan theological and social model as it was passed down to nineteenth-century New England Calvinists like Dwight. The Puritans' relationship to the wilderness, derived from their reading of Scripture, became a theological and physical pursuit to understand themselves and their descendants as the inheritors of the American sacred landscape. This inheritance, however, was a landscape that remained closely tied to a decline in piety and a falling away from morality.[4] For Dwight, the Puritans' attempt to build a moral community was linked to their ability to order the land. This fusion of religious and social ideology with the New England physical landscape grew into a cognitive map for future pilgrims, intended to help them to find their moral place within the physical world. For Dwight, and for the Connecticut Missionary Society, the precedent for linking morality with the landscape that was set in Scripture and then employed by the Puritans remained relevant for their descendants who settled the western frontier.

But there is something else to notice. Dwight wrote his cautionary treatise as a plea to emigrants, not as a sermon to like-minded congregants. While he claimed a common Puritan heritage with the settlers, it is evident from his tone and his perspective that they required moral guidance, or perhaps suasion. According to Dwight, habits, like roads, must be shaped, and his insistence on constructing both properly suggests disinterest or even resistance to this model on the part of the settlers. Significantly, Dwight's description of a convenient road that accommodates homes and farms also reflects his position in the contested issue of the proper way to plan a frontier town. For him, as for most of the Connecticut Missionary Society members, a proper town plan followed a blueprint of an idealized Puritan community. Not only were towns and churches founded simultaneously, but ideally a Puritan town would be surveyed to place the meetinghouse in the physical center of the town on a center green with outlying homes and farms. In this manner, the church remained at the center of Puritans' lives both theologically and spatially. Dwight addressed transplanted "neighbors" whom he believed to be perched on both the moral boundaries of New England Congregationalism and the spatial edges of civilization. His invocation of the moral and spatial aspects of the first generation of Puritan settlers and his insistence on a shared sacred lineage among himself, the settlers, the Israelites, and the Puritans must be understood as a rhetorical strategy to inscribe a particular moral meaning onto a contested frontier landscape.

Questions and Sources

Home missions on the moving American frontier occurred in tandem with mapping, as land surveyors cleared and marked space soon occupied by Christian missionaries. The Connecticut Missionary Society's Plan of Union mission to northeastern Ohio, a space known as Connecticut's Western Reserve or, optimistically, as New Connecticut, illustrates the difficulties of articulating and disseminating spatial and moral values to distant peoples and places.[5] The underlying question throughout this study is, What is the relationship between religion and space? To answer this question I focus on one aspect of the problem: the relationship between moral and spatial order as seen through one home missionary society's attempt to evangelize one region. I adopted this as my primary research question because the subjects of my study—missionaries, home society trustees, and settlers—were themselves preoccupied with the relationship between moral and spatial values. The link between moral discourse and the physical landscape is prominent in Protestant frontier missionaries' letters and diaries, particularly in the ways in which they used landscape imagery to express religious ideas and conflicts. For example, one missionary lamented the Western Reserve settlers' disinterest in religious matters in a letter to the home society, stating that "our fields + farms lie unfenced, untilled, unsaved."[6] Here is illustrated the direct relationship between uncultivated landscapes and souls, and the echoes of Puritan concern for using fences to manage the land properly and to maintain boundaries to enclose the community of believers.

Simon Schama in *Landscape and Memory* argues that "landscapes are culture before they are nature," and this observation held true for the northeastern section of Ohio in the early nineteenth century. New Connecticut was constituted first in the minds of those who constructed it from faraway places. Their imaginary rendering, drawn first in the abstract, took on mythic proportions accommodating the landscape metaphors of a howling wilderness and a garden paradise, before any one of the interested parties whom I examine in this study set foot into the territory. To make sense of the disjuncture between imagination and reality and how that operates through efforts to claim physical and moral space, I have employed the concept of mapping. At some points I examine drawn maps, and in other instances I use the term *mapping* to speak broadly about creating imaginary models and imposing them upon places and sometimes people.

From the most literal uses to the most metaphorical mapping, this study is always concerned with the physical and moral landscape.[7]

As I thought about the connections between moral and spatial order that are present in missionary letters and publications, three themes emerged. The first is the connection between spatial and religious control of the frontier through the creation of models, or "maps," of piety and behavior. A second and related theme is the missionaries' dual aim to create moral communities and to shape the physical landscape. To understand this desire and how it was implemented, I have paid attention to the relationship between bodies and religious practices. I found that missionaries, settlers, travelers, and the Connecticut Missionary Society's trustees were very interested in bodily responses to religious exercises and the descriptions of the spaces where religious practices took place. Eyewitness accounts of both the extent of the bodily manifestations of religious fervor and the location where religious excitement occurred allowed the Hartford-based trustees to assess the validity of frontier religious practices. Beyond religious practices, the missionaries and the home society were also interested in how people behaved in their daily life. The subject of "habits" surfaces in many of the discussions about moral and spatial order. The missionaries and their sponsoring society seemed convinced that proper moral habits could be practiced only in orderly spaces. A third theme is the instability of the Western Reserve as a mission site. The Connecticut Missionary Society promoted the Western Reserve as a New Connecticut, and the territory was viewed by land surveyors, missionaries, settlers, and travel writers as a blank space that needed to be mapped and defined. Through the course of my research on the Connecticut Missionary Society's mission to the Western Reserve, I realized that I needed to broaden the scope of the study to include nonmissionary institutions and people who held a primary interest in shaping and describing the physical landscape. That impulse is apparent not only in the missions-related materials but also in documents from the Connecticut Land Company, diaries and letters of land surveyors and land agents, maps and private and published travel diaries.

I am aware that my material intersects with broader discussions of foreign and domestic missions, religion on the American frontier, and revivalism. While I am indebted to the excellent scholarship that has addressed crucial issues of the theological groundwork for American missions, or the social, economic, and political factors that led to unique forms of revivalism on the frontier, I am not seeking to expand on those issues. I am motivated by other questions. This is not to say that I have chosen to ignore the scores of secondary literature on these topics or that I have avoided some basic organizing categories because they did not interest me. My ideas developed both from finding what I did not expect in the primary sources and from realizing that I had to formulate categories that would help me to make sense of what I had read. A case in point is the topic of conversion. It might bewilder readers familiar with other treatments of nineteenth-century Protestant missionaries that the subjects of my study and I write very little on the topic of conversion. Occasionally these missionary letters mention a "revival time" or a sacramental occasion when many hearts were turned toward God; only rarely, however, do the missionaries mention individual conversion. In fact, the home missionaries in their correspondences with the home society say surprisingly little about personal sin, salvation, and redemption. Of course, this was the topic of the sermons, prayers, and eulogies given by the missionaries on the frontier, but their interest in sin and salvation, as seen in their letters, focused less on individuals and more on the signs deciphered from the landscape that pointed to the community's and the nation's future. From a reading of their letters and journals, it seems as if this group of Protestant home missionaries looked to outer signs of behavior and practice to gain knowledge of the inner beliefs of the settlers. Many of the discernible signs of morality that they reported were imprinted on the landscape. Missionaries believed, for example, that disorganized towns and uncultivated fields generally signaled infertile grounds for their evangelical labor. More than one missionary noted that seeing late autumn pumpkins rotting on the ground proved the inhabitants' laziness and boded poorly for future spiritual harvests. In the minds of the missionaries, settlers who manifested laziness through their crops and fields were unlikely to exert much energy regarding their souls. Salvation, therefore, was literally and figuratively inscribed in the landscape. Not only did the frontier hold redemptive possibilities for the nation, but in the missionaries' minds the landscape itself could be read to assess that state of the inhabitants' souls.

Scholars of Native American missions and foreign missions have argued for many years that American Protestant missionary endeavors operated not simply in the realm of theology but on the most basic level of daily life. Cultural practices such as dressing, hair length, food preparation and consumption, and sexuality became the proving ground of theological beliefs through cultural encounter.[8] It should therefore come as no surprise that home missionaries repeated this process to check the legitimacy of

Euro-Americans' beliefs. Those settlers who maintained Christian habits on the frontier, the missionaries reasoned, were likely to have Christian souls. But if Christian habits were neglected, the missionaries believed, the settlers were likely to fall into "barbarism," a state that missionaries to Native Americans described in great detail.

Plan of Union missionaries strove to hold on to adherents through preaching, prayer, and distribution of religious tracts, but the more subtle aspect of home missionary work involved maintaining community moral boundaries. Boundary maintenance included monitoring individual behavior or "habits," family life, and community action.[9] The Connecticut Missionary Society rhetoric concerned itself with the community of believers at least as much as with individuals. The organization's documents, for example, are filled with moral injunctions that stress the importance of re-creating New England communities, both physically and morally. Specifically, the missionary society constantly reminded settlers, through its publications, of their responsibility to watch over each other and to guard against immorality. A missionary, after all, could do only so much to impress upon people the importance of saving grace, but there was a great deal more that he could do to construct and promote community moral boundaries.

Methods and Relevance for the Study of Religion

My understanding of spatial construction is informed primarily by cultural geographers and social historians who view space not merely as a background but as a readable text.[10] Although most spatial theorists emphasize the political and economic implications of spatial representation, I am interested in the moral implications of power struggles on a religiously constructed landscape. As described by cartographers, missionaries, land speculators, travelers, geographers, and settlers, the Western Reserve embodied contradictory dreams, anxieties, and desires. Some viewed and promoted it as an Edenic second New England, while others saw it as an uninhabitable wilderness on the periphery of civilization. The desire to claim and define the frontier space was expressed by the missionary society through the moral imperative of cultivating the landscape as a first step in creating a godly community. Similarly, the physical layout of roads and towns and the construction of churches and homes provided a litmus test for determining frontier settlers' habits and morals. Shaping the frontier space became a moral agenda for land surveyors, missionaries, and settlers, but it also became a moral indicator for geographers, travel writers, and the Connecticut Missionary Society.

Religious studies scholars have shown interest in space as a category of analysis, but until recently that discussion revolved primarily around Mircea Eliade's theories of sacred space.[11] While many scholars—most notably Jonathan Z. Smith—object to Eliade's universalizing views, particularly that sacred space always intrudes on ordinary space, they continue the discussion around similar questions, such as what constitutes sacred space, where is it to be found, and what does it mean?[12] Yet space remains a useful category, even if theorists disagree on its creation and function in religious traditions and practices. David Chidester and Edward T. Linenthal, in their edited collection *American Sacred Space*, articulate three dominant views of sacred space in contemporary scholarship. First, sacred space is constructed through ritual action and provides an arena for religious performance that often reinforces social and political authority. Second, sacred space provides orientation for understanding an individual's place within a meaningful worldview. Third, sacred space is contested, and its ownership is always invested in power relationships and maneuvers.[13]

But not all religious studies scholars interested in space as an analytic category take up the question of its sacredness. For example, religious historians who study regional demography find meaning in the changing religious affiliation and population on the American landscape, or the regional flavor of religious movements.[14] Other scholars focus on natural or built landscapes as a point of departure to evoke or understand religious sentiments.[15] Still others employ spatial categories to analyze religious movements or to illuminate the richness of religious rhetoric and sacred text.[16] A few scholars have demonstrated the intriguing connections between religion and space by analyzing the religious significance of material culture, from elaborate temples to simple garments.[17] Such work reminds us that finding, claiming, or constructing the sacred leads students not simply to sites and objects but also to embodied practices. Spatial endeavors, even in their most abstract forms, such as mapping imaginary places, are always concerned with the body's position in relationship to the space it inhabits. For scholars of religion, the investigation of embodied spatial practices traditionally has focused on ritual practices or pilgrimages to holy people or sites.[18] The field of inquiry is broadening to include everyday embodied practices in local sites such as homes, as meaningful arenas of religious belief and action.[19] Among the most suggestive studies are those that consider space as a point of cultural and religious contact, exchange, and sometimes conflict.[20] Spaces may be read, therefore, not only as sacred or profane but also as the reflections and reproductions of religious and social desires and anxieties.[21]

While I imagine myself writing for religious studies scholars, I know that conversations extend beyond disciplinary boundaries. I have thus endeavored to communicate with cultural geographers, and with scholars interested in frontiers of all sorts. Specifically, I have tried to attend to the issue of religion and power on an unstable and contested landscape. In one respect I am writing to add to the historical scholarship of the Western Reserve that emphasizes New England's—especially Connecticut's—religious and cultural dominance in the region.[22] These careful local histories often assume a wholesale transfer of New England's religious culture to the Western Reserve or adopt a variety of Frederick Jackson Turner's "frontier thesis" to deny the transplantation of any religious institution.[23] Religious historians, with a few recent exceptions, relate similar stories of frontier religion. Many scholars who have written on religious culture in western settlements in general, and New Connecticut in particular, focus on certain missionaries' relative success or failure in establishing lasting institutions.[24] In the past decade some scholars have questioned the usefulness of the metaphor of transplantation for historical interpretation.[25] Rather than assessing a missionary's success or failure by counting up converts or churches organized, we might think of missionaries making their way among multiple religious expressions in frontier communities. Moving beyond the model of planting religious institutions allows for the consideration of people, sites, and objects and opens the subjects to new questions that might lead us in new directions.

Argument and Organization

I begin the study with the mapping and missionizing of the Western Reserve. In chapter 1 I show connections between spatial division and moral values by focusing on the institutional side of drawing moral landscapes in this frontier space. To do so I compare the Connecticut Land Company's goal to divide the Western Reserve into neat, orderly townships with the Connecticut Missionary Society's aim to construct moral towns in that same region. Both the land company and the missionary society had unrealistic hopes about the malleability of frontier regions and settlers, hopes that were based almost entirely on their nostalgic desire to re-create a perfect New England village or a biblical paradise on the frontier. Drawing similarities between land surveyors and missionaries, I discuss the attempts to create an imaginative geography that merges national expansion with nostalgic religious longings for a lost time and place.

The Connecticut Missionary Society and the Connecticut Land Company sought to inscribe their idealized vision of an orderly moral community on the frontier. The first Western Reserve missionaries also struggled to fit into an idealized model of pious missionary labor on the frontier. In chapter 2 I shift my focus from institutional desires to shape the landscape to personal experiences of the first missionaries sent to New Connecticut. I continue to follow the theme of expectation versus reality as I explore the missionaries' understanding of their labor within the context of a model of frontier missionary piety that linked physical hardship with spiritual maturity. Frontier life proved physically challenging, and the Plan of Union missionaries soon realized that physical stamina and courage, not contemplative moments leading to spiritual growth, were the most important characteristics of a successful frontier missionary.

Similar to their struggles to fit themselves into a preconceived model of frontier piety, missionaries described and defined frontier space from within a particular context that linked physical and moral order. Casting their memories back through biblical and national history, missionaries found meaning in the physical landscape. Not simply moral signs but moral lessons could be drawn from the way that space was organized. More important, shaping the physical space offered a concrete opportunity for missionaries and settlers to re-create an imagined past while moving them closer to a millennial future. In chapter 3 I investigate the physical landscape as a means to discern and articulate moral values. Specifically, I look at the Connecticut Missionary Society's dual interest in shaping the physical landscape to promote moral values and the potential immorality that it feared could occur in nonstructured spaces. The Plan of Union missionaries and the home society hoped to create towns that were replicas of New Haven or other paradigmatic New England towns. In frontier towns that resembled this ideal, the missionaries claimed that the inhabitants maintained proper moral and religious habits. Conversely, in the towns organized differently, the missionaries complained of infidelity, immorality, and licentiousness.

In chapter 4 I examine published travel narratives that illustrate the connections travelers made between physical landscape and morality that extend beyond missionary letters and publications. Unlike the promising reports of New Connecticut printed in promotional land sales literature and missionary publications, these narratives dispute the claim that the Western Reserve constituted a New Connecticut. I read these narratives in the context of Jedidiah Morse's American geographies, a series of geographical texts that also drew a close connection between the physical landscape and morality.

Twenty-nine years after the first Plan of Union missionary entered the Western Reserve, another missionary, John J. Shipherd, arrived in that region hoping to advance God's kingdom on the frontier. In chapter 5 I focus on his successful attempt to do just that. Seeking to attain "gospel simplicity" and to create a covenanted community, Shipherd gathered like-minded people to glorify God in the Ohio wilderness. The founders of the Oberlin Colony and Institute fused theology and landscape to realize their goal of a covenanted community in New Connecticut. The colonists believed that all aspects of planning, including the town survey and home and building construction, reflected their theology and social vision. Ironically, the most successful attempt to re-create Puritan New England on the frontier by a missionary ultimately served as the catalyst to end Connecticut's Plan of Union mission to the Western Reserve.

For American Protestants, missionary activity was part of their collective identity. What began as isolated colonial attempts to convert Native Americans in the seventeenth century eventually grew into a corporate enterprise that spanned the globe.[26] But this is not the story of converting Native Americans or carrying Christianity to foreign lands. This is a story about the Connecticut Missionary Society, an organization that struggled to maintain moral and spatial connections with neighbors, family, friends, and strangers who left New England to live in northeastern Ohio. The primary storytellers are the Congregational and Presbyterian Plan of Union missionaries who were sent by the home society to foster that tenuous link. This is also a story about settlers who were dually concerned with maintaining a bond with New Englanders and with creating new communities with their frontier neighbors, emigrants from other regions who often claimed different religious ties or none at all. Many of the frontier settlers as well as the missionaries found themselves accommodating regional diversity while they simultaneously promoted a theology that flourished only amid cultural and religious homogeneity. The tensions that arose from the Plan of Union missionaries' frustration with competing denominations demonstrate that although missionary efforts in America generally are discussed in terms of conversion, the most constant home missions theme was retention. Retaining congregants who removed to frontier settlements through physical and spiritual ties proved a difficult task for many Protestant missionaries. Preaching, prayer, and instruction played a role in the retention effort. So, too, I argue, home missionary societies hoped to re-create moral communities by marking and bounding physical spaces, making this retention project a spatial effort. While this is the story of one small missionary endeavor, it has wider implications for understanding how individuals and groups articulate religious identity through the imposition of moral and spatial order. By highlighting the moral and spatial aspects of this single missionary endeavor, I trace the formation of religious identity, an identity that takes shape in texts, bodies, and the physical landscape of the Western Reserve.

FIGURE 1. "New Lands." Printed in *Connecticut Courant*, Tuesday, January 4, 1820. Advertisements like this for lands in New Connecticut were printed in Connecticut newspapers throughout the first decades of the nineteenth century. Besides indicating the tract of land, the advertisement also provides information about a mill, a school, a church, and the moral character of the inhabitants.

CHAPTER 1

The Benevolent Design
Mapping the Landscape

Mappers and Missionaries

Before purchasing land in northeastern Ohio, Silas Allen wrote his former classmate Moses Cleaveland in the spring of 1797 requesting a firsthand account of the recently surveyed territory known as Connecticut's Western Reserve. Allen, like so many future settlers, relied upon several regional maps and published travel accounts for descriptions of the western frontier. Because the majority of the printed information promoted land sales and "various reports give various ideas of that country," Allen appealed to Cleaveland's "acknowledged judgment and candor together with the means of information you have had" to provide an accurate assessment of the land, climate, and potential for habitation.[1] Allen considered himself fortunate to be acquainted with Cleaveland, the Western Reserve's chief surveyor, because most emigrants depended on informational fragments culled from sundry sources other than firsthand knowledge. Some would-be western settlers imagined a garden paradise or the re-creation of a perfectly ordered New England village. Others feared an uninhabitable wilderness on the frontier beyond the reach of the civilizing forces of New England. All who migrated to the Western Reserve, however, shared a common mental process of imagining an unknown place and investing it with nostalgic desires. Scriptural longings, national expansion, nostalgic memories of a lost Puritan New England, and providential fulfillment blended together in the imaginary constructions of New Connecticut.

Silas Allen penned his inquiries at a formative moment in this particular region's history. Situated directly west of the Allegheny Mountains, New Connecticut had just become a "frontier." Years before Allen wrote his letter, Native Americans, including Shawnee, Delaware, Erie, Kickapoo, Miami, Muscouten, Ottawa, and Wyandot, traversed the loamy and wooded land. Members of the Erie tribe, called by the French the Cat Nation, who spoke the Iroquois language, were among the earliest inhabitants of villages along the southern shore of Lake Erie; they named the major waterway Cuyahoga, meaning "crooked river." Later they were absorbed by the Iroquois, who subsequently claimed the region by right of conquest. The Muscouten, a seminomadic tribe linked linguistically to the Algonquian, planted corn crops, hunted deer, and listened to preaching by Jesuit missionaries in the seventeenth century. Although Euro-American settlers would later deem the landscape difficult to farm, the dense woods and calm, shallow rivers provided perfect hunting and fishing grounds for many Native Americans. White-tailed deer, black bears, wolves, wild turkey, and squirrels roamed the territory, and bass, catfish, walleye, and perch swam in the rivers. Deer and bear were not only the most important food source but also a valuable trading commodity. By the eighteenth century Native Americans living around the Cuyahoga River encountered Europeans not only through missionary activity but also by participating in the fur trade.

But in 1785 things changed. The United States Congress passed the Land Ordinance that required surveys of all unmapped congressional lands, and two years later the Northwest Ordinance was signed, providing an orderly grid plan for western territories, including the region that would soon be named Ohio. Trading beaver and black raccoon furs with Native Americans who inhabited the region became increasingly less important to Euro-Americans than obtaining these valuable lands. By the time Allen wrote to Cleaveland, surveyors had followed (generally) the Northwest Ordinance and mapped the territory—"New Connecticut"—from the Pennsylvania line west to the Cuyahoga River. The Connecticut Land Company members who jointly owned the region sold lots to speculators and settlers, and the area that had formerly been virtually unknown to Euro-Americans became a place where nostalgic desires for a lost time or utopian hopes for a more perfect future might be realized. Very little of the physical landscape had changed. The Euro-Americans' perception of the area as fertile "new" land available for settlement, however, transformed the space located at the furthest reaches of Euro-American expansion into a frontier. In this particular region, dreams of national expansion merged with desires for providential fulfillment.

While the Connecticut Land Company calculated the area's financial projections, the Connecticut Missionary Society imagined its moral potential by connecting the frontier to biblical stories of Eden and Zion as well as nostalgic memories of the Puritan experiment in New England. Retelling these epics of God's people in the wilderness contextualized the Connecticut Missionary Society's work within Christian and national history. An imaginary geography of an untouched paradise and a sacred narrative about the redemptive possibilities of a promised land were already in place before any surveying or missionizing. "New Connecticut," in other words, was built first in the minds and later in the descriptions of land surveyors, missionaries, and their sponsoring societies.

Constructing such an imaginary space before seeing it is not uncommon. Spatial theorists and cultural geographers assert that the way people describe their environment is always a process of adjusting perceptions to expectations, their imaginary model to their experiential reality. What they expect to see—a howling wilderness or a desert blooming like a rose—determines how they describe that which they do see. Physical landscape such as frontier space becomes meaningful through human perception, and mental maps, like drawn maps, inscribe landscape with human meaning and desires. As the maps were being drawn, the Western Reserve became a place where missionaries, settlers, and travelers could step into biblical history, as well as a space to re-create an idealized version of Puritan New England. Whether the region was described as a new Zion or as a New Connecticut, the Western Reserve provided a place for sacred history to unfold on American soil. The physical landscape, described in both geographical and scriptural terms, therefore, framed the missionary endeavor. Thus *mapping* is an appropriate point of entry into the complex enterprise of missionizing New Connecticut, a place that simultaneously re-created a biblical past and heralded a scriptural future.

The Connecticut Land Company and the Connecticut Missionary Society aimed not to institute a new society in the West but rather to impose their particular vision of Connecticut's social, political, and religious organization onto the landscape.[2] Their joint aspirations correlated a neat landscape with morality and social order. To order the space, the land company utilized the Land Ordinance grid survey, homogenizing the landscape into straight lines and angles. So, too, the missionary society diluted religious and social diversity by emphasizing in its publications the homogeneity of the Connecticut-born settlers. This erasure of contours placed the surveyors and missionaries in the awkward position of fitting terrain and people into idealized categories that neither reflected the bumps and curves of the region nor represented the dispositions and desires of all the inhabitants. Such an ordered space required strong boundaries. Strictly drawn lines demarcated the region so that one could step out of the wilderness and into New Connecticut. Tight moral boundaries maintained cultural and religious homogeneity to distinguish the saints from the sinners. In both spatial and moral terms, boundaries needed to be marked and maintained against a hostile environment. The men who first ventured into the "ordered" space not only recorded and organized information about the landscape and the settlers but also enabled the further expansion of the land company and the missionary society. A neatly ordered space invited settlers and assuaged the fears of potential donors to the missionary society, eastern benefactors who often viewed the frontier as beyond the reach of eastern control.

The land company and the missionary society sought not only to describe the Western Reserve; they also wanted to define it. Both organizations aimed to order the landscape to make the region appealing to prospective land buyers and missionary society donors. Together they participated in a larger process of claiming and promoting the Western Reserve as a New Connecticut. The Connecticut Missionary Society, like its missionaries, however, never presented itself as working with the land company. On the contrary, the society often defined its spiritual labor over against the worldly work of land sellers and buyers in the region. In an 1805 publication the society wrote: "People have been flocking from various parts into the wilderness, for the sake of farms, honors, wealth and worldly good; but the Lord hath planted it, that churches might be gathered unto his name; that worship and praise might be paid unto him from regions."[3] The wilderness drew the attention of many worldly people who exploited the land to increase their own wealth, but, according to the missionary society, God's providential plan for the region was unfolding. Although the society repeatedly stated that it did not share the interests or goals of the land company for the Western Reserve, it is possible to identify some intriguing points of contact. Many of the missionary society members were interested in land sales, and some of the land company members supported the missionary cause. For example, Abel Flint, while holding the position of corresponding secretary of the Connecticut Missionary Society, also authored a surveying manual in 1804.[4] The Reverend Jedidiah Morse, a strong supporter of the Connecticut Missionary Society and Protestant home missions in general, compiled the first geography of the United States in 1789, a text that illustrates his dual commitment to moralizing and to mapping the new nation. These two examples do not prove that the men involved with mapping and missionizing the Western Reserve understood themselves to be working toward a common goal; they do suggest however, that mapping and missionizing operated in a larger context of claiming and defining frontier space.

Sometimes the efforts to map and to missionize coincided in documents that provided interesting assessments of a region's moral and topographical terrain. These publications generally described the advances of several competing denominations on the frontier with accompanying demographic and surveyors' maps. The combination of land description and religious expansion presents a fascinating example of the coextensive aims of mapping and missionizing, even if nineteenth-century land surveyors and missionaries rarely envisioned themselves as involved in the same enterprise. The maps drawn by land surveyors for the Connecticut Land Company and letters written by missionaries for the Connecticut Missionary Society represent discursive attempts to shape space. Both the land surveyors and the missionaries provided a crucial informational link between their sponsoring agencies in the East and the actual site of expansion in the West. Walking the landscape, they sought to fit what they saw into fairly strict models derived from drawn maps and personal expectations. Land surveyors labored to organize the landscape into a neat grid, and missionaries scoured northeastern Ohio in search of the Promised Land. Professionals employed by Connecticut organizations, the surveyors and missionaries crisscrossed western lands in the hopes of gaining financial and religious profits.

While the land surveyors and missionaries attempted to inscribe a set of spatial and moral presumptions onto the Western Reserve, they also erased or exaggerated any deviant landmarks or behavior. Surveyors might have struggled with uneven terrain and mathematical dilemmas, but their product—the map—held implicit claims to accuracy. Likewise, who better than a Connecticut missionary to report on settlers' behavior to a Connecticut audience? The missionary himself might face any number of unusual conflicts and disappointments on the frontier, but the view presented to his sponsors and readers, seen through his "Connecticut eyes," appeared as a credible account of religious life on the western frontier. The Connecticut Missionary Society trustees underscored this point in the *Narrative of Missions* (1813). "The state of the country," they explained, "may be presented in its true light, by the communications of the missionaries whose residence is there."[5] Although engaged in different professions, the land surveyors and missionaries served as mediators who produced maps and letters that defined the landscape and reconciled their absentee employers' expectations with the realities of the frontier. Both groups understood that their positive assessment of the frontier would increase land sales and home missions donations. The missionaries also came to realize that a particular style of writing that balanced frontier drama with "flattering prospects" for salvation of souls was not only welcomed but expected by the home society. The challenge for land surveyors and missionaries was to accurately describe the frontier while providing information that met their employers' expectations. The land company and missionary society in turn gathered the firsthand information and presented it to prospective land buyers and society donors.

Both groups participated in the nostalgic desire to re-create a lost time and place. The Western Reserve became a new home perceived to be rightfully occupied by people who claimed it by imposing their sacred genealogy and national history onto it, a process that involved more than simply emigrating to the territory. As Miriam Peskowitz points out, "To fulfill the desire to return home, one must first posit a certain place as home."[6] In this way, building imaginary "homes" like New Connecticut is part and parcel of the colonialism that erases or displaces people while claiming territory and rewriting history. To exemplify this powerful yet basic connection, one needs only to ask where have the Native Americans gone to if they are not located on the maps and are no longer the object of missionary labor? In imagining the frontier space west of the Alleghenies as a New Connecticut or a Garden of Eden, both the Connecticut Land Company and the Connecticut Missionary Society assumed the privilege of claiming the space as "home."

In this chapter I focus primarily on the institutional side of transforming the territory into a home space, New Connecticut. I consider the Connecticut Land Company's efforts to shape the landscape to resemble a lost New England. I also follow the Connecticut Missionary Society's attempts to fashion the moral landscape to resemble a past Puritan or scriptural home. Balancing two sets of primary sources from the land company and the missionary society, I consider how the landscape and the Native Americans who resided there had to be manipulated in order to create a space that simultaneously tapped into regional nostalgia and scriptural longings. Looking at these disparate texts together reveals the deep connections between mapping and missionizing that participated in the unfolding (or constructing) of what the missionary society would call God's "benevolent design" for the region, the country, and sacred history.

The Connecticut Land Company: Mapping

The mapping of the Western Reserve, or "New Connecticut," resulted from a political agreement between the state of Connecticut and the federal government. The three-million-acre territory constituted the remainder of western lands after Connecticut ceded the bulk of its property to the United States government in 1780. The Connecticut Land Company purchased the land from the state and surveyed it in accordance with the United States' 1785 Land Ordinance, which required that public lands west of the Appalachian Mountains be mapped prior to settlement. The Land Ordinance established that everything north of the Ohio River and west of the Pennsylvania border would be surveyed into squares of townships and ranges. The townships were to be divided into six-square-mile parcels, each containing thirty-six sections (of one square mile, or 640 acres) and ordered north to south, while the ranges were numbered east to west. The ordinance also set aside land—section 16—in every township for the maintenance of schools. This division system determined boundaries prior to legal settlement and without reference to any residing inhabitants or to the natural landscape. This approach reflected the perspective of surveyors, landowners, and the federal government—namely, that land unoccupied by Euro-Americans constituted blank space waiting to be divided. In this respect the grid system that was imposed on the Western Reserve, like those used in the division of many other land parcels, ignored the construction, use, and habitation of the landscape by Native Americans. It also ignored claims of squatters to ownership by right of occupancy. The practice of viewing land as "a tabula rasa" is a common feature of those who conquer and colonize indigenous people, who often are remapped and renamed in the process.[7]

News and maps of this fertile area circulated on the Atlantic Coast and spurred interest in the western territories. Led by Oliver Phillips, thirty-five members of the Connecticut Land Company bought the estimated three million acres of the Western Reserve in 1795 and quickly began advertising the land for sale in Connecticut and Massachusetts newspapers.[8] An 1803 notice in Hartford's *Connecticut Courant* proclaimed that the region "afford[ed] the most pleasing prospects to industrious and enterprising men."[9] On the basis of information culled from printed maps and travelers' land descriptions, a committee of eight representatives granted land deeds apportioned according to each investor's financial contribution. The purchasers acted for themselves and, in a few cases, for interested parties. The final partnership numbered fifty-seven men, including one of the larger shareholders, land surveyor and general agent Moses Cleaveland.[10] Although the members had varying personal reasons for acquiring western property, the Land Company organized itself around land sale for profit. To achieve this, the Association Articles drawn up in 1795 dictated among its immediate goals to extinguish all Indian land claims, to survey the entire Reserve, to decide on the first settlements, and to sell the lots to settlers only.[11]

In the summer of 1796, less than a year after Congress passed the Land Ordinance, Connecticut Land Company surveyors Moses Cleaveland of Canterbury, Connecticut, and Seth Pease of Suffield, Connecticut, laid out a town on the banks of the Cuyahoga River and renamed it in Cleaveland's honor, and Amos Spafford drew the map (figure 2).[12] With the help of six principal surveyors and thirty-five axe, chain, and rod men, Cleaveland surveyed almost one hundred acres and divided the lots around a central town square.[13] Guided by compasses, sketchy maps, and Seth Pease's astronomical expertise, the surveyors walked the region and worked throughout the hot and rainy summer from July to October. On the whole, the surveying was more difficult than they had expected. They slogged through muddy swamps and suffered from dysentery, fever, headaches, cramps, fatigue, and hunger as they carved out six townships of five-square-mile lots (not six-square-mile lots as stated in the Land Ordinance). The men ate what they could scavenge off the land. Gooseberries, raspberries, wintergrew berries, and boiled rattlesnake filled their

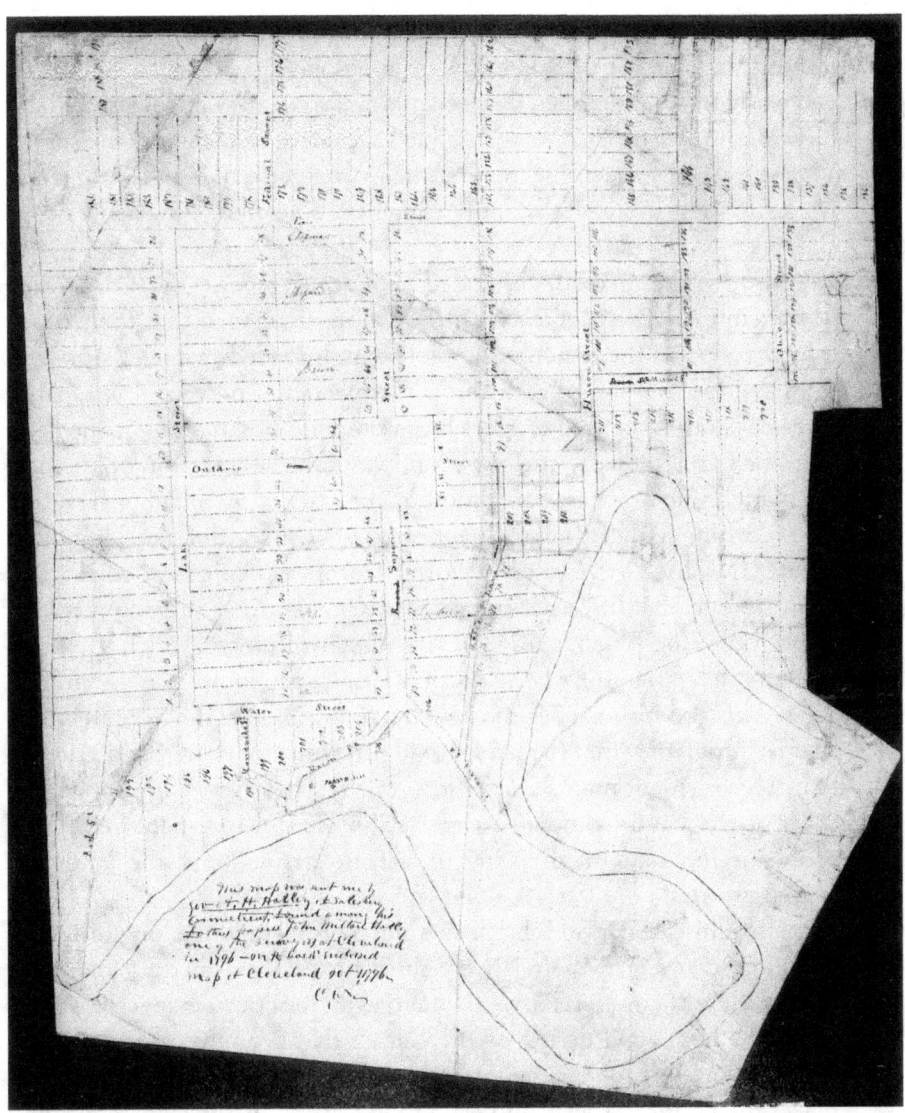

FIGURE 2. Amos Spafford's map of Cleveland (1796). Spafford's map shows the surveyor's attempt to shape the landscape to resemble an idealized model of a Puritan New England town. Courtesy of the Western Reserve Historical Society, Cleveland, Ohio.

stomachs, while concerns about completing the survey occupied their minds. After almost three months of grueling work, through heavy rain and with low food supplies, Cleaveland was forced to sell a township to his crew at one dollar per acre as an added incentive to complete the survey. They named the town Euclid, after the mathematician, and continued to work for a few more weeks, more contented since they now had a financial stake in the land.

Although the surveyors intended to establish a perfect grid according to the land survey specifications, they soon discovered that their rough calculations and the region's uneven terrain impeded that goal. Surveyor John Milton Holley of Salisbury, Connecticut, noted a discrepancy three days into the survey: "Here by a very good observation of the Polar Star at its greatest eastern elongation, we took the variation of the needle (which was 1° 35 east elongation of the star) by a second observation next morning with the ranges it appeared to be 1° 30 (the star elongation) the needle varied 53₍Ä east Mr. Porters compass + mine varied alike."[14] Even though the difference appeared slight, the final survey years later showed that the actual acreage of the Western Reserve, which took into account the variations of the natural landscape, comprised 2.5 million acres. This 500,000-acre error created a financial loss; it also represented a larger problem—that the land would not conform to the rigid grid system. This incident marks a specific moment when New Connecticut fell short of the Land Company's expectations, and it foreshadowed future problems inherent in imposing unrealistic desires onto the landscape (see figure 3).

Such a miscalculation is hardly a unique problem in the long history of mapping, or even in the relatively short history of American mapping. Maps are always interpretative tools and early American maps tell us more about the hopes and desires of the culture that produced the maps than about accurate land representation. A number of early American maps reflect the political, social, and economic features of the landscape, and I will soon examine a couple of these maps that represent the Western Reserve. But first I must consider an early map that reflects moral values. Cartography and moral narrative converge in one of the earliest published New England maps, which appeared in Cotton Mather's 1702 *Magnalia Christi Americana*. In his enormous text describing and defining America, Mather included only one cartographic representation of the region. Although he had dabbled in cartography at Harvard College, it is unlikely that he drew this map, which is based on John Thornton, Robert Morden,

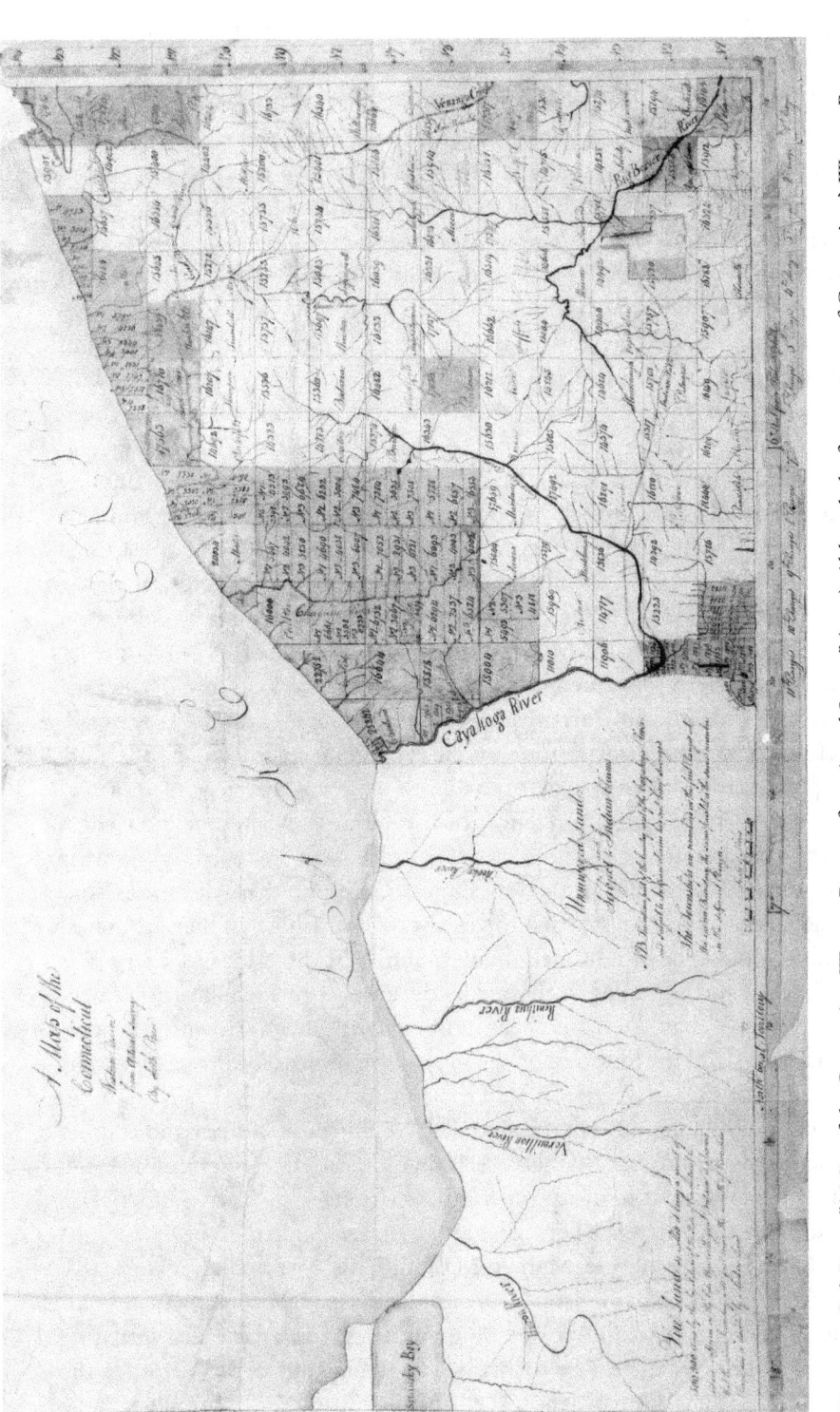

FIGURE 3. Seth Pease, "A Map of the Connecticut Western Reserve, from Actual Survey" (1797). Although the first surveyors of Connecticut's Western Reserve intended to establish a perfect grid, the landscape's contours impeded that goal. Courtesy of the Western Reserve Historical Society, Cleveland, Ohio.

and Philip Lea's 1685 map of the colonies. The "Mather Map" (figure 4) shows the boundaries of New England from Casco Bay to an elongated Long Island, includes vague markings for East New Jersey, and labels an empty expanse "New York." In accordance with colonial English cartographic trends, the most detailed areas are the waterways and the coastal towns in Massachusetts and Connecticut. But the Mather Map distinguishes itself by using meetinghouses to represent New England townships. These tiny icons dotting the landscape illustrate Mather's fusion of sacred historical narrative and mapping.

Later in the text, in a chapter titled "An Ecclesiastical Map of the Country," Mather lists the ministers in the counties of the three New England colonies, Plymouth, Massachusetts, and Connecticut, and comments on the climate and the growth in population as well. Mather's map and narrative belie his eighteenth-century geographical knowledge in at least one remarkable way. In a simultaneously cartographic and rhetorical move, Mather anachronistically separates and highlights Plymouth Colony on the map and in the narrative, even though by the time of its printing, Plymouth had been subsumed by the Massachusetts Bay Colony. This visual and narrative link to Puritanism—albeit outdated—inscribes the small, defunct colony's central position on the expanding colonial map. But more important for Mather was that the success of townships depended primarily on an active clerical presence. In his narrative Mather acknowledges that natural calamity and "the dreadful Indian war" reduced significantly the number of townships in New England. Despite these disastrous conditions, however, he notes that towns always flourish when they are graced with the presence of educated divines. Similarly, those that Mather labels as "decline towns" could be charted by the absence of such illustrious men. "The gospel has evidently been the *making* of our towns," Mather remarked, "and the blessings of the *upper* have been accompanied with the blessings of the *nether-springs*."[15] The statistics about New England settlements and inhabitants reflect the usual factors such as weather and conflict with Native tribes. But Mather asserts that it is the strong clerical presence, rather than natural resources or hostile relations with Native Americans, that made the difference between growth or decline in a township.

The structure of the Mather Map and his corresponding narrative Ecclesiastical Map demonstrates the implicitly spatial character of his religious discourse and the power of mapping to overcome disheartening social realities. Mather inextricably tied New England sacred history to the claiming and marking of landscape. Writing during the politically volatile

FIGURE 4. "An Exact Mapp of New England and New York." This engraving was printed in Cotton Mather's *Magnalia Christi Americana* (1702), illustrating the spatial character of Mather's sacred history of New England. Note that on this map meetinghouses signify New England townships. Courtesy of the Newberry Library, Chicago.

1690s, he made a choice to reinforce the centrality of the Plymouth Colony geographically and rhetorically, thus reeling in his readers' desires to re-create a lost time centered around a Puritan community, and he cast forward the hopes for renewing that early communal state.

Mather's cartography, in all its forms, constitutes the narrative equivalent of what geographer J. B. Harley terms "subliminal geography," the unconscious creation of the center of the universe.[16] Through a historically skewed map and a correlative narrative, Mather guided the readers' mental viewpoint toward Plymouth and away from theological border areas such as Dartmouth, which he describes as "perishing without vision."[17] Still, while Mather asserted the prominent place of his forefathers in New England's redemptive history, he also personally witnessed decline in church membership, theological compromises including the Dedham Half-Way Covenant (1662), and tragedies such as the Salem witch trials. In the eye of this theological and political storm, Mather's ambitious but nonetheless contradictory work reaffirmed his Puritan belief in the chosenness of saints, the authority of Scripture, and New England's central role in God's redemptive plan for humanity. Mather's sacred history set the standard for future narrative maps that would continue to place Puritanism at the center; it also serves as a model for the spatial and moral mapping of the Western Reserve less than one hundred years later.

Before the Land Ordinance grid surveys were executed, Euro-American investors interested in western lands in the late eighteenth century could examine a few reputable maps to ascertain the size and land quality of the Western Reserve. John Mitchell, a British physician and botanist who lived in North America for twenty years, compiled and published "A Map of the British and French Dominions in America, with the Roads, Distances, Limits, and Extent of the Settlements" in 1755.[18] Mitchell relied on information supplied by explorer Christopher Gist and used mathematical equations to locate settlement sites. Mitchell's map provides an example of the political power of maps, in this case, reinforcing British claims to the territory. Mitchell included an Iroquois village on the banks of the Cuyahoga River but neglected to locate Pennsylvania trader George Croghan's trading post in a nearby Seneca village. According to Ohio map historian Thomas H. Smith, this exclusion of the trading post "was a further attempt to strengthen England's claim to the Ohio Country through its alliance with the Iroquois."[19] Mitchell's map can be read as one part of the British attempt to dominate the political landscape.

Besides Mitchell's map, three other important maps informed western speculators, investors, and travelers during this period. Lewis Evans's "General Map of the Middle British Colonies in North America" accompanied a pamphlet of essays concerned with the geography, history, and politics of the region.[20] This map circulated widely through its ten editions from 1755 to 1807.[21] Evans, who relied on traders for topographical information, provided a more detailed map than Mitchell's, including Indian villages such as "Mohicon John's town" and "White Woman's Town"[22] and military forts, as well as information about passage via waterways and on foot. For example, he described the Muskingum River as "all gentle and passable with canoes to the Portage at the Head," while the Quasioto Mountains were judged "30 or 40 Miles right across through which there is not yet any occupied path in these part." One edition of Evans's map, published by Thomas Pownall in 1776, served as a reliable guide on the strenuous journey across the Allegheny Mountains and proved particularly popular with Western Reserve settlers.

Thomas Hutchins's "New Map" (1778) and Abraham Bradley's "Map of the Northern Parts of the United States," which appeared in the third and fourth editions of Jedidiah Morse's *The American Universal Geography*, together provided informational sources for westward expansion. Hutchins, a British officer and mapmaker, was the Chief Surveyor of the first "Seven Ranges" of the Land Ordinance and personally visited the entire western region. His surveying went slower than he had hoped: he and his crew were interrupted many times by the threat of Native American attacks. It took Hutchins two years to survey four ranges (800,000 acres). Even though his men worked by mathematical equation and with surveying instruments such as the sextant to determine the latitude for the baseline, and a circumferentor, a compass that gave readings in degrees, they still made a number of errors. Congress was impatient and wanted the lands surveyed for quick sale, and in the end this pressure proved more important than accuracy. Although Hutchins personally surveyed southern Ohio, his map of the Western Reserve relied on previous mappers such as Evans, as well as on his own personal observations. His mapping style, reminiscent of older surveying techniques, provides colorful details that give the reader a sense of familiarity with the region. Bradley's map outlined the territory according to the 1785 Land Ordinance.[23] This map, the first to delineate clearly the boundaries of New Connecticut, also locates established counties within the Northwest Territory. Bradley's map, however, remains less descriptive of the terrain and more focused on political subdivisions, specifically the Pennsylvania state boundary, the western Indian boundary, and General Anthony Wayne's 1795 Treaty line.

Missionaries also helped to map the region. John Heckewelder's map, drawn from his personal observations and travels, combines a naturalist's approach to the land with political information (figure 5).[24] Heckewelder, a German-born Moravian missionary, founded a mission settlement named Pilgrim's Rest on the banks of the Cuyahoga River in 1786. His map, dated January 12, 1796, plots the terrain and natural landmarks of the region, such as rivers, swamps, muddy banks, and well-trodden paths. The map also delineates the political lines of Indian territories according to the 1795 Treaty of Greenville, which opened Ohio to white settlers.[25] Besides the map's detailed illustrations, Heckewelder includes a written statement in which he describes the region and identifies the banks of the Cuyahoga as the preferable area for settlement. He bases this land-quality assessment on access to water and land routes, richness of soil, and the availability of timber and game. "There are some beautiful small Lakes in this country, with water as clear as Chrystall, + alive with fish. In these Lakes as well as in Cujahaga River water fowl resort in abundance in Spring + Fall."[26] Heckewelder's map, and his written interpretations, created a bridge between a naturalist's approach to land assessment and a political map that located treaty lines.

All of these mapmakers, while claiming a certain amount of scientific objectivity, clearly display through their maps their own perspective and their sponsoring agency's interests in the region. So while the production and interpretation of maps is often evaluated in terms of scientific accuracy, maps are, in the final analysis, representations. All maps, according to geographer J. B. Harley, are shaped by social and political relations, and, I would add, moral endeavors. What is excluded from a map is always as significant as what is included.[27] The empty spaces on maps do not reflect a "reality" of "nothing" between two points; rather, such "blanks" show that nothing of importance to the mapmaker exists between two points. But this is not as innocent or as simple as it at first seems. Blank spaces on maps do not simply reflect gaps in knowledge, but as Simon Ryan points out, these cartographic spaces "actively erase (and legitimize the erasure of) existing social, and geo-cultural formations in preparation for the projection and subsequent emplacement of a new order."[28] Likewise, the marked spaces on maps direct the viewers' attention to places that are of central or peripheral significance to the mapmaker. Reading a map, therefore, alerts

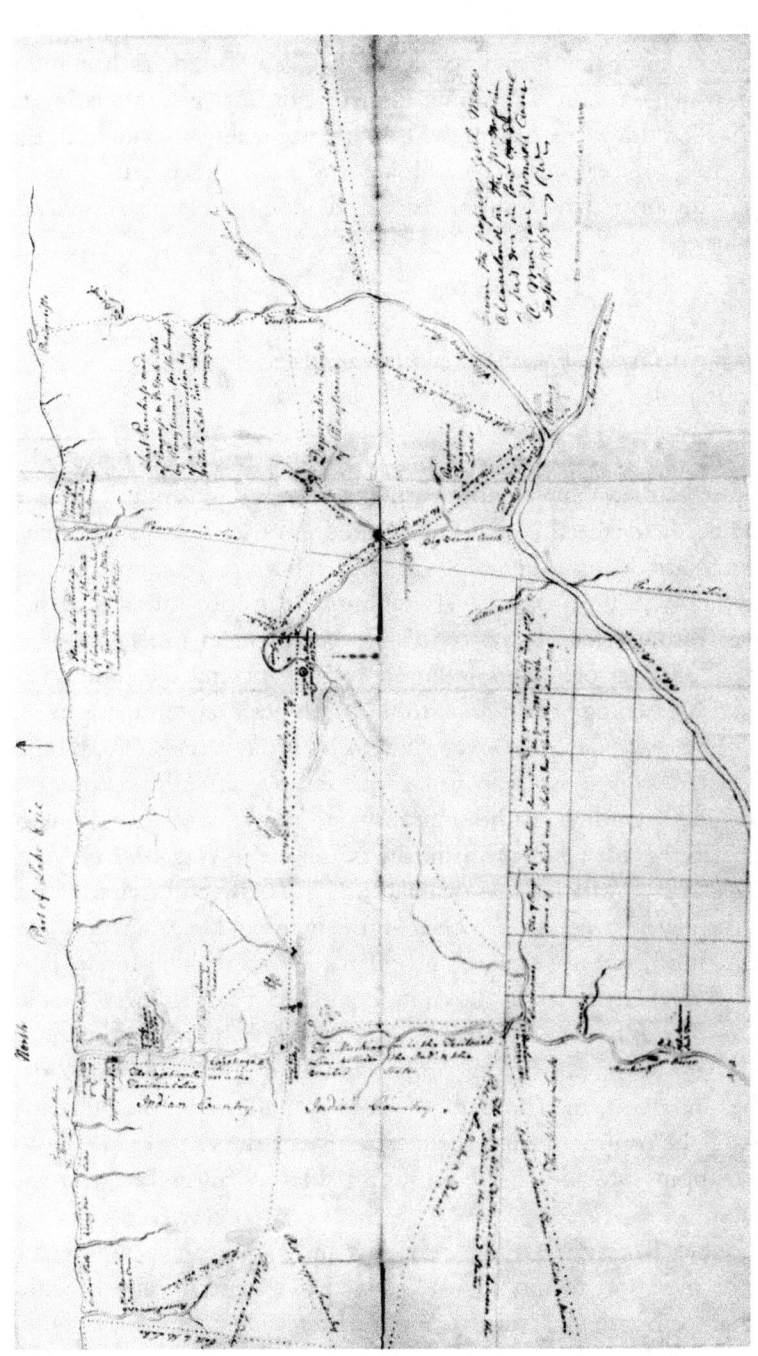

FIGURE 5. "Heckewelder Map" (1796). Moravian missionary John Heckewelder provided information about the political treaty lines and land quality in his map. Courtesy of the Western Reserve Historical Society, Cleveland, Ohio.

us to the perceptions and expectations of the author and the intended audience. Any space that is mapped is not merely a blank backdrop but a canvas on which we paint a meaningful picture of ourselves in relation to the world. That drawn maps represent desire, not reality, is evident in the efforts of the Connecticut Land Company and the Connecticut Missionary Society to control the frontier space and erase the Native Americans who lived there.

"In regard to the Heathen on our borders": Erasing the Natives

Besides rugged landscapes, land surveyors and missionaries also encountered Natives. Nineteenth-century Europeans and Americans typically vilified or idealized Native inhabitants in order to distance themselves from Natives on the genealogical chart. This representational trend, found primarily in European travel literature, developed into a "taming" of Natives through literary portraits showing them as innocents or as noble savages.[29] Cartographers followed suit by moving the position of potentially threatening inhabitants from central positions on maps to the margins. This shift occurred over time and through repeated colonial encounters and conquests. Jean Rotz, for example, articulated the early European understanding of the centrality and power of Native presence when he placed Native Americans in the center of his 1542 *Map of North America and the West Indies*.[30] As contact *increased* between Europeans and Natives, the Native presence *decreased* on the maps and became more idealized, evoking images of nature and plenty. By 1646 Englishman John Speed's well-circulated map of the Americas, *A Prospect of the Most Famous Parts of the World*, removed Native Americans from the map proper and relegated them to the position of romanticized subjects in the decorative cartouches and on the map borders.[31] Speed's map illustrates the European conquest of the continent from the perspective of the victor's side, showing that mapping provides an idiom for articulating cultural contact and conquest.

The contact between Native Americans and Europeans is a poignant example of the effort to modify a territory to fit a preconceived mental map. All early North American mapping occurred within this colonial context. Geoff King notes that the European encounter with Native Americans brought together all the scientific and theological elements that informed mapping throughout the previous centuries.[32] While relations between Natives and settlers in America differed according to time and place, Europeans rarely acknowledged Native land claims and their concomitant land maps or "cartographies."[33] Although often dependent on Native Americans' knowledge of the land, European explorers and cartographers "discovered" and marked what they portrayed as empty space.[34] The Europeans' belief in their ability to draw scientifically accurate maps also signaled an affirmation of the mapmakers' status as authoritative professionals who through mathematical and scientific expertise credibly represented reality.[35] Such maps enabled the Europeans to erase, as it were, Native Americans from the land.

Maps of the Western Reserve followed the general European trend and ignored the indigenous presence either by depicting Native figures on the margins or by erasing them completely from maps. Grid maps of the town of Cleveland drawn in 1798, for example, suggest that no one traversed Ohio before the Connecticut surveyors did, even though Cleaveland wrote in his journal that he negotiated with the Pequa chief of the Masesagoes before starting the survey (see figure 2).[36] Renaming the landscape was part and parcel of claiming it. By 1800, before any of the missionaries in this study stepped into the region, more than thirty of the towns had been surveyed under Cleaveland's direction; a few years later, under Seth Pease, some of these towns had been renamed after Connecticut villages.[37] Cartographic mention of Native American presence was pushed further west. The promise of non-contested, expansive western land constituted the single most important factor for Euro-American settlers and the Connecticut Land Company and Connecticut Missionary Society in their plans for selling, settling, and missionizing the region. Native Americans remained as cultural and religious outposts, visible but not integrated into the Euro-American religious community. In many ways the "poor heathen on our borders" as the missionary society put it, were regarded in much the same way as the frontier wilderness, an indigenous landscape that needed to be leveled in order to make Euro-American settlement possible.

The New Englanders who set out to plan, settle, and missionize the Western Reserve carried with them ambivalent feelings regarding Native inhabitants but clear objectives regarding the land. Connecticut missionaries struggled with the seemingly contradictory biblical imperatives of inward and outward spiritual focus that mirrored the seventeenth-century Puritan theological dilemma. The injunction in Joshua 17 to cut down the forest and build a New Jerusalem inspired the Puritan colony, while the scriptural lamentations of Jeremiah and the Macedonian "Come over and help us" led a faithful few to rescue souls lost in the moral wilderness. The scriptural tension that was never fully resolved as Puritans joined together in covenanted communities while simultaneously praying for Indian conversion was repeated to a lesser degree by Protestant missionaries on the frontier. If Native Americans became invisible or pushed off the map, the conflict over whether to devote energies to missionizing them or Euro-American settlers would be resolved.

Missions to Native Americans presented financial as well as theological problems for the Connecticut Missionary Society, illustrating the complexities of spatial and moral mapping. Native American presence was erased when land surveyors gridded the area following the 1785 National Land Ordinance. Surveyors divided and renamed Native land without reference to the previous inhabitants or their marks on the landscape. From the Euro-American cartographic perspective, the Natives did not exist. But despite the Connecticut Land Company's assurance to would-be settlers that they had "cleared" the land of indigenous peoples, their continual presence was undeniable. For one year, missionary David Bacon worked unsuccessfully among remnants of Indian tribes, mostly Ojibwes, on the borders of the Western Reserve near Lake Erie. The following year he traveled further west, to Lake Michigan, where he tried but failed to found a mission among the Chippewas. About the same time the Connecticut Missionary Society sent Joseph Badger to visit the Wyandot Indians on the outskirts of the reserve to gather information but not to establish a mission. By 1804 Bacon was sent back to the Western Reserve to work among the New England emigrants, Badger labored solely among settlers, and the Connecticut Missionary Society abandoned its efforts among Native Americans in the frontier regions.

The shift from Native American missions to home missions required articulating strong boundaries on the Connecticut Missionary Society's moral map of the region. Simply put, in the minds of the trustees Native Americans no longer resided within the borders. The trustees explained the "painful necessity" of redirecting labor and funds in their 1805 Annual Report: "In regard to the heathen, on our borders, the door does not appear to be opened to carry among them, the good news of life and salvation."[38] The society voiced its concern for the moral well-being of Native inhabitants by including them in the mission statement, but from this point on, it focused primarily on New England emigrants and the creation of a morally ordered community on the frontier. Significantly, the society portrayed Native Americans as living "on our borders," rather than residing inside the Western Reserve. This phrase served to position Native Americans on the fringes of the landscape as well as on the margins of Euro-American imagination of the frontier community.

The Connecticut Missionary Society: Missionizing

Although re-creating Puritan New England or, more improbably, finding the Promised Land in northeastern Ohio might seem misguided, that is exactly what the Connecticut Missionary Society set out to accomplish in the early nineteenth century. Its efforts to do this, however, did not begin with the Western Reserve. The trustees, working through the General Association of Connecticut, had sent Congregational missionaries to minister to former Connecticut citizens living in the newly opened settlements closer to home as early as 1774. The first missionaries toured frontier settlements for four months of preaching, organizing churches, and performing ministerial duties.

The General Association of Connecticut faced numerous obstacles in its efforts to extend Congregational piety and order in the wilderness; the primary challenge involved finding competent clergy to send on missions. Settled New England clergymen in the 1770s seldom accepted a nomination as missionary because of the physical rigor of frontier preaching or their inability to find suitable parish replacements during their absence. Among the missionaries who agreed to tour the frontier towns, only a few satisfied all the requirements of the sponsoring society, and many fell short of the settlers' and the association's expectations. In printed statements the General Association claimed that it was "entirely satisfied with the zeal, faithful and laborious diligence of our brethren in their several missions."[39] But internal correspondence shows that members worried about the missionaries' activities, particularly their failure to correspond promptly with the home organization to apprise it of the status of the new settlements. This problem remained unsolved over the next few decades of missionary labor. The General Association's greatest challenge, however, was its own disorganization. As Connecticut natives continued to move further from Hartford and New Haven, the members resolved to form a more efficient organization aimed "to Christianize the Heathen in North America, and to support and promote Christian Knowledge in the new settlements, within the United States."[40] After setbacks caused by the Revolutionary War and the general disorganization of missionary efforts, the Connecticut Missionary Society officially formed on June 21, 1798, in Hebron, Connecticut, and quickly dispatched missionaries to New York, Delaware, Vermont, and Pennsylvania.

From its inception and throughout its existence, the Connecticut Missionary Society faced the same difficulty as the General Association in finding qualified missionaries. During the first years of the society's organization, religious awakenings increased throughout New England, and settled clergy were either unwilling or unable to leave their home congregations. Young men graduating from colleges and later seminaries—young men who constituted the most promising pool for missionary candidates, generally chose to fill pulpits in newly organized churches in the old settlements rather than to accept contracts to missionize the frontier. And even when the revivals subsided in the East and the western territories became more settled and travel less daunting, the Connecticut Missionary Society continued to struggle to find suitable missionaries. The problem was endlessly discussed in communications among the missionaries in the field, the sponsoring society, the settlers, and the society's donors.

Another early disappointment for the missionary society, as I have already indicated, involved its unsuccessful mission to Native Americans. Like Puritan and eighteenth-century Congregational missionaries, the men sent by the Connecticut Missionary Society made few lasting inroads among Native Americans. As efforts to bring Christianity to Native populations met with repeated failure, the Connecticut Missionary Society narrowed its focus to the Euro-American inhabitants of the new settlements. With the exception of a few rugged and committed missionaries such as David Bacon in Ohio, the majority of the missionaries commissioned through the Connecticut Missionary Society worked among displaced New England frontier settlers. By June 1805 the Connecticut Missionary Society officially ended its mission to Native Americans. This colossal failure was quickly forgotten as the society increased its interest in a three-million-acre tract of land in northeastern Ohio called the Western Reserve, or "New Connecticut."[41]

The Connecticut Missionary Society was part of a growing trend at the beginning of the nineteenth century toward state-level, interdenominational benevolent societies. The New York Missionary Society (1796) and the Massachusetts Missionary Society (1799) also formed from smaller groups to establish churches in frontier settlements. Minor doctrinal differences were set aside to evangelize the western territories. The Connecticut Missionary Society was so concerned about its success in the frontier settlements that in 1801 the trustees joined forces with the Presbyterians in what became known as the Plan of Union. This denominational merger sought to combine manpower and finances to spread the gospel to frontier settlers. The union between the General Association of Connecticut and the General Assembly of the Presbyterian Church aimed to reach similar theological and missionary goals and enabled both religious groups to cover more territory in the missionary field.[42] Following this plan, the missionaries would organize Congregational, Presbyterian, or "mixed" churches, sometimes termed "Presbygational," depending on the settlers' wishes. The Plan of Union covered the entire Northwest, but only in the Western Reserve were the majority of the churches organized according to Congregational form. In practice, denominational distinctions were subordinated to the greater cause, as all three types of churches were part of the Western Reserve Synod. It was not until the third decade of settlement that denominational interests and internal squabbles would split the Presbyterians and Congregationalists and end the Plan of Union in New Connecticut.

The Connecticut Missionary Society's motivations for missionizing the frontier inhabitants arose from biblical and national memory. Scriptural injunctions such as the Great Commission to "make disciples of all nations" inspired and legitimated missionary endeavors.[43] Of equal importance was the trustees' firm belief that America would play a redemptive role in God's divine plan for human salvation. The seventeenth-century Puritan experience in the New World, their "errand into the wilderness," joined two goals that carried over into the nineteenth-century Protestant imagination: to sustain a morally exemplary society while actively seeking the salvation of others. Although God's divine plan remained hidden from human eyes, the Puritans understood that they had special obligations for carrying out that plan and that the landscape they inhabited would also serve to bring about world redemption. Early missionaries such as John Eliot, Eleazor Wheelock, and Experience Mayhew sought to civilize as well as evangelize Native Americans by organizing into "praying towns" or later mixed Native and Euro-American communities. Others, like David Brainerd, were concerned less with extending cultural values than with preaching the gospel.[44] Although the evangelism efforts were not entirely successful, the links between Puritan scriptural interpretation, national destiny, and missionizing were boldly stamped on the seal of the Massachusetts Bay Colony.[45] This network of associations lingered in the collective memories of nineteenth-century Protestant evangelicals such as the Connecticut Missionary Society trustees.

From their perspective in the first decades of the nineteenth century, the Connecticut Missionary Society's trustees did not need to refer all the way back to Scripture or even to Puritan New England to justify their missionary endeavor. They glanced back only a generation, to the eighteenth-century revivals that provided the impulse for home missionary labor. The theological justification for American missions in the eighteenth century came out of the New England revivals of the 1740s and 1750s, a movement that divided Congregationalists and Presbyterians over questions about divine sovereignty, human ability to affect grace, and millennial expectancy. Although the revivals were cause for great joy and optimism, they also provoked concern regarding the fervor triggered during conversion experiences. Jonathan Edwards, the central figure in the early debates about the purpose and credibility of revivals, expressed his anxieties about the emotive quality of revivals in *Some Thoughts Concerning the Present Revival of Religion in New England*. Edwards adhered to the Calvinist tenet that an individual could do nothing to effect saving grace. He could not help but notice, however, the effects that forceful preaching, such as his own "Sinners in the Hands of an Angry God," had on the spiritual progress of his congregants. Sermons that vividly described the horrific sufferings that sinners would endure eternally in hell clearly aroused deep convictions and concerns among his listeners about the spiritual state of their souls. The embodied responses to this and other revivalists' preaching through moans, cries, wringing of hands, and dramatic bodily gestures of fear and anxiety provided physical evidence that the sermons affected the listeners. Edwards perceived that the preaching stirred sinners to pay closer attention to the state of their souls, but the preaching, he reasoned, could not inspire individuals to attain grace through any merit or work of their own.

The dramatic response to his preaching that Edwards observed in his eighteenth-century Northampton church he believed signaled the dawning of this new age. He, like his Puritan predecessors, envisioned America as the site for God's fulfillment of biblical prophecies. Edwards and his students at Yale promoted a postmillennial vision in which they saw a protracted battle occurring on earth between the forces of good and evil that ultimately would result in the triumph of good and the inauguration of a Golden Age. According to this theological perspective, the Golden Age, while spiritually driven, would occur on the physical earth and transform both people and the world. The emotional responses to his preaching that he witnessed confirmed his suspicion that the millennium was at hand and that the redemption of the world had begun in Northampton, Massachusetts. Those who agreed with Edwards were labeled New Lights and tended to emphasize human agency and missionary action to help bring about a new age. Although they believed that ultimately God controlled human history, New Lights also preached that God acted through the church. While Old Lights cautioned against these evangelical tendencies that seemed to lead to self-interest, New Lights—later called New Divinity men under the theological reworking of one of Edwards's students, Samuel Hopkins—walked a thin line between a traditional Calvinist theology of human depravity and God's sovereignty and an evangelical theology that promoted "disinterested benevolence" as a characteristic sign of a regenerate soul. To achieve this spiritual goal, one needed to sacrifice all worldly comforts for the salvation of others. Self-interest had to be erased to achieve true Christian virtue. Within this theological context, the missionary exemplified the most radical form of "disinterested benevolence."

While the increasingly popular New Divinity movement seemed a liberalizing tendency to the traditional Calvinists, the New Divinity clergy espoused a thoroughly conservative social agenda in comparison to the more recent religious movements that were emerging at this time. New Divinity men affirmed the Puritan past and the commitment to a community gathered around shared moral values. Missionary work was one element of a larger reform formula to produce a moral nation. The six clergy and six laymen who were elected trustees of the Connecticut Missionary Society in 1798 counted themselves among the most politically and economically influential of the New Divinity men. All twelve officers came from the ranks of leading Connecticut citizens and five of the trustees—Jonathan Brace, Jonathan Davenport, Roger Newberry, Hemen Swift, and Jonathan Treadwell—held positions in the Federalist Connecticut government.[46] Most of the missionaries hired by the Connecticut Missionary Society also were followers of Edwards and the New Divinity movement. These men, with their religious and cultural roots in Puritanism, viewed the nation as suffering a moral declension in which they sounded a call to return to a purer religious and communal beginning. The problem with this view was that the Plan of Union missionaries dispatched to frontier communities found competition from missionaries of other denominations, including Methodists, Baptists, and Universalists—

missionaries who also sought to save the nation through their own evangelistic efforts. The greater challenge for Plan of Union missionaries, however, was to instill a sense of community by re-creating a Puritan ideal among the migrating New England population. For as the physical boundaries of the religious community remained fluid and people moved further away from families, friends, and institutions, the spiritual boundaries also stretched and often snapped.

The Connecticut Missionary Society's approach to missionizing the frontier combined practicality with lofty moral goals. By the turn of the century the western territory appeared to expand daily, and migration from New England increased rapidly. In Connecticut and on the frontier, the missionary society struggled with the growing anti-clerical and anti-authoritarian feelings that emerged in postrevolutionary America. Itinerants from many religious groups canvassed the furthest boundary outposts, as denominations competed first to locate and then to fix religious space.[47] Methodists circuited the frontier efficiently, and other religious groups such as Baptists, Universalists, and Campbellites attracted converts. The Connecticut Missionary Society aimed not only to evangelize the frontier settlers but to do it more effectively than preachers from competing denominations.

Lofty goals, however, do not pay the bills. The Connecticut Missionary Society knew that its vision for extensive western missionary labor could not succeed without a strong financial base, so the trustees petitioned for support from Connecticut's General Assembly and were granted an annual statewide collection for their cause. The society continued to send missionaries on four- to six-month itinerating tours, but with the increase in funds and state support they pushed missionaries further west for extended periods of time, usually one year. The first missionaries to travel to settlements in Pennsylvania reported immediately that a greater effort should be exerted to meet the frontier's spiritual and social needs. The missionaries, however, were not the only easterners to voice concerns about the population on the frontier. By 1800 the Connecticut Land Company recognized that a strong missionary presence served as an additional incentive for Connecticut buyers interested in western lands. The Land Company's anxiety over poor land sales and its promotion of the Western Reserve as "New Connecticut" spurred it to request that the missionary society send Congregational missionaries to that region. For its part, the missionary society fostered an image of a particular kind of community that fused landscape and morality, much like an "ideal" New England town.

"Sprightly towns" and "numerous churches which gem the whole landscape": Spatial Nostalgia

To construct mentally a typical New England town in the Western Reserve, the Connecticut Missionary Society trustees conjured a visual image of a central green with a church and house lots around its edges. Their imaginations held fast to this symbolic landscape that combined order, morality, family, and community even though few New England villages in the seventeenth century or in the nineteenth century replicated that form.[48] This idealized vision of New England focused on fertile, developed areas like the Connecticut River Valley. Connecticut Missionary Society trustee and Yale president Timothy Dwight, for example, described the pleasing view of the Connecticut River Valley in his *Travels in New England and New York*, noting that "a perfect neatness and brilliancy is everywhere diffused." Dotted throughout the ordered landscape were "sprightly towns" and "numerous churches which gem the whole landscape." Historian J. B. Jackson regards Dwight's relationship to the landscape as specifically religious. Jackson argues that "perfection or completeness resided not in the landscape itself, but in the spirit that had brought it into being and continued to animate it."[49] This spirit exuded from the Connecticut Missionary Society,[50] for which beauty was found in a neat landscape—one, Jackson points out, that reflected the moral or ethical perfection to which all its inhabitants presumably aspired. To order the space, the Land Company utilized the American grid survey to shape the landscape into straight lines and angles. In a similar vein, the missionary society downplayed religious and regional diversity by emphasizing the supposed cultural homogeneity of western settlers. An ordered landscape represented spiritual unity.

But spiritual union did not necessarily signify cultural homogeneity. Seventeenth-century Puritans covenanted together through theological beliefs for mutual protection against the wilderness, but they had emigrated from different regions of England, mostly commercial centers in the South and East, carrying these regional customs and practices to New England. Just as Puritan New England always contained dissenting religious views, the built landscape of homes and public buildings also reflected regional distinctions. David Grayson Allen demonstrates that Puritans held on to English regional particularities in architecture and agricultural practices even after the social and economic reasons dissipated for these particular formulations in New England. Furthermore, although most Puritan towns replicated English towns as an open-field village, an incorporated borough, or an enclosed farm, diversity existed even within those three categories.[51] Nevertheless, in the midst of this visual diversity, the desire for the paradigmatic seventeenth-century New England village still fired the imagination of nineteenth-century New Englanders.[52]

The vision articulated by Timothy Dwight of "sprightly towns" found the ideal cartographic representation in James Wadsworth's 1748 "A Plan of the Town of New Haven."[53] Originally surveyed by town planner John Brockett in 1638, New Haven's "nine squares" constitute a cartographic metaphor for the ideal New England village (figure 6).[54] At the town's inception the marketplace was located on the center green, but by the time of William Lyon's 1806 redrawing, the green housed a meetinghouse, court, jail, and schoolhouse. Following English patterns, house lots lined the green, with common arable land beyond the domiciles.[55] This English technique for structuring a town space took on distinct meanings in New England. The primary difference arose from the theological and social agency that inspired Puritans to form communities there. Rather than living in a community because of birth or social and economic obligations, Puritans chose to live in covenant with one another. While the villages and towns of Puritans replicated English surveying formulas, they rejected some rules and maintained a symbolic and structural cohesion that reflected their "New" England lives.[56]

There was, however, social and religious stratification in New England towns. The New Haven map exemplifies the hierarchy through the drawn and written details that accompany it. The size and construction of homes suggest the importance of status within the community. Jared Ingersoll, for example, was a lawyer who lived in Lot 37, one street off the town green, in a two-story home with a chimney, many windows, and an addition to the left side of his house. Not surprisingly, his home is not as grand as that of Yale College president Thomas Clapp, but it is immense compared to Widow Lyon's modest house situated on the green, directly across from the central structure, the meetinghouse. While Ingersoll's large house reflects his economic standing, the widow's home might indicate religious or social prominence. Or its size and site might indicate her ambiguous social position as a propertied woman living outside of a Puritan patriarchal household. In this view, the widow's home might signal social, economic, and religious deviance—a "heterotopic space" on the New Haven map.[57] This is unlikely, however: the widow and her home cannot be

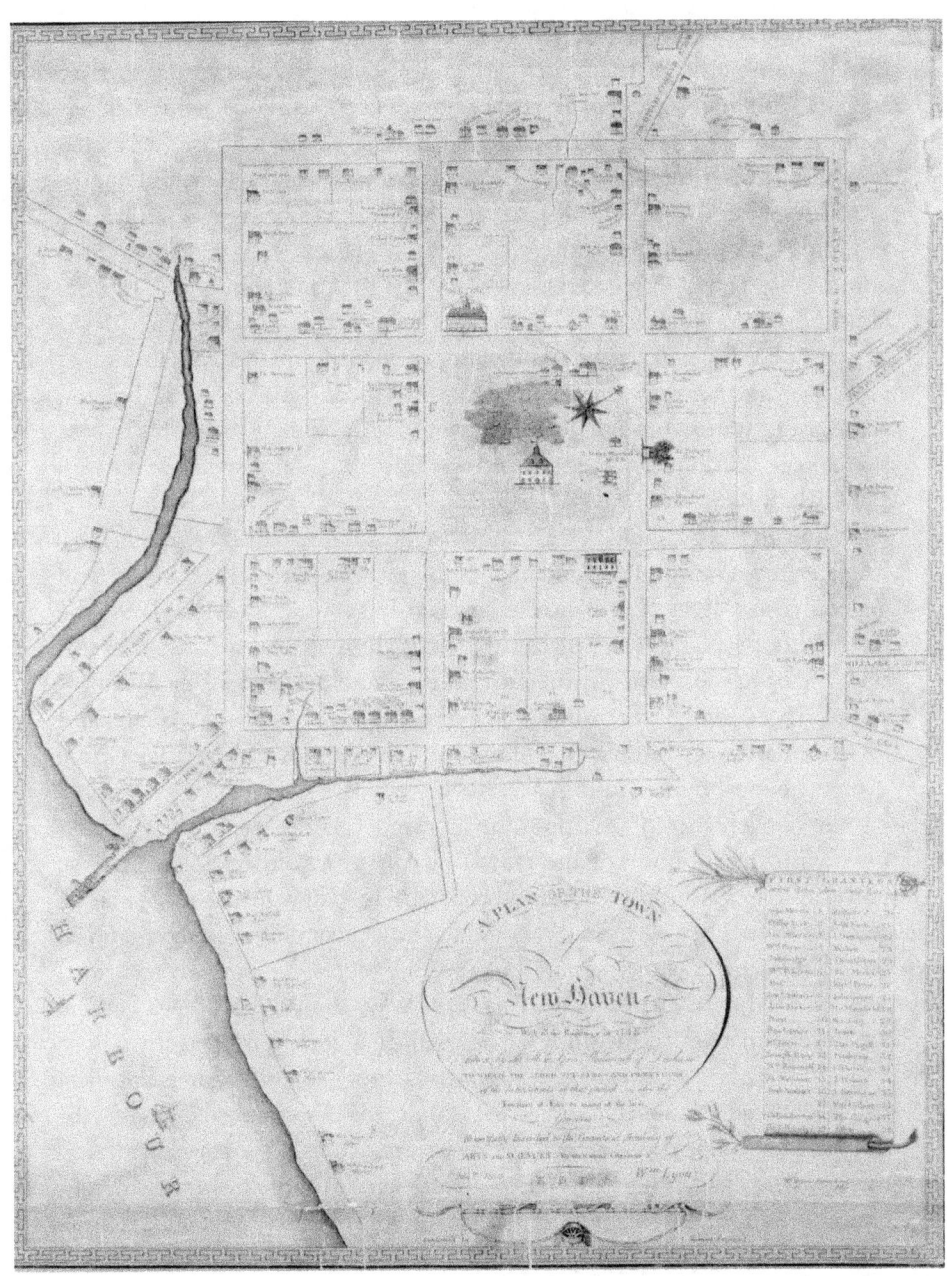

FIGURE 6. James Wadsworth's "A Plan of the Town of New Haven" (1748). This map provides the blueprint for the type of idealized old Connecticut town that surveyors and missionaries attempted to replicate in New Connecticut. Courtesy of Map Collection, Yale University Library, New Haven.

understood as deviant, since she had been married and had suffered the loss of a husband; she therefore held a respectable position within Puritan society. Unlike the siting of the other homes and businesses, which clearly represent Puritan social norms, the site of the widow's house marks her ambiguous position as a single, propertied female residing within a patriarchal social and theological structure. Rather than being hidden on the margins, her home is positioned in the visual center of town, allowing the community an unobstructed view of it and the opportunity to offer her constant care and supervision; this is reflected in the positioning of the structure on the map.[58] The significance of identifying individuals' homes and drawing them to scale extends beyond locating property rights and showcasing status through a decorative art form. The widow, the lawyer, the college president, and the meetinghouse all occupy specific spots on the Puritan social and theological map.

While the New Haven map shows a neat, square survey, most New England towns accommodated geography rather than geometry. The land generally was divided into house lots, cattle ground, and farmland; the largest and best lands were distributed according to wealth, size of family, number of cattle, status in the community, and any other social or economic issue deemed important. Village greens were not always square, and lot boundaries conformed to the natural environment. Nevertheless, the geometric ideal remained in place.[59]

The convergence of the desire to re-create an idealized New England town with the adoption of the 1785 Land Survey Ordinance illustrates the powerful relationship between landscape and ideology. Just as maps can be read as ideological assertions rather than as exact geographic representations, built landscapes such as homes and meetinghouses are similarly inscribed with cultural meanings. There are as many ways to read landscapes as there are to read maps.[60] In his study of eighteenth-century Virginia, Rhys Isaac argued that the space carved out by backwoods Baptists for evangelical revivals altered the social and cultural landscape. In contrast to the established social authority, evangelicals constituted the lower social and economic classes and gathered in alternative spaces to forge a competing religious authority that resulted in a strong political base.[61] William Cronon's study of the ecological impact of the European encounter with Native Americans in colonial New England exemplifies how landscape may be read as simultaneously an arena of power and one of negotiation. Through traveler descriptions, official records, and ecological evidence—such as vegetation, tree growth patterns, and water depositories—Cronon traces the conflicting land practices of Native Americans and Europeans.[62] The landscape is neither passive nor neutral, although often depicted as such. Just as settlers carried their cultural and spatial assumptions west, the landscape holds its own history and meaning. Laurie Maffly-Kipp demonstrates this in her study of California missionaries and their attempts to mold the physical environment to bolster spiritual goals. She states: "As the clergy strove to replicate a familiar religious environment, the fact that they did so in a different setting dictated that their results would diverge from their model."[63] The built landscape that was under construction during this settlement process accommodated all of these readings. The manner in which space was carved represented assertions and disruptions of social order, and its history of being shaped by previous inhabitants as well as its ecological specificity helped to form new and distinct meanings for the missionaries and the settlers.

New Connecticut symbolized moral, spatial, and nostalgic desires. An early map of the county seat, Huron, elegantly displays the inscription of these longings onto the Western Reserve landscape (see figure 7). Promoting sales and missions by tapping into available mental images and longings for a lost New England enabled the members of the Connecticut Land Company and the Connecticut Missionary Society—as well as future settlers—to participate in the reenactment of the creation of a mythic Puritan community. Unfortunately for some immigrants, the moral and spatial desires that demanded a cohesive community clashed with the realities of poor land sales. Although the majority of the Connecticut Land Company proprietors were from Connecticut, they generally sold their lots in the Western Reserve indiscriminately to anyone who could afford to buy. Henry Champion distinguished himself from most proprietors in the care and interest he took in the potential buyers. "I am not pressed to make sales," he wrote to his land agent, Abraham Skinner. "I wish you to sell only when you can obtain a fair and reasonably good price, and to actual settlers only."[64] Champion's stated concern was to fill his property not only with New Englanders but with New England families.[65] Some proprietors sold all their land at once, some held on to their property, anticipating an increase in land sales, and others distributed land among family and friends.[66] Besides the diverse methods used by the proprietors to sell land, their own holdings were scattered throughout the Western Reserve. Unlike old Connecticut, town composition in New Connecticut varied greatly, and in many cases a significant degree of ethnic, regional, and religious diversity existed. In a few towns, such as Tallmadge, Hudson, Austinburg, Burton, and Painesville, the clear majority of inhabitants had emigrated from New England. Not surprisingly, these towns were the first to establish churches and to welcome Plan of Union missionaries.

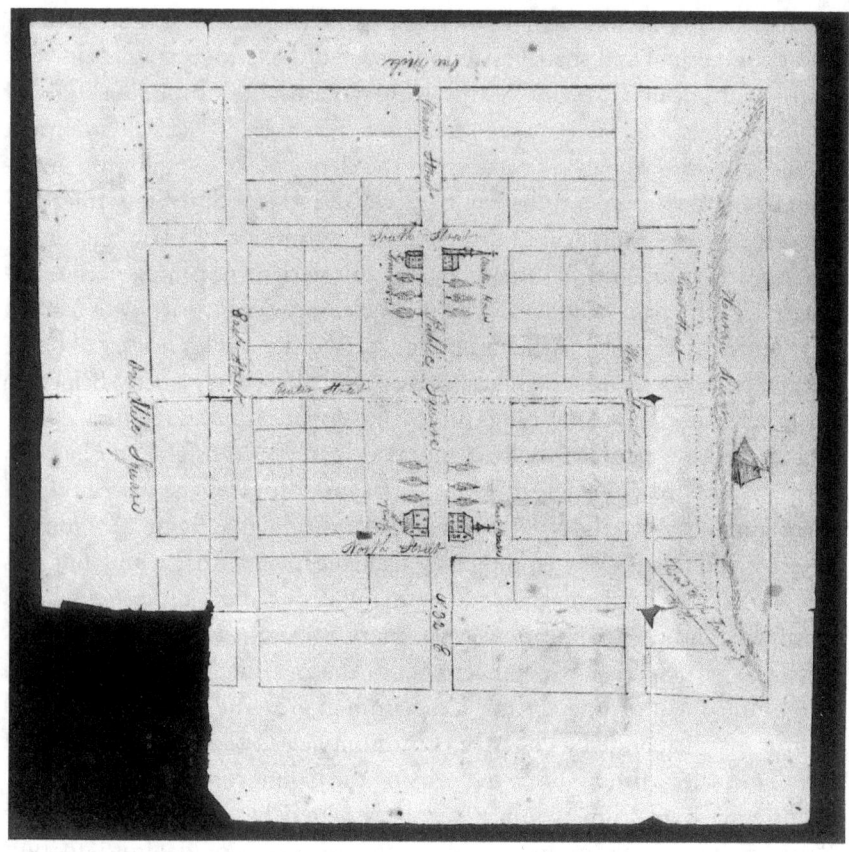

FIGURE 7. Map of county seat, Huron, Ohio. An example of moral mapping that draws in the four pillars of an idealized New England town: meetinghouse, academy, jail, and courthouse. In this map the physical and moral landscape is neatly ordered. Courtesy of the Western Reserve Historical Society, Cleveland.

"The most benevolent designs": Missionary Publications

Just as Western Reserve maps were drawn, circulated, and read in atlases and exploration books, so too were the Connecticut Missionary Society's plans for the region composed and distributed through its printed publications. Three printed forums disseminated the society's agenda for the Western Reserve. The missionary society board of trustees published an annual address that included a *Narrative on the Subject of Missions with a Statement of Funds* that detailed the highlights of the mission year, including excerpts from missionary letters, a list of books sent to frontier inhabitants, and a general plea from the trustees for contributions. The *Connecticut Evangelical Magazine*, published monthly and edited by Protestant clergy involved with the missionary society, printed excerpts from missionary letters and from the annual *Narrative of Missions*. The missionary society also issued and distributed occasional pamphlets, such as an *Address to the Inhabitants of the New Settlements* (1795, 1803, and 1817) and *A Summary of Christian Doctrine and Practice: Designed Especially for the Use of the People in New Settlements of the United States of America* (1804). The home society's publications were devoted to Protestant home missions particularly where Connecticut emigrants settled, and the society relied on missionary correspondences to provide information about frontier religious life for each edition.

New Connecticut provided good copy. "A district of the first importance," it received a great deal of attention from the trustees, primarily because of the number of Connecticut natives who relocated there.[67] Each year, an increasingly larger portion of the missionary society's annual budget, therefore, was dedicated to evangelizing that region. The Western Reserve missionaries' reports were mined for appropriate material that would both legitimate the missionary endeavor and inspire donors to continue to support the home society. These publications provided the reading public with the Connecticut Missionary Society's view of its successes and failures on the frontier. Like a mapmaker who accentuates some areas and diminishes others, the missionary society carefully chose its material to portray the home mission in particular colors.

Missionary letters printed in the *Connecticut Evangelical Magazine* and the society's annual *Narrative of Missions* offered the public firsthand descriptions of life and opportunities in frontier settlements. Besides spreading the gospel, the missionaries served as land prospectors, fundraisers, and foreign correspondents who described the western landscape through Connecticut eyes. In the letters one finds almost as much information about the crops, timber, and soil as about missionary activity. One missionary, for example, wrote glowingly in his 1801 missionary report about the material as well as spiritual features of the region: "Respectable people are flocking in from every quarter. The crops at this season afford the most flattering prospects. A remarkable degree of health prevails throughout the country. The friendly disposition of the Indians banishes all apprehensions of danger from them. If the Lord should make this wilderness as a watered garden by planting and nourishing churches in it, there would be no place more desirable to live in."[68] Seeds sown by humans flourished in this fertile land; now all that was needed was the hand of God to till and plant the moral soil. A missionary's letter in these publications served more purposes than simply reporting saved souls. It forged a link between the missionary and his sponsors; it accounted for the missionary's progress as a type of long-distance time sheet; it described foreign places; it assessed land quality for prospective settlers; and it judged the status and potential of future missionary endeavors.

Similar to the relationship between land surveyors and their maps, missionaries walked religiously uncharted territory and organized their experiences into a narrative that made sense to their readers back home. The Plan of Union missionaries embarked on a continual process of translating their frontier experiences with the expectations of the reading public and the sponsoring society. The missionary's letters, therefore, proved an essential source of information for the home society. Not all of the information in missionaries' letters made it past the editors' desks and into the printed publications. Many letters were lengthy and repetitive; they required editing to fit within the space limits of the journals. In the *Connecticut Evangelical Magazine*, the editor typically lifted quotes from a variety of missionary letters that summarized their efforts in different regions. While spatial constraints such as the number of published pages limited the length of missionary narratives, it was the motivations and goals of the missionary society that ultimately dictated the content of the magazine (figure 8).

The first few publications of the *Connecticut Evangelical Magazine* described missionary efforts on the frontier as a struggle for spatial and moral control of desolate regions. The missionaries not only had to navigate a foreign landscape; they also had to contend with unruly settlers. Neither the missionaries nor the settlers were spared the difficult journey

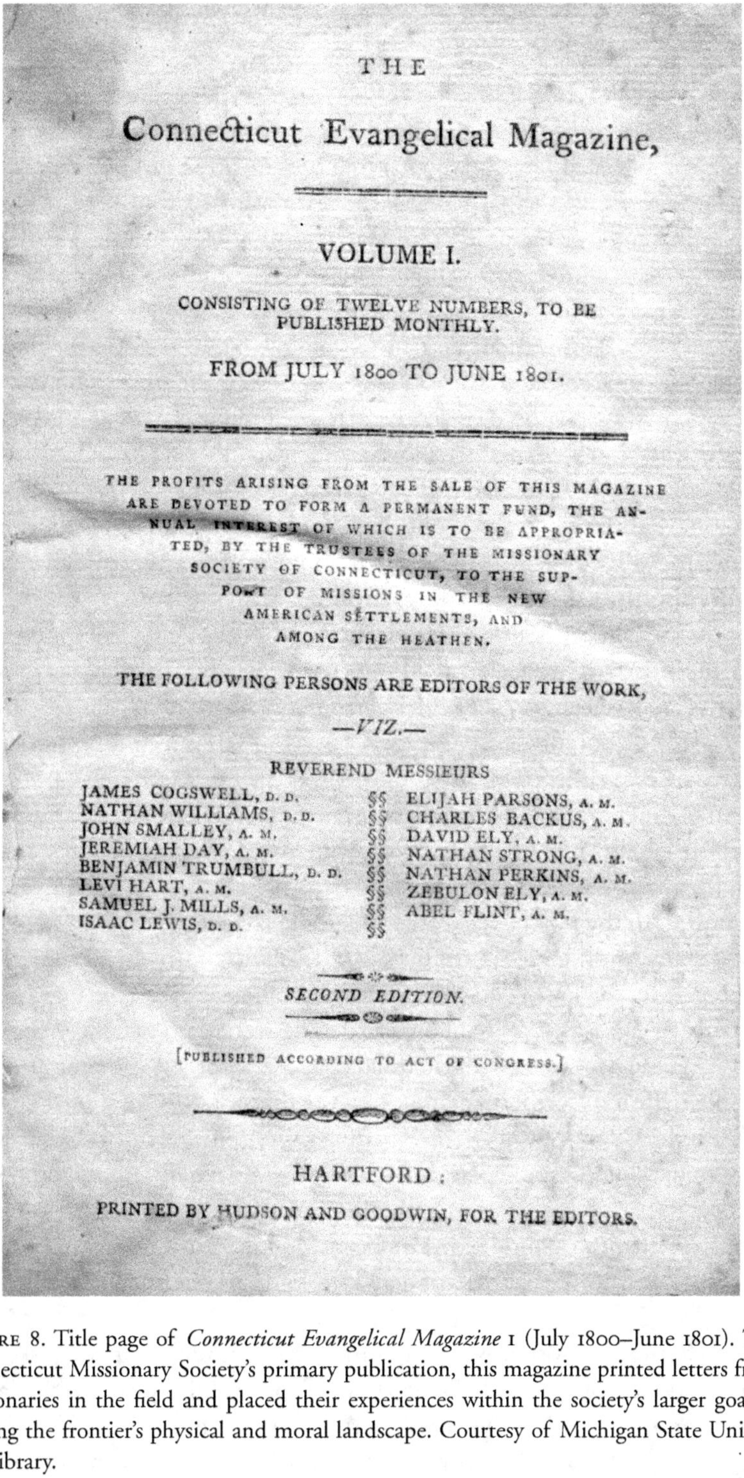

THE
Connecticut Evangelical Magazine,

VOLUME I.

CONSISTING OF TWELVE NUMBERS, TO BE PUBLISHED MONTHLY.

FROM JULY 1800 TO JUNE 1801.

THE PROFITS ARISING FROM THE SALE OF THIS MAGAZINE ARE DEVOTED TO FORM A PERMANENT FUND, THE ANNUAL INTEREST OF WHICH IS TO BE APPROPRIATED, BY THE TRUSTEES OF THE MISSIONARY SOCIETY OF CONNECTICUT, TO THE SUPPORT OF MISSIONS IN THE NEW AMERICAN SETTLEMENTS, AND AMONG THE HEATHEN.

THE FOLLOWING PERSONS ARE EDITORS OF THE WORK,

—VIZ.—

REVEREND MESSIEURS

JAMES COGSWELL, D. D.
NATHAN WILLIAMS, D. D.
JOHN SMALLEY, A. M.
JEREMIAH DAY, A. M.
BENJAMIN TRUMBULL, D. D.
LEVI HART, A. M.
SAMUEL J. MILLS, A. M.
ISAAC LEWIS, D. D.

ELIJAH PARSONS, A. M.
CHARLES BACKUS, A. M.
DAVID ELY, A. M.
NATHAN STRONG, A. M.
NATHAN PERKINS, A. M.
ZEBULON ELY, A. M.
ABEL FLINT, A. M.

SECOND EDITION.

[PUBLISHED ACCORDING TO ACT OF CONGRESS.]

HARTFORD:
PRINTED BY HUDSON AND GOODWIN, FOR THE EDITORS.

FIGURE 8. Title page of *Connecticut Evangelical Magazine* 1 (July 1800–June 1801). The Connecticut Missionary Society's primary publication, this magazine printed letters from missionaries in the field and placed their experiences within the society's larger goal of shaping the frontier's physical and moral landscape. Courtesy of Michigan State University Library.

to the Western Reserve or the everyday hardships of life on the frontier. Along with the treacherous roads, dangerous wild animals, violent rivers, and miserable weather, the western inhabitants often did not welcome the missionaries. This was particularly depressing for Plan of Union missionaries who had hoped to at least find favor among New England settlers. An *unpublished* letter to the missionary society typified the resistance that missionaries faced from Connecticut emigrants. "There are here a number who have left Connecticut desiring to be free from its good regulations," wrote missionary Jonathan Lesslie. "Some of these are in almost every town, + they are opposed to the regular settlement of clergy."[69] Although Lesslie was appalled to discover this resentment, the Connecticut Missionary Society trustees had been alerted to these sentiments during earlier missionary tours in Vermont and New York. Their careful response to the predicament is evident in the printed addresses that were aimed as much at the disgruntled inhabitants of frontier settlements as at the society's supporters. The trustees insisted in their publications that despite rumors that the missionaries were meddling in settlers' affairs, they came to the settlers "with the most benevolent *designs*."[70] Editors of the *Connecticut Evangelical Magazine* acknowledged a level of dissent among settlers but assured the reading public that "notwithstanding the many unfavorable reports which are circulated respecting the feelings of inhabitants of the new settlements towards missionaries" many settlers appreciated the missionaries and expressed thanks to their benefactors in Connecticut.[71] According to the missionaries, many settlers lacked the time and energy to devote to spending an afternoon in Bible instruction when crops needed to be planted or harvested. Missionary Abraham Scott gave up on weekday preaching in the fall of 1807, "as people were then generally very busy and also very backward with their harvest, by reason of frequent rains during the season."[72] Other recent emigrants did not much care for clergy in either old or New Connecticut. The magazine's editors expressed little surprise in hearing these challenges to their mission. Their religious and social goals for frontier communities represented an extension of the control they struggled to maintain within Connecticut. A missionary's report of a friendly reception by settlers signaled not only moral but social order (figure 9).[73]

Spreading the gospel was not simply a matter of saving souls for the Connecticut Missionary Society; it encompassed all aspects of social stability and moral order. The missionary narratives and editorials written in the society's publications wove the theme of religious and political insta-

QUESTIONS.

1. CAN a good man be unwilling that the great, good, wise, just, merciful Jehovah should so plan his operations concerning all creatures, actions and things, as to answer his benevolent purposes?

2. Can the eternal purposes of God be hurtful in the end?

3. Are we afraid that infinite perfection will have too much influence in the affairs of this world?

MIKROS.

If mankind are totally depraved and naturally opposed to God, and are entirely dependent on him to change their hearts, wherein is the propriety of directing them to repent and love God?   M.

MESSRS. EDITORS,

A READER of your useful Magazine wishes for an explanation of Hebrews vi. 4—6. What is that from which if a man fall it is impossible to renew him again to repentance? Can a man partake of the common influences of the spirit of God and his backsliding be fatal? When may a man know that he is under that awful sentence?

AN explanation is desired, by a correspondent, of 1 Corinthians xv. 29, and also of 1 Peter iv. 6.

Religious Intelligence.

MISSIONARIES.

Extract of a Letter from the Rev. Joseph Badger Missionary to New Connecticut, dated Young's town, January 8, 1801.

"AFTER a long and tedious journey I arrived at No. 2, on the 1st Range the 30th ult. I went on foot and led my horse nearly 200 miles—the travelling being excessively bad, owing principally to the season of the year.

"After passing the mountains and arriving in Washington county, I passed through and near to, about twenty Presbyterian congregations, where for two years past, there has been in the most of them a pretty general serious awakening. God has been pleased to carry on his work in convincing and hopefully converting many hundred souls in these parts. The awakening extended nearly 80 miles from east to west. A number of new settlements north-west of the Ohio, extending nearly to the eastern bounds of New Connecticut, were visited in a special manner, and there yet remain many instances of serious awakening. By what I can learn, both from ministers and people, the work has been generally free from enthusiasm; but powerful in humbling the proud heart, and in bringing it to be swallowed up in God's will.

"God has done great things for his church in this country. About six years ago there were several young men hopefully brought into Christ's kingdom. By the advice of a few pious and learned ministers, a number gave themselves to study. An academic school was established, where the languages and arts and sciences are thoroughly taught. There have been sixteen or seventeen very worthy and pious ministers raised up in this school. It was thought by many, when they saw such a number entering on the ministry, there would be no places for them; but the late awakening has opened places enough. The settlements are making with such rapidity and so many congregations forming, that

FIGURE 9. *Connecticut Evangelical Magazine* 1 (March 1801): 358. Missionary Joseph Badger's first letter published in the *Connecticut Evangelical Magazine*. Courtesy of Michigan State University Library.

bility throughout accounts of missionary labor with cautionary or didactic tales. The frontier settlers were routinely described as being both spatially and morally disorderly. The editors stressed the importance of instituting religious practices as a concrete approach to re-creating their vision of Connecticut religion and society on the frontier, and they interpreted any opposition to this endeavor as subversive not only of religious order but also of social and political stability.

For the Connecticut Missionary Society trustees, dissent sprang up on the periphery of controlled space. The editors generally rebutted hostility to their missions by referring to the growing number of Connecticut natives inhabiting the frontier, thereby hoping to dispel the notion that dissent arose from within. From their perspective, the antidote for this disease required a strong infusion of like-minded people. The flaw in their logic stemmed from the conviction that Connecticut emigrants were religiously and politically united and that the majority of Western Reserve settlers came from Connecticut. Although the home missionary society envisioned a religiously homogeneous region, the Western Reserve proved to be a fertile mission ground for various itinerant preachers and rival religious movements.[74] In 1819 missionary Simeon Woodruff preached a Sabbath sermon in Palmyra and reported that besides Methodists and Universalists there was also a Baptist church "divided into two, so that there are sometimes 4 meetings in the town on the same day."[75] Offering alternative religious options, these "dissenters" simultaneously evinced power by their presence on the land and by their challenge to the Plan of Union missionaries.

Religious "dissenters" threatened not only the settlers' souls but also the future welfare of the nation. The Connecticut Missionary Society's strategy to promote stability on the frontier targeted political and religious dissenters or "sectarianism." All twelve of the trustees, six clergymen and six laymen, believed that the maintenance of the established social order was inextricably linked to moral order. The missionary society saw its task as comprehensive and urgent. Fueled by a growing anxiety over the increased presence of preachers from competing denominations, the Connecticut Missionary Society urged Connecticut citizens to contribute to the missionary cause. Missionary Harvey Coe confirmed this need and reasoned that sending more missionaries to the Western Reserve would prevent the spread of religious sectarianism. The dearth of missionaries, he wrote, "will have the tendency to invite in preachers of other denominations which are numerous in this country, and many of them very erroneous."[76]

The primary way to maintain order, according to the missionary society, was to fight sectarianism by establishing religious institutions.

In the 1802 *Narrative of Missions*, the trustees stressed the importance of their endeavor by stating: "The civil and political well-being of societies no less than the present and future happiness of individuals depends much on religious institutions."[77] Among the missionary society's chief concerns was the western settlers' virtual invisibility from "the public eye." To minimize the opportunity for lawlessness and corruption, the society urged the settlers to establish civil and religious institutions.[78] It counseled emigrants to replicate Connecticut society in all aspects, particularly observing the Sabbath through public and private worship, forming churches, and encouraging missionaries to preach. The trustees viewed their actions regarding western settlements as setting the precedent for future generations, and they warned Connecticut residents that the moral and national future depended upon quick action on the part of the Plan of Union missionaries. While politics, finances, and the establishment of denominational strongholds on the frontier framed the missionary society's efforts, the moral and religious plight of the settlers guided its vision.

This vision focused on a particular understanding of landscape. Basic assumptions about the relationship between spatial and moral order provide a context for the Connecticut Missionary Society's conception of its work in frontier space. There were theological traditions that linked moral action to the landscape and conditioned the sponsoring society to have certain expectations of missionary labor on the frontier. Like their Puritan predecessors, Plan of Union missionaries and the trustees relied on biblical images describing the frontier as Zion, Eden, a garden, the wilderness, and a desert, calling to mind scriptural references regarding humanity's proper relationship to the natural world.[79] Also like the Puritans, the missionaries needed to balance their theological convictions of themselves as inheritors of the Promised Land and their identities as pilgrims still in exile in that same land. These contradictory biblical images and self-identities nevertheless worked together to reinforce the readers' belief in God's plan for creation and humanity's role in sacred history. In some instances the frontier resembled the desert; it was a place of isolation and temptation. In other instances the frontier was transformed into a garden by the cultivating hands of missionaries. But the most important chapter of sacred history recalled through these environmental metaphors was American national history. Pilgrims had peopled the wilderness in biblical and national history following the prophecies that Zion would one day be restored. Calling themselves Israelites, the New England Puritans articulated their purpose for inhabiting the wilderness by emphasizing the millennial hope of building Zion in the New World. This notion that the American landscape provided both hardship and redemption for individuals and the nation continued into the nineteenth century. Surrounded by biblical imagery, the work of the missionaries on the frontier became firmly situated in a sacred and national history.

In New Connecticut, physical geography was symbolic geography, representing both scriptural and national desires. The depiction of the Western Reserve as Zion illustrates the joining together of biblical and national themes. Zion recalled the Israelites' exile in Babylon and their nostalgic desire to return to their homeland. In this biblical account the Israelites returned to Zion only after they repented for their transgressions in a foreign land and then were redeemed by God; and the call to build Zion that was repeated in the missionary publications echoes the dual scriptural themes of repentance and redemption. After an account of a successful missionary season in which "the Lord hath been remarkably building up Zion and appearing in his glory," the editors of the *Connecticut Evangelical Magazine* noted that settlers showed serious attention to religious matters. This occasion proved that God continued to act in history.[80] For the Connecticut Missionary Society the frontier was a battleground, a field on which to fight competing religious groups. Further, it provided a second chance to cleanse the nation of its collective sins and build a godly community following the Puritan blueprint. Building Zion connected nineteenth-century missionaries to seventeenth-century pilgrims who sought to construct a godly community in the wilderness. Zion represented the goal of returning to a perfect biblical place of religious and political freedom; it also signified the Connecticut Missionary Society's nostalgic desire to re-create an idealized version of Puritan New England on the frontier.

The metaphorical image of the frontier as a garden, inspired by biblical injunctions of stewardship of or dominion over the landscape, found expression in spatial and moral ordering of the Western Reserve. Sometimes the missionary society viewed and promoted the frontier as Eden, a garden paradise apart from the rest of the world. At other times it became a garden by God's grace and missionary cultivation. An excerpted letter from missionary John Seward, printed in a *Narrative of Missions*, echoes this theme: "All who feel interested in the prosperity of Zion will rejoice to hear that the wilderness is become like Eden, and the desert like a garden of the Lord."[81] Missionaries picked up this metaphor and tended to describe themselves as gardeners or farmers cultivating spiritual fields. Jonathan Lesslie explains that where a missionary settles, "he from the rude state of nature is an instrument of clearing and fencing a garden for the Lord."[82] Before hearing the missionary preach, the settlers resembled nature in its "rude state." According to Lesslie, settlers as well as the land need to be "cleared" and "fenced"; no longer a disorganized "landscape," the orderly settler is now a productive member of the Lord's garden. Missionaries used what to them was a positive agricultural metaphor even when their optimism failed. "It is a dismal time in this quarter," wrote John Seward in the fall of 1812. "Our fields + farms lie unfenced, untilled, unsaved."[83] Like Lesslie, Seward linked salvation to a specific type of land use that fenced and cultivated farms. Fields, like souls, needed strong boundaries and intervention through cultivation.

Creating and maintaining moral boundaries were at the root of these scriptural metaphors of garden and Eden. The missionaries' and their sponsoring society's desires to claim and define the frontier space were expressed by the moral imperative of landscape cultivation as a first step in the creation of a godly community. This relationship that was expressed by John Seward in terms of untilled and unsaved fields proved to be more than a helpful metaphor for "harvesting" souls. The trustees believed that improving the wilderness involved both physical cultivation and moral cultivation; further, they believed that these two activities must work together: "The immense *material* wilderness is rapidly falling by the cultivator's hand. Where is the friend of Christ who can view with indifference not the obligation only, but the desirableness of doing whatever is commanded for the effectual subjugation of the vast *moral* wilderness?"[84] The home society did not simply employ environmental metaphors to articulate its designs on the region; the trustees understood that there was a direct link between an ordered landscape and a moral community. The physical layout of roads and towns, and later the construction of churches and homes, provided a litmus test for determining the habits and morals of the frontier settlers. The missionary society believed that the construction of orderly towns promoted and evidenced a moral community. Conversely, towns that were planned in a disorderly fashion indicated to the missionaries that the settlers were likely either to break religious bonds or to become simply "irreligious." Shaping the frontier space became a moral agenda for land surveyors, missionaries, and some settlers and a moral barometer for the Connecticut Missionary Society.

Describing New Connecticut as the wilderness or a desert evoked biblical images of the Israelites' wandering before entering Canaan and of Jesus' forty days spent in the wilderness. Both scriptural stories refer to the wilderness as a place that tempted followers to turn away from God. The Connecticut Missionary Society provided ample evidence for its readers that the frontier wilderness was a haven for evil forces that sought to subvert missionary endeavors. The new settlements were plagued constantly by "false teachers" and all stripes of opponents. "Naturally," the editors commented in 1811, "all mankind love to embrace those delusions, by which, 'with cunning craftiness' such teachers 'lie in wait to deceive.'"[85] Even in places where missionaries found serious attention to their preaching and ministrations, the society noted that "errorists of various kinds crowd into places where seriousness prevails, to turn people away from the truth."[86] The most vulnerable places, according to the society, were located on the periphery of the Western Reserve. Missionary letters published by the sponsoring society attested to the fact that settlements on the boundaries of the Western Reserve were spatially disorganized and generally immoral. After a few years as a missionary to New Connecticut, Abraham Scott branched out to Belmont, Columbiana, and Jefferson Counties, south of the border. There he found "the general state of people deplorable, as to religion. They have little preaching of gospel truth. The Sabbath is, consequently, disregarded and profaned."[87] Scott draws here a connection between hearing preaching and practicing moral behavior, in this instance, observing the Sabbath. For those readers who worried about the effectiveness of missionary labor on the frontier, this example of the breakdown of society, beginning with neglecting the "habit" of observing the Sabbath, might have encouraged their financial commitment to missions even when missionary field reports sounded bleak. Missionary Jonathan Lesslie echoed this connection two years later. In the 1814 *Narrative of Missions* the trustees summarized his missionary report: "In those towns, where missionaries have been most generally received, the state of society was the best. . . . On the other hand, good habits were not acquired where the gospel and its institutions were lightly esteemed; and if they ever existed, they became soon extinguished."[88] People who did not welcome Plan of Union missionaries were unlikely to practice "good Habits." Transforming the wilderness required constant vigilance on the part of missionaries and settlers to instill "good habits" and to fight the temptations they faced so far from watchful Connecticut society.

The missionary society also combined metaphors of wilderness and desert to emphasize the isolation and distance between settlers and their friends and families in the East when seeking funds to continue missionary labor. In the *Connecticut Evangelical Magazine* of March 1805, the society wrote an extensive summary of the good effects of charitable donations in the new settlements. The gifts, they claimed, had been received gratefully, and through God's grace and missionary labor, "the wilderness and the solitary place have been made glad, and the desert hath blossomed as a rose."[89]

So, too, the editors combined the metaphor of children and wilderness to describe the frontier settlers and portray the society or its emissaries as protective mothers. In a plea for donations in 1812, the editors wrote that settlements that have benefited from missionary labor "have been so far nursed by the Missionary Society" and have responded favorably to that "spiritual food." The vulnerable "infants" were dependent on the home society for basic sustenance. Therefore, "without the fostering care of this Society they must despond"; they would starve without support.[90] While missionaries made valiant efforts, these souls might soon languish in the wilderness and be left to plead "come over and help us" in vain.[91] Souls crying out in the wilderness needed to be answered by charitable donations. The impulse to missionize wilderness "children," the society reminded its readers, was not only a part of their sacred history but also their state's history. Recalling the colonial Connecticut missionaries who attempted to convert Native Americans, the trustees exclaimed, "Such has been the character of the people of this State since the days of our fathers, who immigrated here, and multitudes have been enriched with gospel blessings through their benevolence."[92] The Connecticut Missionary Society, settlers, and donors were gathered into a large family through an illustrious common ancestry. "Maternal" instincts demanded that the home society and the donors care for their vulnerable "children."

The wilderness also called to mind the Puritans' experiences in which the landscape held both promise and peril. The New World wilderness provided a place for God to unfold the divine plan but also furnished a redemptive landscape for the suffering of true Christians. In both instances, labeling the frontier a wilderness recalled the Puritan experiment and joined the society's donors and the settlers through common memory and spiritual ancestry. In all of the printed publications, the Connecticut Missionary Society urged the frontier settlers and the New England subscribers to remember their attachments to each other as "brethren and friends." This bond was described as familial, institutional, and moral. "With some of you we have been well acquainted. Once you were our neighbors and counsellors. You belonged to our congregations; you were members of our churches."[93] The missionary society also appealed to an attachment through "common origin" in New England sacred history. "Our fathers were your fathers. They were the pious pilgrims, who first came to New England, and laid the foundations of all our invaluable civil, literary, moral, and religious institutions."[94] The settlers were described as new pilgrims who "brought with them an attachment to those religious institutions" found in Connecticut but needed help laying down these invaluable foundations in their new settlements.[95] Surely, the society reasoned with eastern donors, they deserved the advantages of similar institutions as they peopled the wilderness. In time, the society reminded western settlers, abiding by these institutions would improve their condition and ultimately further the kingdom of God. The settlers and the subscribers to the Connecticut Missionary Society's literature were compelled to support the home mission because of the ties that bound them together.

This strong attachment was based not only on a shared past but also on a common future, which remained in jeopardy. In an 1803 *Address to the Inhabitants of the New Settlements* the society warned frontier settlers that they had reached "a most important juncture" and that their actions would affect not only themselves but also future generations.[96] This particular publication focused on family government as the cornerstone of a godly society. The missionary society urged settlers to maintain family religion by sanctifying the Sabbath, supporting public worship, reading Scripture, refraining from moral vices, and instilling all of these habits in children. The problem, the missionary society warned, was the lack of moral surveillance in frontier communities. The frontier settlers were living beyond the watchful gaze of eastern society, and the missionary society feared that without public scrutiny, the inhabitants would fall into immoral beliefs and practices.

Fourteen years later another published *Address to Emigrants* repeated this warning: "How different are the circumstances of people, the moment that they find themselves planted down, almost alone in the wilderness, and perhaps a thousand miles from all their former acquaintance. *Here no public eye sees them.*"[97] People who maintained sobriety and lived lives of upstanding character among the watchful eyes of friends in New England could easily be reduced to unruly beings hidden from the view and rules of home. "This we are certain," the society asserted, "is not idle theory. Human depravity is ever impatient of restraints. It requires strong barriers, to keep it within any tolerable bounds."[98] After comparing the frontier inhabitants' wilderness plight to those of the Israelites and the Pilgrims, and detailing the steps to the creation of a moral society, the society forged a conceptual link between morality and landscape. "The early habits of a people," the society warned, "are like the first roads in a new country, which it is extremely inconvenient to alter, after the inhabitants have long been accustomed to them, and have built their houses and shaped their farms by them."[99] According to the missionary society, the maintenance of moral habits needed to be re-created on the frontier to ensure moral and social order in the present and future. Habits, like roads, were nearly impossible to alter once they had been established.

The emigrants who heeded the Connecticut Missionary Society's warnings found themselves in a precarious position, burdened with the hopes and fears of an entire community. While some frontier settlers sought new lives in the western settlements, many more hoped to maintain a strong connection to their eastern homes. The Western Reserve—as Zion, Eden, a garden, the wilderness, or a desert—was a region that accommodated the nostalgia for an idealized biblical and national past and the desire for an imagined future. Both the Connecticut Land Company and the Connecticut Missionary Society participated in ordering the landscape to realize this vision. The land surveyors and missionaries found themselves in the awkward position of matching these desires to the realities they observed firsthand in frontier space. Unfortunately for the society, the blueprint for a morally ordered society in the wilderness, drawn so vividly in its imagination, could never be successfully inscribed on the frontier.

For almost twenty years Connecticut's leading citizens had organized the mapping, sale, and settlement of the Western Reserve, and during those years they read and heard mostly discouraging reports from that quarter. Settlement moved more slowly than predicted, and individuals appeared scattered throughout the wilderness. The first group of missionaries sent to the Western Reserve complained of disease, poverty, extreme conditions, and a general disinterest among settlers in religious matters. Describing his experience as a missionary among Connecticut emigrants in New Connecticut, Ezekiel J. Chapman wrote: "A great degree of stupidity prevailed, and but little encouragement was given to missionaries."[100] The editors of the *Connecticut Evangelical Magazine* redacted Chapman's and the other missionaries' disappointment to shape the public vision of the Western Reserve as a New Connecticut. The actual encounter with the natural and moral landscape of the Western Reserve, of course, made a different impression.

From the institutional documents examined here, it would seem that the imprint of New England values onto the landscape was a foregone conclusion and that this grand endeavor would end in success. Like a house of cards, however, this imaginary structure conjured in the minds of the land company and missionary society members remained vulnerable to the slightest pressure of "reality." Both the people who entered the region and the landscape itself resisted such strict maps. In chapter 2 the focus moves from the institutional preparation of the "New Connecticut" to the reality of missionary life in the Western Reserve. In pursuing this topic, I focus on the figure of the Plan of Union missionary. Here the disjuncture will become apparent between the "New Connecticut" as mapped by the Connecticut Missionary Society and the missionaries' experiences that led to changing the conceptions of the missionary "self."

Over the next few decades of the nineteenth century, the Western Reserve would become a home for many more New England emigrants seeking a New Connecticut or a Garden of Eden. These individuals, however, would rely on tools other than those employed by the land company and the missionary society. The home organizations maintained a keen interest in the region, and the Connecticut Missionary Society continued an active involvement in the hope of transforming the area from a wilderness to a redemptive landscape. But the work from this point forward shifted from institutions into the hands of the people who moved to the region. To keep an eye on how these emigrants created real homes in a predetermined space, the Connecticut Missionary Society dispatched missionaries to oversee the project. The missionaries themselves faced difficulties in reconciling their fantasies with the reality of frontier work. But the sponsoring society's trustees had little foresight about the emotional well-being of their employees; their eyes were set on the task at hand. And when the first missionary ventured to the Western Reserve, the Connecticut Missionary Society held its breath, hoping that the "house of cards" would stand.

Chapter 2

Models of Piety
Protestant Missionaries on the Frontier

When Thomas Robbins set off to Connecticut's Western Reserve in northeastern Ohio on August 25, 1803, he carried with him a set of explicit and implicit instructions. The day before the journey he felt "considerably unwell" and up to the last minute he admitted a temptation "to shrink from the great work I am about to undertake"; yet Robbins called on God's strength, mounted his horse, and rode through Salisbury, Connecticut, into New York State.[1] As the son and grandson of prominent Connecticut clergymen, he not only brought clearly defined expectations from his sponsoring home society, but he also bore the weight of the lionized Protestant missionaries who had labored before him. All the information that he amassed before leaving—theological readings after college, an admonishing sermon and charge from his own father at his ordination, imaginative missionary biographies, and secondhand stories from missionary friends and relatives—shaped his expectations of missionary work.[2] Engaged as a teacher, a supply preacher, a theological student, and a short-term missionary to New York during the seven years after his college graduation, Robbins turned down opportunities for settled pastorates to accept a call as a missionary to the Western Reserve. He might have imagined a heroic adventure ahead of him in which he would emulate the trials and glories of the celebrated missionaries who sacrificed personal comfort for the salvation of souls; he encountered instead the unromantic reality of missionary life and labor on the nineteenth-century American frontier, which reflected more clearly tribulations than triumphs. The most daunting challenge that Robbins faced, however, was to fit his missionary labor into a model of piety in a manner that remained consistent with the expectations of his sponsoring society no matter what he faced on the frontier.

Now I move away from the mapping and mental preparations of the landscape by the land company and the missionary society to consider the experiences of the first Plan of Union missionaries in the Western Reserve. It would be expected that, as representatives of the home society, they would produce reports that confirmed the success of their employer's organization of the frontier by affirming that the Western Reserve was a Promised Land or a New Connecticut. Instead, the first missionaries realized almost immediately that the Connecticut Missionary Society's moral map of the Western Reserve did not accurately represent life in the frontier communities. And when they pointed out the flaws in the design, the home society ignored their suggestions for modifying the plan and sent out another representative to redraw the moral map of the region. In the end, the missionaries, not the mental construction of New Connecticut, were blamed for any discrepancies between imagination and reality. Before I return to mapping in the last section of this chapter, I will look at the early missionaries' personal struggles to reconcile their own preconceptions of missionary labor with their actual work on the frontier and how those experiences led to changes in the construction of the missionary "self."

The first four missionaries sent to the Western Reserve between 1800 and 1806—Joseph Badger, Thomas Robbins, David Bacon, and Ezekiel Chapman—struggled with the natural and moral landscape. The physical environment posed daily threats to their health and to the well-being of the home mission. Thomas Robbins found this to be true from the start. Because of illness and poor riding conditions, his 834-mile journey from Norfolk, Connecticut, to the Western Reserve lasted three grueling months. All three missionaries expressed surprise at the inclement weather and extreme frontier conditions, and also at the settlers' general ambivalence about their missionary labors. Traveling over the rugged frontier terrain, the missionaries viewed the physical environment as a moral canvas stretched before them. While the majesty and beauty of the frontier demonstrated God's creative power and benevolence, it was an orderly, productive landscape that evidenced moral order. Morality could be deciphered in straight roads, cultivated fields, and blossoming meadows. Building a moral community on the frontier required physical and spiritual stamina that recalled both the Israelites' redemptive history and the Puritans' experiment in the New World. A missionary stepped into sacred time by assigning scriptural value to the frontier—by rendering it Zion, a garden, the wilderness, or a desert. When he described the space as "New Connecticut," he was also recollecting the attempts of Puritan New England to construct a godly community in America. The missionary could trace a direct line backward from himself to the pilgrims and view his labor as a new chapter in God's redemptive history on American soil. Walking in frontier space, the missionary recognized the visible landmarks from these narratives and became a part of sacred and national history. While the physical environment provided certain challenges, they were viewed positively. For missionaries, the frontier not only provided a moral canvas or a place to step into biblical and national history, it also provided an arena in which to face physical obstacles that would lead to spiritual gains.

Missionaries dispatched to the Western Reserve by the Connecticut Missionary Society in the early nineteenth century followed a model of missionary piety and labor that they gleaned by reading the lives of popular missionary heroes, primarily young, single, soul-searching missionaries to Native Americans. Drawing from these narratives, frontier missionaries could discern God's hand in mundane daily activities and in the unfolding of their own spiritual lives. While there were numerous examples of faithful missionaries, David Brainerd—a sickly but contemplative man—proved the most popular among Protestant missionaries in the nineteenth century.[3] Western Reserve missionaries familiar with this model of piety wrote letters to the home society that imitated the emphasis on the physical challenges of frontier missions found in stories about Brainerd. But the missionary experience in the field and the issues of family, social status, competing denominations, and harmony that plagued the earliest missionaries in the Western Reserve taught the nineteenth-century missionaries that a "young David Brainerd" rarely succeeded on the nineteenth-century American frontier. These missionaries sought to redefine the character of a successful frontier missionary, but, as we shall see, they were ultimately judged against the Brainerd model of piety, which remained popular but was no longer practical for a Plan of Union frontier missionary.

Brainerd's trials, both physical and spiritual, became noteworthy because he displayed signs of holiness through his humility and self-sacrifice in pursuing the missionary cause. Although his efforts had few lasting effects, his labor was memorialized in a popular autobiography edited after his death by Jonathan Edwards. The book served as a devotional text and inspirational travel companion for countless domestic and foreign missionaries.[4] In Brainerd, Edwards found what historian Joseph Conforti aptly describes as a spiritual "case study": the renegade missionary showing signs of true religious affections.[5] Brainerd's self-sacrifice and self-effacing piety exemplified "disinterested benevolence," a quality prized by nineteenth-century evangelicals. Conforti shows that by the nineteenth century the *Life of Brainerd* became an "archetype" for missionary memoirs and continued to "shape missionary sensibility."[6]

The details of the biography are as follows. The *Life of Brainerd* presents a man who gave his life for the missionary cause and yet continued to scrutinize his soul for signs of holiness, even on his deathbed. As a missionary, the number of conversions he won remained low, but Brainerd himself was a success: his life advanced spiritually, as seen in his display of disinterested benevolence.[7] Brainerd's willingness to suffer for God's plan led Edwards to caution readers and potential emulators against such extremes and to temper Brainerd's enthusiasm for hardship. "Another imperfection in Mr. Brainerd, which may be observed in the following account of his life," Edwards warned, "was his being *excessive in his labors*; not taking due care to proportion his fatigues to his strength."[8] Whether Edwards pointed to a problem inherent within Protestant missionary culture or predicted the effect of the biography on future missionaries is difficult to discern. What remains clear is that David Brainerd's lasting appeal lay in his excessive physical and spiritual devotion to the missionary cause.

Western Reserve missionaries could sympathize with Brainerd's hardships and isolation, but they soon found limits to what could be imitated from David Brainerd's short life.[9] First and foremost, their missions differed. Brainerd sought to reach Native Americans, but his would-be emulators struggled to hold on to Protestant Euro-Americans on the frontier. For these men, the need to educate and the desire to "civilize" were merely theoretical discussions; in their practical strategies they sought to retain church members rather than convert Native Americans. Although on one level that task seemed less complicated, the frontier settlers' rejection of former religious ties signaled more frightening and deeper ramifications than any encountered with Native Americans. Instead of advocating a radical theological shift from a previous life, as in Native missions, the home missionaries endeavored to remind the settlers of the religious and social benefits of instituting a particular type of Protestantism on the frontier. These missionaries could not maintain that failure arose from insurmountable language and cultural barriers, obstacles that had proved impassable for Brainerd. As Western Reserve missionaries preached Calvinist tenets and tried to replicate eastern towns and churches in the western settlements, displaced New Englanders and settlers from other regions and denominations made religious choices based on their previous experience and understanding.

Brainerd's missionary work among Native Americans differed significantly from the labor of men sent by the Connecticut Missionary Society, yet his model of piety continued to influence missionaries. Further, the correspondences between Western Reserve missionaries and the home society demonstrate that the hallmark signs of Brainerd's spiritual maturity—humility, soul-searching piety, and self-denial—were failing attributes on the frontier. Surprisingly, even his personal characteristics—he was a young, single, and ailing man—were deemed inappropriate qualities for a Plan of Union frontier missionary by settlers and missionaries alike. Missionaries laboring in frontier settlements had little time to scrutinize their souls and showed impatience with those missionaries who did. Physical hardship was not transformed into spiritual gains in missionary letters, and selfless labor was rarely esteemed.

Though Brainerd did not represent the reality of Western Reserve missionary life and labor (and one could easily argue that Edwards's highly edited memoir failed to accurately portray Brainerd's missionary labor), his model did have real effects on missionaries and the larger missionary culture.[10] The home missionaries came to understand themselves and their work in light of Brainerd's life. At the same time, the sponsoring missionary society and the interested reading public expected a successful frontier missionary to resemble David Brainerd. Western Reserve settler Eliphalet Austin expressed this understanding of the missionary prototype when he championed Congregational home missionary Ezekiel J. Chapman as "a young David Brainerd."[11] It becomes clear that when missionaries suspected something was flawed because their expectations did not match their experiences, they vacillated between blaming themselves and questioning the model of piety.

"I find I can preach, if I can ride": Missionary Letters

Through the letters of nineteenth-century missionaries, we know their travails and their struggles to live up to Brainerd. American home missionaries of this era drew from a rich literary and cultural tradition that taught proper missionary behavior and letter-writing techniques. Letters served a particular purpose within the cultural economy of missionaries' lives, enabling them to present themselves to family, congregations, clergy, and the sponsoring society through excerpts from their letters that were published in missionary journals. Here the expectations of the larger community emerge through narrative and style conventions, as well as representations of the missionary "self" in each missionary's description of his personal experiences.[12]

The missionaries sent out by the New England missionary societies shared common experiences, education, theological preparation, and social status. By the nineteenth century the majority of Congregational missionaries did not come from the upper echelon of New England society, but they understood themselves as acting within a specific arena of expectations, as enumerated above. At this time, as Donald Scott has argued, the status of New England clergy was in flux. What was in the eighteenth century a "sacred office" reserved for socially established and educated men had evolved into a profession open to men of many ranks.[13] Young, spiritually awakened men who aspired to this vocation responded to the growing need for clergy as piety and religious fervor increased in the early nineteenth century. These men, whatever their financial situation might have been, believed that college, as well as advanced theological reading, constituted an important part of their ministerial training. Although some could afford or gain entrance to Yale or Harvard, many more attended newer provincial colleges, such as Amherst or Bowdoin, as scholarship students, or they worked for their tuition. Of the twenty-nine missionaries sent to the Western Reserve between 1798 and 1818, for example, nine graduated from Yale, five from Williams, and most others from provincial colleges.[14] Before the founding of Andover Seminary in 1808, Congregational ministerial candidates devoted a couple of years after college graduation to private theological study in a professor's or minister's home.[15]

The Congregational and Presbyterian ministerial training produced a similar writing style and tone among the missionaries; specifically, Western Reserve missionary letters resembled each other because the missionaries modeled themselves on the pious prototypes depicted in missionary memoirs. These biographies, with their tales of trials and successes, provided a blueprint for missionary labor. Missionaries wrote in a manner that imitated these prototypes and simultaneously appealed to the reading public and affirmed their positions as faithful missionaries.

But Joseph Badger and Thomas Robbins soon realized that a successful frontier missionary had to reject the idealized Brainerd model of piety and adopt new methods for missionizing the frontier (see figures 10 and 11). The disjuncture between ideal and real surfaces appeared throughout missionary letters, precisely where affirmation of this model would be expected. For example, missionaries Badger, Robbins, and Chapman felt unprepared for the physical rigors and were disappointed by the lackluster reception in New Connecticut. Their reaction is striking, given that the missionaries were familiar with the model of piety that grew out of the physical hardships and disappointments that plagued Brainerd's missionary tours; we would expect to read of the anticipation of physical challenges and of interest in receiving the spiritual benefits of such hardships. In fact, the Western Reserve missionaries agonized over the lack of time they could devote to personal prayer and study because of physical exhaustion. Missionizing in the town of Warren, Ohio, for a few months, Thomas Robbins admitted that frontier labor was not what he had envisioned. "I find my work more laborious and toilsome than I expected," he complained in a letter to Abel Flint, the corresponding secretary. "I have much less time to devote to reading, writing, or in any way for myself, than I had contemplated."[16] Robbins affirms that frontier missionary work was indeed physically difficult, and the rigors neither allowed the missionary time to contemplate his labor nor occasioned spiritual inspiration.

Some of these stylistic and narrative differences represented the constraints of missionary letters written from the field, as opposed to the discourse of highly edited memoirs.[17] Although the letters did conform to a distinct style (a report, not a biography), they were nonetheless part of a larger Protestant missionary genre. Since missionary biographies created expectations of a typical missionary and his tour, members of the missionary culture read the letters from the Western Reserve within that narrative context. When missionaries recorded spiritual gains, they generally wrote eyewitness accounts detailing the religious fervor that they saw rather than reporting what they themselves experienced. Thomas Robbins filled pages of an 1804 letter to his parents describing a sacramental occa-

FIGURE 10. Engraving of Thomas Robbins, from the *Diary of Thomas Robbins, D.D. 1796–1825*, vol. 1. Robbins was one of the first missionaries dispatched by the Connecticut Missionary Society to the Western Reserve. Courtesy of Michigan State University Library.

FIGURE 11. Engraving of Joseph Badger. Although his relationship with the Connecticut Missionary Society deteriorated, missionary Joseph Badger was the first and certainly one of the most influential missionaries to the Western Reserve. Courtesy of the Presbyterian Historical Society, Presbyterian Church (U.S.A.), Philadelphia.

sion that he attended in Pennsylvania where he saw "unusual outpourings of the spirit." He wrote so vividly to his parents about the "falling down" and the remarkable signs of revival that he witnessed that his sister Sarah told him in her reply that the family hoped "to hear something perticularly [*sic*] concerning yourself" in the next epistle.[18] Robbins's letter, written to his family and not to the sponsoring society, nevertheless maintains a reporter's style and lacks substantial personal details to satisfy familial readers. A missionary's failure to mention his own spiritual progress in letters to his family from the field was a conspicuous omission, for it deviated from the Brainerd model.

The letters, however, did more than reflect a larger missionary genre; they also responded to specific guidelines from the sponsoring society regarding proper missionary correspondence. The Connecticut Missionary Society, for example, provided explicit instructions as to proper missionary conduct, including the importance of written correspondence. At its May 1801 meeting the society's board of trustees prepared an instructional letter for all frontier missionaries, in which they dictated the appropriate intervals between letters and the descriptive details deemed proper for inclusion. The trustees suggested that missionaries look to the gospel examples of Timothy and Titus when preaching and reminded them to remain "near to God" because of the "magnitude, high importance, and difficulty of their mission."[19] Missionary Thomas Robbins received such a letter from Secretary Abel Flint in 1803. According to Flint, the society required each missionary to send detailed reports of preaching, administering the sacraments, and establishing churches. In addition, the board expected a register of baptisms. These statistics, along with a narrative account, were to be sent to Hartford, Connecticut, every three months. Although Flint does not prescribe a particular set of behaviors, he enjoins Robbins always to "consider the expectations, anxieties and hopes of those who have generously contributed to the support of the missionaries" and to be careful of the "observing eye of adversaries" who desire the occasion "to think and speak evil of the design on which you are sent."[20] Further, the missionaries remained aware that their letters would be excerpted and circulated in the society's printed publications, for all interested parties to consider.

While the Connecticut Missionary Society gave its men explicit directions for missionary letters, missionaries also followed unstated instructions requiring them to maintain a narrative balance between anticipated success in the field and the continuing need for greater missionary labor. Thomas Robbins perfected this narrative balance and employed it in most of the letters he sent to the missionary society and to his family in Norfolk, Connecticut. His letter of 1804 to the Connecticut Missionary Society mentions the success of Methodists and other competing religious groups on the frontier. After noting the gains of Methodists in the region, however, he maintains that, for Congregationalists, "the prospects of religion in the country, though gloomy in some respects, are by no means discouraging. I think a holy God has given us some reason to believe that he does and will have some compassion for New Connecticut."[21] Two years earlier, the less eloquent missionary Joseph Badger used an optimistic land sales metaphor when he reported that for the missionary society "the prospects are flattering" on the Western Reserve but added bluntly, "I really want a fellow laborer in this great wilderness, and I think the cause of God loudly calls for one."[22] Ezekiel Chapman decried the "stupidity" of settlers while praising the region as "healthful, the inhabitants in general robust, + in good worldly circumstances. In short, nothing but religion is necessary to make N[ew] C[onnecticut] as agreeable a country for living in as any in the world."[23] The repetition of this narrative balance in the majority of Western Reserve missionary letters provided a positive interpretation of missionary activity for Connecticut readers even when there were no apparent successes to count. In these particular cases the landscape promised greater rewards than missionary efforts with settlers. More important, the narrative balance encouraged Connecticut citizens to continue to support home missions. Since the missionaries provided an authoritative informational link between the East and the frontier, it was crucial that they closely follow this writing pattern. Balancing the positive and negative aspects of the land and the mission was a simpler task for the missionaries than tracking the progress of their souls through the ebbs and flows of missionary life and labor.

Western Reserve missionaries also wrote extensively about physical difficulties, but they rarely described the personal spiritual benefits of such trials. They did not chart their own spiritual progress in contemplative passages; rather, they focused on practical material concerns—money, food, shelter, illness, and the statistical results of missionary labor. Physical strength, good health, and maturity were essential for tackling these problems. After a few months in the field, most missionaries tended to agree with Joseph Badger's assessment: "It appears to me that if two or three ministers of strong healthy constitution, who have been settled in the ministry six or eight years; men of *sound sentiment + piety* . . . they would be of more use than three times the number of young inexperienced preachers."[24] The frontier, according to Badger, was not the place to acquire ministerial skills or to mature spiritually. In other words, Badger called for missionaries who did not resemble David Brainerd.

The landscape played not an edifying but an adversarial role in the missionary letters. The letters include the narrative extremes of frontier trials and contrast these with the banality of riding through the muddy wilderness alone for days on end. Missionaries wrote wearied explanations of why they failed to cover as much ground as the sponsoring society expected. Joseph Badger was not unusual in his insistence that the physical drain of frontier missionizing was worse than the home society could imagine. "The distance of the settlements from each other, the badness of the roads & in many instances no roads or marked trees, & some times if a little belated to tie up the horse & lie in the woods, is fatiguing & uncomfortable beyond your conception."[25] Traditional modes of religious activity and piety—sermons, testimonies, scriptural readings—were interspersed with commentary on agricultural activities and frontier living, such as riding on bumpy roads, planting crops, and erecting homes. This evolving formula for frontier missionary letters blurred distinctions between religious and secular activity, for any mission activity became sacred as part of the whole missionary experience. Riding to a distant town became a pilgrimage, and finding shelter along the way a sign of God's protective grace. Striking an odd hybrid form between John Bunyan's *The Pilgrim's Progress* and a classic adventure tale, frontier missionary letters depicted hardship and the lessons learned through trying experiences. The missionaries were quick to observe the outward manifestations of divine providence—a river easily crossed or a destination reached before dark—but they were less inclined to examine introspectively their spiritual strife in their correspondences with the missionary society. While they replicated many of Brainerd's physical challenges in these cases, they did not imitate his spiritual growth.

Links between the physical and spiritual aspects of frontier missionary life were complex. Western Reserve missionaries wrote vividly about hair-raising struggles with the natural environment interspersed with welcome moments of reprieve. This was not simply to imitate frontier missionary heroes like Brainerd. The missionaries quickly realized that in the minds of Western Reserve settlers, their ability to face the frontier physical elements indicated their potential to fight frontier spiritual battles. A successful and respected missionary, therefore, needed to excel at both tasks. Matching physical and spiritual battles also provided colorful narratives that were often excerpted and printed in the sponsoring society's journal, the *Connecticut Evangelical Magazine*.[26] Missionary Joseph Badger, for example, became infamous among New Connecticut settlers and other missionaries for his harrowing, if highly exaggerated, tales. A much-discussed incident in which Badger claimed to have spent the night in a tree with a bear sleeping at its base prompted Thomas Robbins to remark blithely: "The people do as well as they can by me; altho' I have found out that I cannot roll up log houses, ride rivers, and *fight bears* like Mr. Badger."[27] Physical and spiritual tests, while prevalent in Western Reserve letters, rarely suggested the missionaries' own spiritual progress. The battles they recount take place externally with the "enemies of religion" rather than internally.

The connection between the physical and the spiritual in frontier missions did not simply involve rival preachers or finding renewal through the physical environment. Preaching itself became a physical endeavor for the Plan of Union missionaries. They complained of preaching under physically challenging circumstances such as after exhausting journeys, in inclement weather, and without adequate rest or food. They were so often ill and suffering from exhaustion that they judged their ability to preach on their physical constitution. After describing his slow recovery from a fever, Thomas Robbins explained to his parents: "I find I can preach, if I can ride."[28] In this particular case, he did not claim to be exhorting to large crowds. Rather, he preached "to a few people, in a private house, who are serious and attentive."[29] Plan of Union missionaries, while generally not as emotive as other Protestant frontier missionaries such as Methodists and Baptists, found preaching to be a physically draining experience but not a gauge for their own spiritual stamina.

Not all Protestant home missionaries found frontier labor so taxing. Methodist preacher Peter Cartwright ridiculed the "eastern missionaries" as ineffective and mocked their tendency to exaggerate their sufferings. In his autobiography, Cartwright asserted that ill-prepared eastern missionaries sent "doleful tidings" back home filled with "wailings and lamentations over the moral waste and destitute condition of the West."[30] Such exaggerations, Cartwright explained, were published as fact in missionary journals to boost donations. The problem, according to Cartwright, was neither the western landscape nor the frontier inhabitants but the eastern missionaries' preaching style. "The great mass of our Western people wanted a preacher who could mount a stump, a block, or an old log, or stand in the bed of a wagon, and without note or manuscript, quote, expound, and apply the word of God to the hearts and consciences of the people."³¹ Unlike the success of Methodists, "the result of these eastern missionaries was not very flattering."³²

Cartwright's characterization of the ineffectual eastern frontier missionary illustrates a common sentiment held among western settlers, who often questioned the authority of Plan of Union missionaries to preach on the frontier. Sometimes these objections came from unlikely quarters. Missionaries, for example, were quick to report challenges by influential citizens against the sponsoring society. Missionary Ezekiel Chapman, for example, felt particularly discouraged by the "principal men of New Connecticut" who not only championed infidelity but also "unmercifully and indecently slander missionaries." To avoid any personal responsibility for the antipathy, he adds that these men "vent their curses against the society which employs and sends them."³³ Joseph Badger also reports that "Mr. Abbot a violent deist says he does not want to be insulted by Connecticut sending missionaries."³⁴ This besieged writing style surfaced repeatedly as missionaries echoed Brainerd and other Christian literary examples of religious trials and dangerous encounters that threatened the establishment of God's kingdom. Besides providing specific information requested by home missionary societies, such as numbers, dates, and miles, missionaries demonstrated a familiarity with the expected tone and content of their letters through these repeated narrative anecdotes and sequences. What distinguishes these letters was the subtle questioning of the Brainerd model of physical hardship and spiritual gain even as the missionaries continued to be informed by convictions inspired by Brainerd. Other disruptions to the Brainerd model of piety emerged in missionary letters around the issues of family obligations and social distinctions and harmony among missionaries. The experiences of Joseph Badger, Thomas Robbins, and Ezekiel Chapman will illustrate that the weaknesses of the Brainerd model, based as it was on an unmarried young missionary working principally alone, were more apparent to the missionaries in the field than to the trustees back home.

"Difficulties inseparable to a family": *Age, Marital Status, and Missions*

Soon after land surveyors marked out the first ranges and townships on the Western Reserve's eastern border, the Connecticut Missionary Society sent the earnest Joseph Badger of Blandford, Massachusetts, to survey the moral landscape. This appointment came at an opportune moment in

Badger's career. A Revolutionary War veteran who had been preaching for fourteen years, Badger found himself losing a theological battle in his church to congregants who espoused the merits of free grace. By the time of his missionary call in the spring of 1800, Badger's church split; a dissenting Episcopal Society formed, and the exiled clergyman accepted the Connecticut Missionary Society's appointment to western missions. Badger distinguished himself as the first missionary sent to the Western Reserve and as the Connecticut Missionary Society's most disgruntled employee. Badger's voluminous letters and published diary provide invaluable information regarding the early settlement and mission to the Western Reserve. The experiences of this older, healthy, family man point to the shifting model of a successful frontier missionary.

Badger missionized on horseback for almost one year, narrating his travels through letters that note the landscape, its flora and fauna, the type of weather, and the number of families on the land, all features of interest, of course, to a land speculator as well as to a missionary society. The number of families would be noteworthy to the Connecticut Missionary Society, but Badger's eye envisioned other fields. Also to be reaped were the future spiritual fruits of the bountiful land. In his account, Badger interspersed calamity and adventure with thoughtful concern for the religious future of the West. At times his narratives from this first trip took on a highly dramatic tone as he described the West as an arena for a cosmic battle. "I find the theatre of action between Zion's King, and the powers of darkness," he wrote in the spring of 1801, "extends throughout this deep forest. Satan has set up his standard here with variegated colours."[35] Many settlers, Badger reported, mocked religious practice; in the midst of "dissenters" and "irreligionists," however, a small but sincere group of ten men and sixteen women joined together to form the Western Reserve's first Congregational Church in Austinburg. The treacherous conditions and unenthusiastic settlers, according to Badger, paled in the glow of the Austinburg victory. Although the overall religious situation remained precarious for missionary work, Badger felt that the prospects for the land—both religiously and economically—were excellent. Not only did he confess that he "like[d] the country better than I expected," but showing as much interest in the land as in religion, he remarked that he had "not seen ten acres of land, that with any propriety could be called poor land."[36]

Badger's first impressions of the plentiful land changed when he was unable to provide for his own family. At the completion of his first tour, the missionary society trustees invited Badger to return to the Western

Reserve as a resident missionary at a fixed salary of seven dollars per week. The six-hundred-mile trip west through New York and Pennsylvania in the winter of 1802 with his wife and six children began Badger's long ministry in the Western Reserve, one that was marked by financial and physical difficulties as well as by his mounting bitterness toward the Connecticut Missionary Society. Badger's optimistic rendering of the frontier had reflected—at least partially—his position as a single male missionary, similar to that of David Brainerd. Other than the obligation to send reports to the missionary society, he had been responsible only for himself during his first frontier excursion. While it is difficult to imagine that Badger would have been unprepared for the unique difficulties of family frontier living, he nonetheless expressed astonishment about obstacles facing family emigration and settlement; he was also indignant that the missionary society neither acknowledged nor understood his arduous situation. "If I would have realized & known the difficulties, fatigues, & expence of moving my family to this country before I sat out," Badger lamented, "I should have stayed in New England, or have attempted a shorter remove. Gentlemen, who ride in this country, have no adequate idea of the difficulties inseparable to a family."[37] Presumably the gentlemen to whom Badger refers were the missionary society members or other single missionaries who were free from family responsibilities.

Badger's resentment disrupted the Brainerd model of humility and acceptance of severe circumstances. According to the Connecticut Missionary Society, he failed to maintain a proper "Christian temper." Beyond a dispositional difference from Brainerd, Badger's complaints point to the fact that the missionary model was based on the experience of a single man; it was not flexible enough to include a missionary family. Also, it did not recognize Badger's distinct needs as one who had made a long-term commitment to missionary labor. "It has been astonishing to me," Badger wrote, "that the board should consider the field that I was placed in . . . as requiring no more support than those missionaries who were out only for two or three months at a time, & most through an old settled country."[38] Looking back on his experiences, a bitter Badger reports to the missionary society: "My wife and children severely felt the want of clothing for decency and comfort." In response to the trustees' criticism that he spent too much time with domestic affairs and too little time devoted to missionary labors, he queried, "Did they expect I would drop my family among the trees, without cover; and enter the field of labour?"[39] Badger's correspondences became so sharp that the missionary society refused to communicate with him until he resumed a proper tone and attitude in his letters. Fully aware of the expectations that trustees held regarding the tone and content of missionary correspondences, Badger wrote a follow-up letter that could only be described as impudent. "If my Christian temper is to be measured, by my acknowledging that I have been wholly in the wrong," he responded, "it will doubtless in their view be totally wanting."[40] Badger doubted that his temper would ever satisfy the trustees, as he insisted that he and his family had been treated cruelly by the Connecticut Missionary Society. "Had I understood, that I had to deal with a corporate body of land speculators, or any other sort of sharpers; I should have laid no weight on any or all the outdoor observations, the whole company might have made."[41]

Badger received praise from many settlers who considered him to be an ideal frontier missionary, but he clearly did not fit the Brainerd model of piety. He was not prone to illness like Robbins, and he had more life experience than missionary Ezekiel Chapman. He was neither ailing, nor young, nor single. He did not write contemplative passages in his diary or letters, and he never recorded spiritual benefits derived from physical hardship. One could hardly portray Badger as an example of disinterested benevolence, as he was constantly tortured by his own self-representation. Rather than lose his sense of self in the larger missionary enterprise, Badger wrote pages and pages to the Connecticut Missionary Society insisting that he had been unappreciated and at times misrepresented, and that no missionary had ever suffered more than he.[42]

"I have no prospect of being popular": Social Status and Missionary Labor

Although Badger directed the force of his anger toward the home society, other missionaries did not completely escape his ire. The significance of this animosity resided in the missionary culture. Because the participants in the New England Congregational missionary culture expected a common set of educational, familial, and social standards, which revolved around a privileged, educated class, the community did not accommodate economic differences. Although an increasing number of missionaries in the nineteenth century came from modest families, the culture valued theological education that remained closely linked to an elite missionary culture. On the one hand the missionary culture ignored status, while on the other missionaries were acutely aware of social and economic distinctions among themselves. For example, when Badger considered the privileged life that he believed Thomas Robbins had lived before his mission, and the social advantages that he maintained through his prominent Connecticut family, he did not feel inclined to promote a friendship with Robbins. Neither did Robbins care to foster a personal allegiance with Badger.

This social and economically based animosity probably did not register in the trustees' minds when they chose Robbins to assist Badger. Within the missionary culture, Badger and Robbins appeared well suited for each other. Both men were educated at Yale, espoused Federalist politics, and expressed a strong commitment to Congregationalism.[43] But Badger lacked Robbins's social refinement, and he attacked what he perceived to be Robbins's shallow popularity in the West. In one letter Badger told the trustees: "I am constrained to believe that his highest aim is to render himself popular, let what come of the Redeemer's cause."[44] Ultimately, Badger's jealousy emerged from the knowledge that, unlike Robbins's, his own financial resources were limited, and if the mission were to fail, he would be destitute; Robbins, by contrast, would fill his grandfather's pulpit, which stood vacant pending his return to Connecticut.[45] This tension signaled another break from the Brainerd model. These Western Reserve missionaries labored under the Plan of Union, a merger between Presbyterians and Congregationalists that required them to work in the spirit of harmony. Any personal or theological differences between missionaries, even those of the same denomination, needed to be erased to present a unified front.

Despite the missionary culture's official disregard of status, social position was a great advantage, as the success of Robbins illustrates. The Robbins family, with its close-knit relationships and Congregational lineage, exemplifies a post–Revolutionary War family immersed in New England missionary culture. The son and grandson of prominent clergymen, Robbins, as well as his brothers and cousins, studied theology in the hope of continuing the venerable family tradition. Besides the material help that the family provided (sending clothes, books, and money), Robbins's extended family gave emotional support through letters. While Robbins felt the distance between the Western Reserve and his parents' home in Norfolk, Connecticut, his family bridged the physical distance through constant letter writing. The family maintained a conversational network centralized in their Connecticut home, a network of family, friends, relatives, other missionaries, and settled clergy. His father, Ammi Robbins, often mentioned in his letters to Thomas that the family depended on this communication so that "we may thus converse & communicate our love, our tender affections to each other, tho' rivers & mountains, plains & forests intervene."[46] Although he expressed pride in Robbins's missionary work, he often cautioned his son against physical excesses and encouraged him in all of his correspondences to consider returning home. After hearing of his son's slow recovery from a grave illness, he praised God's mercy and begged his son, "But don't *overdo*—and if your state of health is such that you can't continue . . . had you not better return before Winter?"[47] Robbins's letters were also read in his Connecticut church and passed along among friends and family.

The influence of his letters extended beyond comforting his parents to inspiring young missionaries and promoting the missionary cause. In this way Robbins continued the missionary tradition of providing firsthand testimony to the drama of frontier missions. After reading a particularly descriptive letter, Samuel P. Robbins, a young cousin of Thomas's known for his lack of direction, was inspired to accept a missionary call to Wilkes-Barre, Pennsylvania. Reflecting on all the privileges he took for granted in the East, and the unknown learning possibilities presented to him beyond college as a missionary in the West, he declared: "Missionaries, I think, are in one of the best schools in the world. But, O, what a dull scholar am I."[48]

Robbins and Badger wrote to the society about missionary concerns and the general state of religion in New Connecticut, but much of their correspondence concerned complaints against each other. Badger betrayed a monumental jealousy of Robbins's popularity with settlers and spared no details in his criticisms of Robbins as one of what he called the ineffectual "missionary boys." In a scathing 1806 letter to the board, Badger attacked Robbins's personal conduct and a preaching style that he believed was "contrary to the aim and design of the society." Robbins's reputation, according to Badger, was as a "medling imprudent man" whose attitudes and actions injured the missionary cause. "If to inquire out the progress of the settlements + the number of inhabitants in the county + attend to the politics current among us; will answer the objects of the mission," Badger remarked, "he is the right man." Of course Badger did not believe this and found fault in Robbins's habit of discussing politics on the Sabbath, pandering to a "polite" crowd, playing backgammon, and above all expressing a superior New England attitude that alienated settlers from different regions. Badger also reported Robbins's refusal to demean himself by distributing missionary tracts, quoting him as stating, "I'm not going to peddle missionary books," and he accused Robbins of rallying settlers against him. Fueling the missionary society's fears of disharmony between the eastern missionaries and frontier settlers, Badger asserted that Robbins created discord through his clear New England bias.[49] On one telling occasion, according to Badger, Robbins toasted to the hope of future "Yankie" settlement on the Western Reserve. "Most of the people being from other parts," Badger reported, "fealt the insult + speak with contempt, of such impertinent distinctions."[50]

Badger's wild accusations widened the division between himself and Robbins. Rather than providing the united front desired by the missionary society, Badger emphasized character, social status, and even age differences. His choice of complaining about Robbins's toast is noteworthy, because he maligned Robbins for promoting "Yankie" culture. Neither Badger nor the missionary society opposed this endeavor; on the contrary, they were working to re-create Connecticut on the frontier. Badger found fault not with Robbins's sentiments but with his impolitic blatant espousal of New England superiority that appeared to be linked to social and economic privilege.[51] The point of Badger's criticism was not only that Robbins focused on the worldly concerns of politics but that his interests served to divide settlers and ultimately hurt the missionary cause. In the context of the Brainerd model that both men inherited, Badger portrays Robbins as the antithesis of the missionary hero: proud, self-interested, and impious.

Badger also questioned the sincerity of Robbins's preaching. Badger observed that, rather than speaking from a firm doctrinal position, Robbins "calculates his sermon as almanack makers do their work for different meridians. Where he knows people will distinguish between truth + error: between matter + sound—he indeavors to preach to please— + when he is where he apprehends people will be pleased with smoothe things, he exactly meets their tast [sic]."[52] While Robbins's preaching style and content proved palatable to many settlers, Badger perceived that his own was unsavory. "I have no prospect of being popular," he admitted, "I have such a habbit [sic] of preaching what some people call dry Calvinism."[53] Badger complained that "most people are fond of smooth things, they are best suited with sermons dressed and cooked so nicely, as to have the salt loose [sic] all its savor."[54] Badger's attempt to invert his jealousy of Robbins's popularity by asserting the "salt" of his orthodoxy was not lost on the missionary society, which sent out letters to both missionaries urging reconciliation and cooperation in the future. The physical strain of frontier missionizing and the quarrels over popular opinion left little time for Badger and Robbins to examine their own souls.

"Book knowledge is not all": The Heart, Not the Head

One of the few topics on which Badger and Robbins agreed was missionary Ezekiel J. Chapman's incompetence as a frontier missionary. Neither doubted his piety, but each was bowled over by his naiveté and uncanny ability to embarrass himself in front of settlers. While it was obvious to Badger and Robbins that a successful frontier missionary needed to speak extemporaneously and to engage in impromptu debates with hecklers, Chapman always preached with notes and adamantly refused to debate challengers who attended his meetings. Chapman's passivity toward opponents, Badger and Robbins warned, harmed the missionary cause more than the Connecticut Missionary Society could imagine. A western missionary, Badger explained, must be ready at all times to engage in theological combat, "grasping the weapon at the time & place for the encounter."[55] Any opponent who questions orthodoxy must immediately "be made to feel like he is a blockhead, & the bystanders will feel so too."[56] Robbins agreed that "an indispensable qualification," for a frontier missionary, "is that he be able to speak at once, and generally right to questions + subjects that he nor any other person thought of before."[57] Besides verbal acuity, a successful missionary needed common sense, a quality that Reverend Chapman woefully lacked. Or as Robbins summarized, "book knowledge is not all."[58] In what Robbins referred to as Mr. Chapman's "most unfortunate slip," Chapman demonstrated his ignorance when he asked some settlers why they placed troughs under maple trees; when he was told that they were for sap, Chapman "replied he thought they were set there to catch acorns."[59]

Badger and Robbins's criticism of Chapman signals another break from the missionary model. On the frontier the missionaries found that they needed to watch each other carefully and reprimand those among them who were ineffective. Their attention turned outward to watch others rather than inward to scrutinize themselves. Chapman failed in Badger's and Robbins's eyes in his reluctance to accept their criticism and in his inability to develop new skills adapted to the frontier. What is particularly striking about Chapman's failure is that he was the missionary that Western Reserve settler Eliphalet Austin praised as "a young David Brainerd." Badger, in so many words, echoed this praise by describing Chapman as "labouring to his utmost, and I doubt not but with more *meekness, humility* and *Christian love* than is found in men of any age or appearance." Unfortunately for Chapman and the missionary society, "his *youth, timidity* and *inexperience* about human affairs and human nature, render him totally unfit for the place he is in now."[60] In other words, the missionary who most closely reflected the Brainerd missionary model was both ineffectual and disrespected on the frontier.

Witnessing the failure of a missionary who "would make an excellent minister in some Connecticut congregation" placed Badger and Robbins in the authoritative position to send instructions back to the Connecticut Missionary Society.[61] Their ability to monitor each other's successes and failures allowed missionaries to exert some influence on the missionary society and to create a new model missionary. Badger and Robbins believed that their authority to do so was based on their frontier experiences. While they desired more missionaries to assist them, they "were of the opinion that it is better not to have any than one who is not right."[62] The problem was defining and finding the "right" frontier missionary. Badger and Robbins maintained that although the Connecticut Missionary Society might have been capable of judging theological preparation, it was incapable of ascertaining frontier readiness. Each wrote letters for a span of two years that began as emotional pleas and later evolved into instructional mandates about what qualifications the home society should consider when selecting western missionaries. Badger reminded the trustees, "It is not every pious amiable young man that will do for a missionary here."[63] Through their detailed prerequisites, which included preaching without notes, the ability to engage in impromptu disputes, emotional maturity, and some physical strength, Badger and Robbins showed the home society that its missionary model remained unsuited to the realities of frontier missionary labor.

Badger and Robbins were not the only people on the frontier who expressed strong opinions to the Connecticut Missionary Society regarding effective and appropriate missionaries. Western Reserve settlers also joined the conversation. A lengthy letter-writing campaign resulted from the growing and obvious antagonism between Badger and Robbins. Many settlers familiar with the missionaries wrote to the home society supporting or opposing each man. Settler Lyman Potter questioned Thomas Robbins's qualifications because he was young, lacked experience, and was "stuffed up with vain conceit." In Potter's view, Robbins "would do more good in some small parish in Conecticutt [*sic*] under the inspection of good teachers in the ministry."[64] Hosea Wilcox wrote to the board complaining that he had questioned Badger's behavior during a religious exercise and Badger "came to me in a threatening attitude and demanded of me to sign a paper as a recantation of what I had said."[65] When Badger threatened to retire from the Connecticut Missionary Society because of low pay, settler David Hudson wrote a letter on his behalf describing him as a man with all the necessary missionary qualifications, being a "man of years" who could boldly "withstand and put to silence the hardiest gainsayers." This was an important quality, Hudson explains, because in his opinion many of the settlers were "disposed to browbeat and ridicule a young and inexperienced boy."[66] This flow of communication demonstrates that the settlers who appreciated the presence of missionaries and acknowledged the Connecticut Missionary Society's position by reporting problems to Hartford believed that their desires and assessments were equally as important as those of the Connecticut Missionary Society. It also reveals that although New Connecticut was fashioned after old Connecticut, the average missionary, trained back East, proved unsuccessful in the West. The Brainerd model of piety did not work for Western Reserve missionaries. As early as the first six years of settlement, both the missionaries and the settlers realized what the Connecticut Missionary Society did not: the Western Reserve was no Connecticut.

The instructions given by the missionaries in the field to the missionary society in Connecticut signaled one example of a shift in the power dynamic between the eastern missionary society and the western missionaries. Although the missionaries and settlers acknowledged the society's status by addressing concerns about missionaries to the board, they simultaneously were questioning the home society's ability to choose proper missionaries. Badger and Robbins believed that if the society ignored their instructions the mission would fail. Their experiences ultimately refashioned the Brainerd missionary model into one more suited to the nineteenth-century frontier. Though suffering and fatigue would always be present, the contemplative, slow, inward spiritual growth so valued by New England clergymen was ridiculed by frontier settlers, and ultimately by most western missionaries. A young, soul-searching man was less desirable than a mature, physically active missionary. Furthermore, while the missionaries continued to accept annual appointments, the missionary society sought long-term commitments that changed the terms of missionary labor.

"Born and raised in the woods": Homegrown Missionaries

By 1806 the Connecticut Missionary Society decided that something had to change. For six years it had contended with missionary infighting, ambiguous reports from settlers and missionaries, and what appeared to the society to be a growing success among rival religious groups, particularly Methodists. These problems were compounded by the modest success among the Connecticut missionaries. Though emigration to the Western Reserve continued to grow, Badger, Robbins, and Chapman had founded only seven churches, in Austinburg, Hudson, Richfield, Vernon, Vienna, Canfield, and Warren. While this poor record appeared to the sponsoring society to be evidence of missionary failings, it partially reflected the region's settlement patterns. Of the 1,100 families that settled in the Western Reserve from 1800 to 1806, only 450 families emigrated from New England. More troubling for the missionary society, of those 450 families, few chose to join a Plan of Union church.[67] Although the Connecticut Missionary Society asserted in its publications that Connecticut natives constituted the majority of Western Reserve settlers, fewer than half the families living there in 1806 had emigrated from New England. Missionaries like Robbins and Chapman, who asserted New England superiority, were preaching to a minority.

These depressing figures led the missionary society to reconsider its approach to frontier missions, including its profile of the ideal missionary. After six years of receiving missionary reports that simultaneously celebrated missionary success and cautioned against infidelity and "stupidity" among frontier settlers, the missionary society deemed that the proper first step in rectifying the failing missions was to gain accurate information regarding the religious climate of the Western Reserve. Rather than relying on the missionaries' perspectives, the society's board of trustees sent former missionary Calvin Chapin, a Connecticut Missionary Society trustee, to survey the moral landscape and to report to the society with recommendations. When the home society informed Badger that Chapin would be sent to assess the strengths and weaknesses of the missionaries' labors, Badger retorted: "I am glad Mr. Chapin is coming; doubtless his independent fortune requires more pay, in this advanced period of settlement in the country, than my poverty did in difficult times."[68] Badger's response to the trustees illustrated the deterioration of his relationship to the society but also hinted at a growing rift between those living in the "mission field" and those watching from their comfortable positions in the East. Chapin toured the region from July to October and informed the trustees that the flaws in their mission resided not in the plan but in the particular missionaries. Chapin amassed evidence against the missionaries as he traveled and spoke with settlers and submitted a detailed report that outlined their failings, based primarily on personal character.

Chapin's easiest target was Badger, who by 1806 had alienated himself from the Connecticut Missionary Society through vituperative letters, a resignation, and even a threat to sue the society for back pay.[69] Badger's irascible personality likely harmed the missionary cause, and both Chapin and the trustees were probably predisposed to blame him before Chapin's tour. Robbins, however, with his elegant prose and strong clerical family, was not so easily discredited. Chapin was careful not to criticize Robbins directly but to highlight the infighting between Robbins and Badger and to use Badger's complaints against Robbins as examples of Robbins's poor judgment. Chapin's objections to Ezekiel Chapman echoed those voiced by Badger and Robbins concerning his inappropriate preparation and character for frontier missions. Through conversations with settlers and some clergymen located near the Pennsylvania border, Chapin tied Robbins's and Badger's failings to strong political sentiments and to a personal animosity between them that damaged the missionary society's interest in promoting a unified cause. Both men worked under the Plan of Union, but while Robbins maintained an allegiance to Congregationalism, Badger had found favor with the Presbyterians. The problem for the missionary society was that the missionaries' mandate called for the promotion of unity under the Plan of Union, not for the assertion of the superiority of one denomination over another.

Chapin received the bulk of his information about the Western Reserve missionaries from "trans-Alleganean clergy" who complained of theological and political conflicts that soured them on Badger, Robbins, and Chapman. These Pennsylvania men sympathized more with Badger, since "they had, *as Presbyterians*, received some treatment from him [Robbins], through his zeal for Congregationalism, which strongly prejudiced their minds."[70] This view on their part represented a benefit for the Pennsylvania clergy. But from Chapin's perspective Badger had become "a zealous advocate of Presbyterianism." Acting against the expressed wishes of the missionary society, "he defended their modes and forms among Congregationalists."[71] The men had theologically positioned themselves against each other, creating a wedge in the missionary society's hopes for a unified cause under the 1801 Plan of Union. Robbins's commitment to Congregationalism extended beyond theology, however, to a belief in the superiority of New England culture. Robbins admits in his diary, published years later, that many of the "principal people" opposed him and "circulated false and ungenerous reports about me, with regard to an interference in the late election."[72] Each man negotiated his religious and cultural biases in specific ways. Badger was forthright regarding his disdain for some individuals and avoided those whom he considered disreputable, but Robbins acquired the reputation of being a "tattler—telling publicly abroad the feelings of failings which he saw in their families, while they were hospitably entertaining him in their home."[73]

Although they grew apart theologically, Badger and Robbins were political allies in a time and place when "Federalism was extremely unpopular."[74] Just as their social manners differed, their political styles were also distinct. Badger used his pulpit to openly reproach men whom he opposed. He would "single them out, as unprincipled men, without calling names—and would reprove and discipline them as such, in terms that all present knew how to apply."[75] Although Robbins promoted Congregationalism, he associated with people of conflicting political and sometimes religious positions. This promiscuous socializing led Badger to complain to the missionary society about what he believed was Robbins's indiscretion. In his defense, Robbins explained, "My practice has been to endeavor to conciliate the favor of the leading characters here."[76] Nonetheless, the Connecticut Missionary Society wrote to censor his behavior, and he responded by claiming to trustee Nathan Strong, "I have wholly done with politics. I don't know but little & say less upon the subject. I find it no self-denial. It is not generally a subject of conversation as in New England."[77] By the time Chapin arrived on the Western Reserve, the general mood toward the Connecticut missionaries and their sponsoring society combined suspicion and exasperation. Political opponents whom missionaries labeled as republicans and Jeffersonians managed to discredit both Badger and Robbins and called attention to what they believed were the unstated political leanings of the Connecticut Missionary Society. Chapin reported that many settlers believed that the missionary society "was an electioneering institution, founded and supported for the purposes of reviving fallen and hated Federalism."[78]

The question of missionary character was vital for both Badger and Robbins. Before his tour, Chapin was not convinced that eastern-trained missionaries represented a problem for the Western Reserve. Writing from Liberty, New Connecticut, he noted that there were plenty of opportunities in New Connecticut and that young ministers, "need no peculiar qualification. . . . The same things that will make a good + useful minister in the old settlements will make one here. He must be *brave, discreet, intelligent + pious*. This is about the sum total."[79] After a few months of surveying the region, Chapin had changed his opinions. If the missionary society desired to continue the mission to the Western Reserve, he reasoned, it needed to find effective missionaries who would not create a rift between Presbyterians and Congregationalists. These men needed to have physical strength and stamina, as well as an ability to preach under unfavorable circumstances and in a style appropriate to the frontier. The only good candidates, in Chapin's opinion, were western-born clergymen who were "from their childhood, accustomed to that *manner* of preaching, which seems most acceptable + usefull among people in the wilderness."[80] These men, "born + raised in the woods" were more suitable for the frontier's rugged conditions than the Connecticut missionaries; and, as Chapin pointed out, "the log cabins + commonly reckoned hard fare of new settlements do not terrify them."[81]

Besides dispositional qualifications, the Pennsylvania clergy whom Chapin found suitable for the mission were Presbyterians. Selecting missionaries from one denomination, he reasoned, would dispense with interdenominational feuds between missionaries. While relying solely on Presbyterians to carry the gospel and uphold the Plan of Union may not have been ideal for the Connecticut Missionary Society, by 1806 the organization had little choice. Chapin's tour confirmed the trustees' fears that the Congregational missionaries had made few inroads into the frontier settlements. The meager success, the society believed, would soon be lost if they continued to send the eastern-trained Congregational missionaries. With some reluctance the missionary society chose Pennsylvania clergyman Thomas E. Hughes to act as the western agent in procuring western-born missionaries to serve for the home society.

Chapin's moral survey of the Western Reserve, while complete, was grim. The eastern missionaries had managed to alienate themselves based on politics and denominational affiliation, the two issues that the missionary society had requested them to avoid. Rather than setting an example of selfless labor and brotherly love, the missionaries exhibited infighting, jealousy, and frustration toward each other, which rendered them ineffective and made them ultimately a divisive element in terms of the cause. Touring the region helped Chapin to assess the moral situation and to suggest strategies for the future. After sifting through all of his information, he decided that the solution to the Connecticut Missionary Society's problem remained not in rethinking the goals of the Western Reserve missionary endeavor but in finding more-appropriate missionaries for frontier settlements.

What remains significant about Chapin's tour is his findings. After traveling the region, talking with countless settlers, gathering evidence, making charts of church members in various towns, and sifting through all the complaints against the Connecticut missionaries, he focused his vision of the problems and solutions for the failing mission within narrow parameters. Rather than questioning the viability of the Connecticut Missionary Society's being involved in western missions at all, or even suggesting modifications to its overall goals, Chapin found fault in the missionaries' character. The results of Chapin's moral survey indicated neither that the settlers rejected the Plan of Union missionaries nor that missionizing the western territory presented too many obstacles for the New England–centered society but that eastern-trained missionaries were neither dispositionally suited nor properly trained to missionize effectively on the frontier. The year 1806 could have been the time when the Connecticut Missionary Society reassessed its abilities and redirected its energy elsewhere, but the trustees agreed with Chapin, and for the next six years they employed western Presbyterian clergymen. And these men exacerbated divisions in the Western Reserve rather than overcoming them.

Chapin never took sides with either Badger or Robbins. In fact, the only issue on which all three agreed was their mutual condemnation of Ezekiel J. Chapman. When Chapin asserted that western-born clergy were better suited to frontier missionizing, he emphasized their physical stamina and their likelihood to survive deprivations, not their inner piety and sufferings for the missionary cause. In doing so he signaled the impractical nature of the Brainerd model for Protestant frontier missionaries. It would be simplistic, however, to argue the immediate deterioration of one model of piety and the quick substitution of another. On the contrary, Protestant frontier missionaries continued to understand their labor from within a discourse that valorized David Brainerd even as their experiences contradicted that model of piety.

Up to this point the focus has been on how the home institutions imagined and prepared New Connecticut, and how missionaries struggled to reconcile their fantasies of missionary labor with the reality of the Western Reserve. All of the parties involved, however, understood that their success ultimately depended on the cooperation of the frontier settlers. And so now the focus shifts to those settlers. The next chapter will once again demonstrate a disjuncture between New Connecticut as mapped by the Connecticut Missionary Society and the actual Western Reserve, this time as inhabited by the settlers. Rather than show how the reality of living in the landscape affected the conception of the missionary "self," I will broaden the investigation to include how the physical space challenged moral values associated with the body, the town, and the household.

The Plan of Union missionaries scrutinized the lives of Western Reserve settlers, finding signs of morality and immorality at every turn. Retaining adherents who removed to frontier settlements through physical and spiritual ties proved a difficult task for these missionaries. Besides preaching, praying, and instructing, this effort included a spatial component, because the home missionary society hoped also to re-create religious communities by marking and organizing physical and moral spaces. The two primary ways in which missionaries sought to hold on to adherents were through ordering the physical landscape and ordering the moral landscape. The home missionaries believed that the construction of orderly towns promoted *and* evidenced a moral community. Conversely, towns that evolved in a disorderly fashion indicated to the missionaries that the settlers were likely either to break religious bonds or simply to become "irreligious." The missionaries viewed moral behavior as both a sign of piety and a means to instill piety. Therefore, they looked for bodily signs of moral order. During religious occasions, moral behavior translated to seriousness, solemnity, and respectful attention to preaching. Outside of religious occasions, moral behavior signified larger issues of moral order, including restraint from drunkenness, profanity, laziness, adultery, gambling, and other common vices. The Plan of Union missionaries also understood their responsibility as agents who actively promoted moral order through preaching, distributing pamphlets, and visiting homes. For frontier Protestant home missionaries, retaining adherents was intimately linked to the physical and moral landscape.

CHAPTER 3

The Moral Garden of the Western World
Bodies, Towns, and Families

In the winter of 1805 the Connecticut Missionary Society received the disturbing information that a Western Reserve missionary, Joseph Badger, allegedly introduced and supported a practice called "the kiss of charity" in his religious assemblies.[1] Badger had labored in northeastern Ohio under the Plan of Union for three years as a home missionary. His efforts had met with limited success, partly because of the extreme hardship of frontier missionizing and partly because of his irascible personality. It did not therefore come as a surprise to the trustees of the home society that Badger found himself in the middle of a controversy with frontier settlers. It was, however, deeply disturbing that the accusations of impropriety against Badger were of such a sensual nature.

Neither Badger nor his supporters denied his active involvement in the practice they called "charity kisses." The questions for everyone concerned remained: what was the nature of the kisses; when did they occur; why were they given; to whom; and most important, where did they land? Badger admitted that he did on occasion practice these kisses, but he claimed they were a sign of friendship only, exchanged upon parting and returning among friends and *not* during religious services. His supporters confirmed that on heated sacramental occasions men and women mixed freely and touched one another often, but did not express spiritual joy by kissing. Badger's accusers, by contrast, swore that the kissing occurred with abandon during religious events. The sponsoring society suspected that the kisses were improper regardless of where or when they were practiced and queried all participants and witnesses extensively through letters. This controversy began the long-distance discussion between old Connecticut and New Connecticut about how to map the relationship between moral bodies and moral spaces on the Western Reserve.

Historical precedents did exist for drawing a close connection between revivalistic fervor and promiscuity. American Puritans and their descendants had a history of linking heresy or heretical behavior with a rhetoric of sexual disorder. Quakers, Antinomians, and those accused of witchcraft, for example, were often depicted as being sexually as well as theologically deviant.[2] These "heretics" were feared primarily because of their challenge to the religious and social order, but they were denounced in sexual terms. Charles Chauncy, like many other clergy opposed to the revivals of the 1720s and 1740s, cautioned against religious excesses that he feared aroused the "passions" and led to indecent behavior, including licentiousness.[3] Itinerant preachers, as Susan Juster has shown, were routinely described as harlots who seduced men and especially young women into compromising theological positions. The antirevivalists' denunciations of such "promiscuous" preaching were replete with sexual imagery.[4] The revivalists' preaching style and the tenor of their services were depicted as sexually charged gatherings where those present moaned, cried, and were overcome by intense physical sensations that accompanied conversion.

The suspicion that religious excitement led to sexual deviance and social disorder was thus firmly in place by the nineteenth century. The task of the home missionary society was to determine if the kiss was a sign of sexual "disorder," which would in turn be an indication of social disorder. And like Badger and the Connecticut Missionary Society, many of the settlers understood that the stakes were high. A committee from Badger's congregation wrote to the Connecticut Missionary Society to explain the "unusual" but not "disorderly" behavior that sometimes occurred during religious occasions and the measured steps that they had taken to ensure propriety. In an attempt to locate the action outside of human sexual expression and desire, they emphasized that kissing was a ritualized greeting among congregants, rather than a spontaneous response to effective preaching. Badger explained that he had picked up the habit from Pennsylvania Presbyterians, who, he maintained, developed the practice as a bodily sign of Christian fellowship. Further, he averred, the "charity kiss" was grounded in New Testament Scripture: Paul enjoins Christians to "salute one another with a holy kiss."[5]

Kissing, according to Badger, did not represent sexual disorder. Instead, the practice demonstrated the unity among his fledgling congregation. A crucial point for the Connecticut Missionary Society was whether or not these kisses were exchanged during ecstatic moments of religious renewal. Although some settlers asserted that kisses were not given under such circumstances, the missionary society was understandably perplexed; in the same letters religious gatherings were described in which many men and women were "taken into the laps of others and held like children for hours, totally helpless." Even though the congregants were careful to segregate the sexes, "it fell out many times that the women were taken care of by men. It so happened that Mr. Badger took care of some of the females both of his own children and others several times, when not engaged with public exercises—and we think with propriety."[6] Badger's church committee asked for the missionary society's understanding and patience, declaring their "situation in this church to be very initial and difficult; being almost all young members . . . who need the strictest watch and discipline."[7] While the members contended that they were being watchful of their young members, they also assured the missionary society that they were training them in good habits as "they have not been the subjects of faithful discipline, in the churches from whence they came."[8] While some of their emotive behavior might have smacked of disorderliness to the sponsoring society, Badger's congregants maintained that religious renewal never dissolved into sensual ecstasy by the means of a kiss.

Not all the people present, however, supported Badger and his holy kisses. Western Reserve settler Hosea Wilcox observed that the "kissing" Badger compelled him to sign a confession stating that he had unjustly slandered the missionary by suggesting the impropriety of Badger's kissing habits. In another letter, Badger countered this accusation by explaining to the Connecticut Missionary Society that Wilcox had voluntarily recanted his statement, begging God's and Badger's forgiveness. But in a confidential letter to the missionary society Wilcox confirmed that congregants were not only in the habit of kissing; if the kiss of charity were simply a mark of friendship, as Badger claimed, "it would have been extended to males as well as females which was by no means the case, neither was it given to many of the elderly Sisters."[9] Badger maintained that the kisses were a sign of civility, not disorder, and that his accusers arose from an angry faction, who reproached him unfairly and ultimately threatened the "Redeemer's cause" in the West.

The correspondence between the frontier settlers and the Connecticut Missionary Society about "the kiss" reveals a particular set of anxieties that emerged when this bodily practice was incorporated into a transitional and religious space. The most obvious concern involved the connection between a borderline sexual act and religious communion. The kiss remained an ambiguous act *only* if its interpreters invested it with diverse meanings. Was it practiced simply to greet the faithful, or was it a sign of excessive emotionalism believed to be common among rival religious denominations? Perhaps more vexing for the missionary society, the propriety of the kiss could not easily be determined: it was sanctioned and practiced not by a splinter group in the newly formed church but by a Plan of Union missionary himself. Badger defended the practice as a mark of civility, friendship, and piety; he thus placed the kiss within the framework that the missionary society desired: it was part of building a moral community. But the Connecticut Missionary Society worried that any bodily manifestations of religious fervor both led to moral disorder and brought Badger's congregation closer to accepting not just the practices but also the tenets of rival frontier denominations; it would lead to the destruction of the carefully planned and "mapped" New Connecticut.

The controversy surrounding Badger's kiss points us once more to the disjuncture between "New Connecticut" as mapped by the Connecticut Missionary Society and the actual Western Reserve. This chapter will explore further this separation. Rather than show how the separation between the imaginary and the real altered conceptions of the missionary "self," it will examine how the frontier, as a landscape under mental and physical construction, produced dramatic transformations in values associated with the body, the town, and the household. This chapter will thus extend the analysis from a consideration of the Plan of Union missionary to a broader examination of frontier society.

"Nurseries of piety": Body, Town, and Family

The shifts in religious bodily expression exemplified through the "kiss of charity" in Badger's congregation signaled a host of changes that accompanied the spatial reconfiguration of this transitional frontier landscape. This transitional moment and place allowed for a certain amount of freedom and experimentation in both moral and bodily behavior. But to examine how body practices change, we must first recognize that the biological body is a social construct subject to historical and cultural modifications, rather than an essential or static unit that remains unchanged over time.[10] In other words, people map their bodies in the same way that they map space. Feminist theorists have offered some of the most interesting examples of the body as an evolving and contested space, and these are instructive for interpreting the significance of religious actions like charity kisses.[11] What these theorists demonstrate is the intimate connection between cultural understandings of the body and daily practices. They contend that cultural rules dictate how a "normative" body looks, acts, dresses, procreates, and receives discipline; all such rules reflect power relationships.[12] For religious men and women, notions about the body are invested with sacred authority, and sacred texts sanction specifically "male" and "female" behaviors as ordained by God.[13] For example, one important aspect of membership in a religious community is that individuals inherit and practice theological knowledge about the body. Any challenge or modification to that order represents a direct affront to religious tradition, sacred text, and divine authority. The stakes were thus high for the Connecticut Missionary Society, and the society worried that the unorthodox practice of "kissing" signaled potential problems, including the loss of adherents to rival denominations that encouraged bodily responses during religious occasions.

Nowhere were these fears rendered more probable than in the bodily expressions and intermixing of the sexes during frontier revivals. Like the revivals of the 1720s and 1740s, the emotive quality of frontier revivals—crying, fainting, and joyous ecstasy—made the missionaries and their sponsoring society nervous, for it became increasingly difficult for missionaries to draw a line between religious renewal and social disorder. In this context, the unbounded space of outdoor frontier religious meetings erased the physical barriers to religious emotionalism, allowing a space for large gatherings of people and for grand gestures and movement; further, the society feared that there was little clerical control over the worship service. Missionary Thomas Robbins reported that he was not surprised that during revivals "some matters of prudence and propriety were overlooked." The impropriety that "naturally arises from the bodily exercise," according to Robbins, "is too great a familiarity between the sexes." Moreover, Robbins notes, "Badger was unable to regulate the behavior because he and his family were involved intimately in the practice."[14] This "familiarity between the sexes," which could lead to moral and social disorder, formed the epicenter of the missionary society's anxiety. While charity kisses remained undefined as moral practices, the body itself became a landscape on which the missionaries could "map"—that is to say, simultaneously inscribe and promote—moral order.

The missionaries who labored with the cultural understanding of the redemptive possibilities of shaping the spatial and moral landscape also understood themselves to be at risk of being transformed by that same environment. The significance of Badger's kiss signaled conflicting attitudes regarding the body in relationship to religious practices that emerged on the frontier. The context of this action—the simultaneous construction of moral habits and built landscapes—sheds light on the connection that the missionary society drew between moral bodies and spaces. From the society's perspective, without the proper built environment, bodies might act in immoral ways. The practice of the "kiss" and the controversy surrounding it telescoped the moral and spatial issues that missionaries and settlers faced during the next two decades of settlement. Questions of how a moral person looks, acts, and expresses herself arose as settlers created a built environment in the wilderness. What would be the physical shape of the frontier, and how would it impact morality? To answer these questions, the settlers, the missionaries, and the missionary society juggled their preconceptions of western landscape; for some this evoked a nostalgic desire to rebuild an imaginary, Puritan community by shaping moral bodies and moral spaces.

The sign of a moral community for the missionary society was an orderly landscape. Straight roads, central greens, and neat fields all indicated morality. These material features, though, remained meaningless without human cooperation. For missionaries, bodily signs of piety demonstrated the relationship between physical and moral order. If straight roads evidenced a moral community, solemnity, sobriety, and industriousness confirmed individual morality. Along with these qualities, a moral person devoted adequate time to work, domestic responsibilities, and Sabbath observance. All of these duties had their proper time and place.

Bodies operated in consecrated time. The Sabbath, according to the sponsoring society, remained a time of family prayer and Scripture reading among moral people residing in the Western Reserve. Missionaries urged settlers to refrain from worldly amusements and secular work on that sacred day. Dancing, playing games, talking politics, and tending crops distracted people from God and sometimes, according to missionaries, led to more serious forms of vice such as idleness, drunkenness, profanity, and adultery. As early as 1802, Ezekiel Chapman reported the "alarming omen" of inhabitants who passed the Sabbath in "hunting fishing, visiting or in idleness."[15] A few years later, Abraham Scott reported that in many towns in the Western Reserve the Sabbath was a day for "visiting, trading, and particularly in this season of the year of hunting, and also in some instances of attending to daily secular business."[16] Simeon Woodruff notes in an 1814 letter to the home society that when he preached in Palmyra, only a few heard him, "the people having generally assembled at a public house to see a puppet show."[17] In Aurora "the subject of making cheese on the Sabbath was brought up. Some were for continuing the unquestionable + wicked practice + some were convinced it was wrong."[18] Missionaries tried to impress upon settlers the importance of behaving properly on the Sabbath, reminding them to preserve sacred time. Although many inhabitants ignored the Sabbath through their bodies as well as their minds, of greater concern to the missionaries were those who behaved improperly while "remembering" the Sabbath or on religious occasions.

The disruption of sacred time and sacred space as well as the embodied demonstrations of religious fervor were, in the minds of the Plan of Union missionaries, the result of the presence of competing religious groups. Baptists, Methodists, and Universalists also missionized the Western Reserve settlements and upset sacred time and space by holding religious meetings at odd hours and in nontraditional spaces. As one scholar has argued, post–Revolutionary War revivalistic groups that worshiped out-of-doors wrested control from the established clergy in New England, whose clerical power was tied to physical buildings such as meetinghouses. They also challenged the social station solidified in pew fees by mixing congregants indiscriminately.[19] Besides challenging clerical authority and social station, the itinerant preachers gathered congregants in homes, fields, and forests, sanctifying new spaces that could not easily be mapped or controlled. For the first few years of settlement in New Connecticut, the Plan of Union missionaries operated in ways similar to itinerants, but they worked toward the ideal of a settled pastorate. Claiming preaching space was a critical concern that in a short time would be concretized in physical buildings. The Connecticut Missionary Society's obsession with plotting town greens and placing its churches on one side of the square re-created its vision of a New England landscape on the frontier by fixing its place in the town's center. The trustees' insistence that moral order was connected to the spatial order of a town square reflected their uneasiness with the moral and spatial disorder caused by itinerant circuits.

As the previous chapter showed, the Connecticut Missionary Society attempted to reassert its control over the Western Reserve by "remapping" the region. Following Chapin's moral survey, the Connecticut Missionary Society decided to send only Pennsylvania-born missionaries to serve in the Western Reserve; "home grown" missionaries replaced the New England missionaries. By the spring of 1809, however, a promising group of New England clergymen showed interest in the area, and the missionary society sent a number of them to missionize, with the goal of settling in the region.[20] But the New England missionaries who moved to the Western Reserve during this second wave of settlement and missionizing held a different relationship to New Connecticut than those who came before them. Although hired as missionaries, they moved to the Western Reserve to eventually assume settled pastorates. Giles Cowles of Farmington, Connecticut, John Seward of Granville, Massachusetts, Simeon Woodruff of Litchfield, Connecticut, William Hanford of Norwalk, Connecticut, and Randolph Stone of Bristol, Connecticut, were among the most prominent and prolific missionaries who relocated to the Western Reserve with their families. All five remained in that region at least thirty years. Other New England missionaries, like Jonathan Lesslie, who settled in the Western Reserve for shorter periods also viewed their vocation as a permanent rather than a temporary tour. Although their struggles mirrored those of Badger, Robbins, and Chapman, they understood themselves differently; they were settlers, not short-term missionaries. Lesslie exemplified this changed attitude when, after ten years of residing in the Western Reserve, he explained to the Connecticut Missionary Society, "I am attached to New Connecticut, when I am out of it I feel from home." Although Lesslie admitted that the region had its faults, he still believed that it was "the moral garden of the Western world."[21]

This moral garden constituted a hothouse for religious and social experimentation. In the face of such diversity, the Connecticut Missionary Society enjoined the settlers to attend to their own spiritual welfare by cultivating proper moral habits, and the society often used spatial language in urging vigilance. Drawing a parallel between spatial and moral order, the missionary society issued an *Address to the Emigrants from Connecticut* (figure 12), reminding settlers that "settling a new state is in many respects like laying out and building a great city."[22] Their decisions and actions were crucial to the moral shape of the region. "If those who first break ground make the streets narrow and crooked; if they build without taste or forethought, a shape, a physiognomy is thereby given to a town, many important features that will remain forever."[23] The route to happiness and salvation was clear. It depended on strict Sabbath observance, the establishment of public worship through church formation, and finding the financial means to support a clergyman and religious institutions.

The missionary society trustees acknowledged that such measures required sacrifice, and they offered suggestions for procuring money. They reasoned that sums could be raised if settlers stopped their use of "ardent spirits," if youths refrained from amusements, and if everyone agreed to make "little retrenchments, in the expenses of your tables, furniture, and apparel." Finally, they believed that each person could redeem a few hours' labor to establish a common religious fund. For those who felt that these sacrifices were too much, the trustees asked, "What is time to eternity? What are house and lands and goods compared with spiritual blessings in heavenly places, in Christ Jesus?"[24] But this list of suggestions, easily accomplished in "civilized" Connecticut, would have sounded quite impractical to frontier people. Labeling the loss of a piece of furniture as a "little retrenchment" not only betrayed the society's misperceptions regarding frontier life but also belittled the importance of basic sustenance and activities that provided food, shelter, and clothing. The missionary society trustees, however, had little concern for the material well-being of settlers; their eyes focused instead on spiritual goals that they believed could be realized only through moral order. In this and other communications with settlers and missionaries, the sponsoring society encouraged Western Reserve inhabitants to develop moral habits and a "tasteful physiognomy."

The missionary society's plea to the settlers was inspired by a vision of a religiously and politically fused nation. Individual salvation, family order, and political stability are here inextricably linked. The missionary society warned settlers repeatedly that they held the moral future of themselves, their families, and the nation in their hands. "We cannot help regarding every man of you, as the representative of thousands who are yet to be born. The moral dangers to which you are exposed alarm us. You stand at the head of two ways, one of which leads to honour and happiness, and the other to misery and ruin."[25] The home society urged settlers to accept the ideology that strong family government, each house being ruled by a benevolent and just father, was the cornerstone of an orderly society.

The Connecticut Missionary Society's desire to strengthen the links

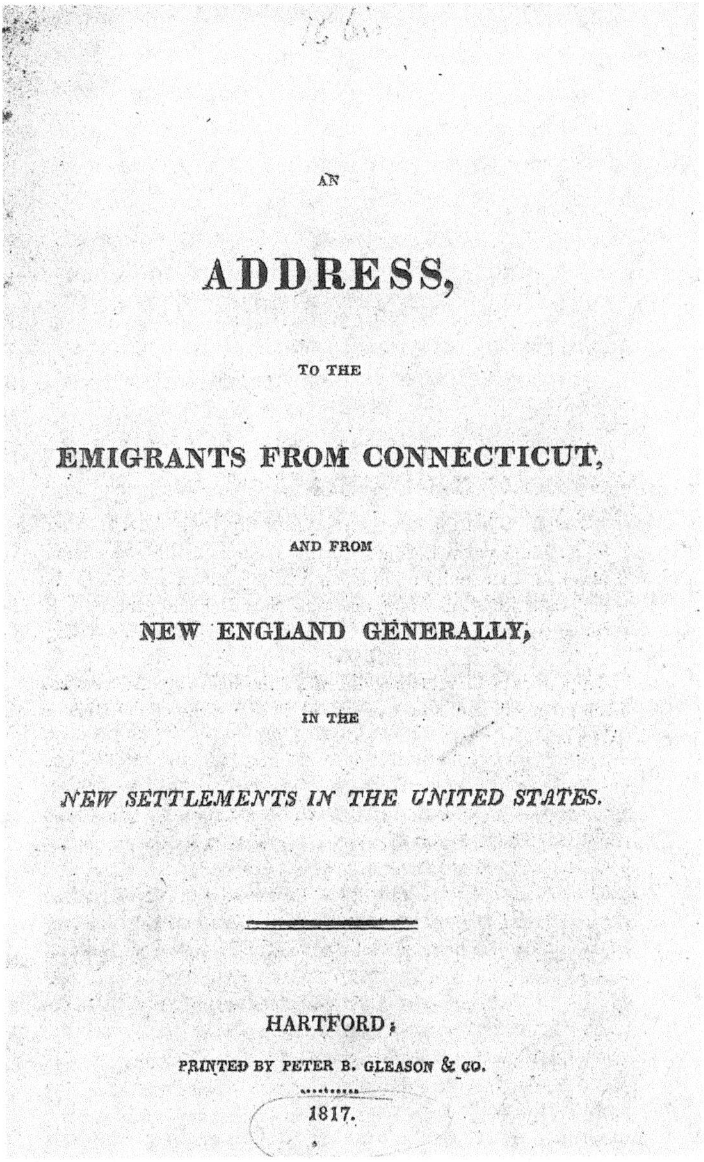

AN

ADDRESS,

TO THE

EMIGRANTS FROM CONNECTICUT,

AND FROM

NEW ENGLAND GENERALLY,

IN THE

NEW SETTLEMENTS IN THE UNITED STATES.

HARTFORD;
PRINTED BY PETER B. GLEASON & CO.
1817.

FIGURE 12. Front page of *An Address to the Emigrants from Connecticut, and from New England Generally, in the New Settlements in the United States* (Hartford: Peter B. Gleason and Company, 1817). In this publication the trustees of the Connecticut Missionary Society reminded the emigrants in New Connecticut that "settling a new state is in many respects like laying out and building a great city." The features of the moral and physical landscape once shaped will remain forever. Courtesy of the Connecticut Conference Archives, United Church of Christ, Hartford.

between family and government reflected a larger trend within nineteenth-century Protestant evangelical culture.[26] Parental advice books, childrearing literature, and children's instruction manuals were abundant at this time, and both clergy and laypeople attempted to harness the political power of the family. An early example of this type of literature was Philip Doddridge's 1799 advice manual for fathers, *A Plain and Serious Address to the Master of the Family an the Important Subject of Family Religion*, which was reprinted and distributed by the Connecticut Missionary Society. Doddridge implored Christian fathers to gather the family for nightly Scripture reading, prayer, and religious instruction so that homes may "become nurseries of piety."[27] He held that family prayer could eradicate most social ills. "But do you imagine, that if reading the scriptures and family prayer were introduced into the houses of some of your neighbors, drunkenness and lewdness, and cursing and swearing, and profaning the Lord's day would not, like so many *evil demons*, be quickly driven out?"[28] The Connecticut Missionary Society's conviction that "families well disciplined and instructed are pillars of both Church and State"[29] increased over the next few decades, on what the missionary society perceived to be a disorderly frontier. And the "disorderly" frontier was the target of the society's moralizing doctrine.

The charge to adopt New England habits was directed not only toward settlers but also at New England–born and Western-born missionaries, who, for almost a decade, had struggled to maintain amicable relationships among themselves. The class antagonism that characterized conflicts between Joseph Badger and Thomas Robbins in the early years of settlement was transformed into regional and cultural antagonism. Connecticut-born missionary Jonathan Lesslie voiced this conflict when he responded to Pennsylvania-born missionary Thomas A. Hughes, who accused Lesslie of favoring and promoting New England manners and customs to Western Reserve settlers. Lesslie's thoughts and actions could not have disturbed the missionary society; they expressed clearly the ideological and moral instructions given by the society to New England missionaries. And Lesslie notes that because of the vagueness of the accusation, he became "a strenuous advocate for the modes and customs of New England." In reference to the accusations of Hughes, Lesslie remained unaware of his transgression: "If it be their mode of farming, I have recommended it to the Pennsylvanians. Their manner of laying out and settling their towns I have said is most convenient. Their industry and economical manner of living I have spoken favorably of. That public spirit which they manifest in educating their children, + the regulation which they have in their schools I have recommended to the Pennsylvanians + even urged them to imitation."[30] Where, Lesslie asked the missionary society, lay the fault in his reasoning?

Jonathan Lesslie's letter reflects fundamental convictions about the organization of space: not only are physical and moral construction linked, but the ideal for both is manifest in New England towns. Plan of Union missionaries drew a correspondence between changes in the physical landscape and moral changes; they were able to assess their success and failure by looking at the landscape. Further, Lesslie's love of order extended beyond spatial arrangement and moral advice to the actual organization of his handwritten missionary accounts. Every three months he sent a detailed narrative to Hartford that included a map of the towns that he visited with a column for the range number, the town number, the town name, and the number of sermons he delivered in each town. This map, like a naturalist's typology, neatly organized the 2,426 miles he traveled and the 134 sermons he preached (figure 13).[31] Although Lesslie did not achieve social harmony with many of his fellow missionaries, he remained a model Plan of Union missionary by scrupulously charting moral order onto the landscape, a "map" that the Connecticut Missionary Society could easily discern.

"A considerable phalanx of infidelity": Religious Rivalry and the Body

The Western Reserve enticed a variety of travelers and preachers who left footprints all over the Connecticut Missionary Society's map. The religious competition between rival groups as well as the growing diversity among members of a single religious group complicated the tasks and goals of the Plan of Union missionaries on the frontier. Although the Connecticut Missionary Society continued to claim in its publications that New England settlers dominated the region, the missionary letters described growing religious and regional diversity. In the town of Canfield, missionary Randolph Stone reported "sectarian feelings running high in this place, there being no less than a Presbyterian, Episcopalian, Methodist, Baptist, + Dutch Reformed Church."[32] In the spring of 1814 Simeon Woodruff noticed "a considerable number of Universalists" in Palmyra.[33] Five years later he complained that although he "preached to [a]

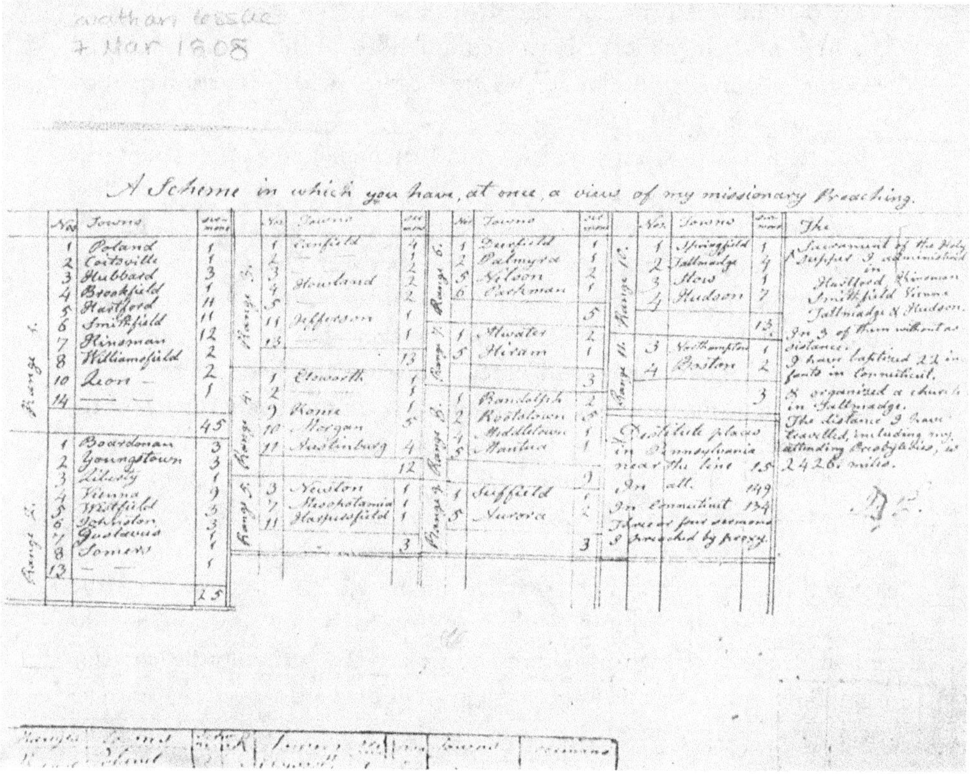

A Scheme in which you have, at once, a view of my missionary Preaching.

The Sacrament of the Holy Supper I administered in Hartford, Hinsman, Smithfield, Vienna, Tallmadge & Hudson. In 3 of them without a distance. I have baptized 22 infants in Connecticut. I organized a church in Tallmadge. The distance I have travelled, including my attending Presbyteries, is 2426 miles.

FIGURE 13. "A Scheme in which you have, at once, a view of my missionary Preaching." A page of a letter from Jonathan Lesslie to Connecticut Missionary Society Trustees, March 7, 1808. This scheme attached to missionary Jonathan Lesslie's 1807 letter to the sponsoring society illustrates the careful mapping of his missionary labor. Courtesy of the Connecticut Conference Archives, United Church of Christ, Hartford.

pretty full meeting" there, "there is a Methodist Ch.h in this town + also a Baptist one, which is divided into two, so there are sometimes 4 meetings in the town on the same day."[34]

Regional and cultural differences challenged the missionary effort to "map" New England moral and physical order. Connecticut Missionary Society envoys John Schermerhorn and Samuel J. Mills toured the Western Reserve in 1814 and found that "those from New Jersey and Pennsylvania, particularly of Scotch and Irish descent," supported the Plan of Union missionary cause through their interest in schools and maintaining preaching. Presumably these settlers were Presbyterians and therefore part of the Plan of Union. Schermerhorn and Mills did not hold other settlers such as "those of German extraction, together with immigrants from Maryland, Virginia and Kentucky," in such high esteem. Their settlement patterns and general habits appeared to Schermerhorn and Mills at odds with New England ways. Besides their lack of enthusiasm for Plan of Union missionaries, they "too fondly cherish[ed] that high toned and licentious spirit, which will suffer neither contradiction nor opposition, and which is equally inconsistent with civil and religious order."[35]

The Connecticut Missionary Society heard of disorderly behavior all over the Western Reserve, and the trustees decried all types of pernicious acts reported to them by missionaries. Settlers living beyond the gaze of Connecticut eyes and in the company of "heretics" and "infidels" tended to drink, profane the Sabbath, commit adultery, and live generally ungodly lives. But the trustees were particularly concerned about the harmful influences of sectarian groups that also canvassed the Western Reserve. Missionary accounts published in the *Connecticut Evangelical Magazine* and in the *Narrative of Missions* acknowledged the presence of rival religious groups in the Western Reserve, particularly those they termed "false teachers," such as Baptists, Methodists, and Universalists. These were dangerous influences for spiritually vulnerable and easily deceived people. Giles Cowles warned that "heretics were diligent, and in some places too successful in the propagation of their delusions."[36] Spiritual vulnerability was presented in these narratives in two main forms. First, recently awakened souls were viewed as particularly vulnerable to false teachings. Second, individuals never exposed to religious doctrine were also highly susceptible to the "unsound" theology of sectarian religious groups.

While Joseph Badger and Thomas Robbins concerned themselves with identifying the right sort of Plan of Union missionary for western settlements, the second generation of missionaries looked closely at preachers from other denominations to identify how they were able to attract frontier settlers. The infighting between Presbyterians and Congregationalists, which had characterized the first-generation missionaries, decreased in the face of competition with these other religious groups. The anxiety produced by rivalry emerged in discussions about enthusiastic revivals and threats to family order. Hence, the question of what sort of man is most fit to missionize the frontier resurfaced as Plan of Union missionaries registered the growth of rival denominations.

Numerous religious groups passed through the Western Reserve, but the Baptists, Methodists, and Universalists posed the greatest danger to the Presbyterian and Congregational missionaries. Although these three rival groups divided on theological lines, they were united in the eyes of Plan of Union missionaries; Baptists, Methodists, and Universalists were "dissenters," lumped together as an unholy trinity of immorality and disorder in the Western Reserve.[37] The conflation of these three groups in Plan of Union missionary letters and publications signified the general presence of "infidelity."

The "dissenters" formed a alarming sectarian triumvirate, far more formidable when depicted together than separately. After visiting one town in the Western Reserve, missionary Giles Cowles alerted the Connecticut Missionary Society to subversive religious tendencies, stating that in one town the inhabitants were "chiefly Baptists, Methodists, and Universalists with a few Congregationalists—+ greatly in need of instruction."[38] John Seward complained often about "sectarian influences" in the Western Reserve. He was outraged by the rapid progress of a nearby Universalist society that had organized and sent one member "with the zeal of a persecuting Saul" to Vermont to hire a preacher "who is a workman + *not* a boy."[39] The criticism, reminiscent of the type of complaint aired against the first Plan of Union missionaries, is now repeated by a missionary himself.

Baptists, Methodists, and Universalists threatened the Plan of Union missionaries' goals because they dashed the hopes of a homogeneous culture on the Western Reserve. What the missionary society could not admit was that these alternative theologies held value for many Western Reserve settlers. In response, the Connecticut Missionary Society insisted that the sectarian threat arose not because settlers preferred a certain theological doctrine but, as one Plan of Union missionary put it, because they desired to hear any religious doctrine preached: "The great call for preaching, and scarcity of it, will have a tendency to invite in preachers of other denominations, which are numerous in this country and very erroneous. Many who do not correspond with them in sentiment, will go to hear them preach, rather than not attend public worship."[40] The sponsoring society viewed the success of sectarians as the result of either the absence of Plan of Union missionaries or the theological tricks played by rivals to deceive the vulnerable settlers.

The Connecticut Missionary Society was acutely aware of the popularity of "pretended" ministers spreading "false doctrine" and highlighted the threat in its annual *Narrative of Missions*. Editorial pleas connected the necessity for increased donations to the settlers' vulnerability to unsound doctrine. As early as 1811 the editor explained that "in the new settlements especially, false teachers are numerous. Naturally, all mankind love to embrace those delusions, by which, 'with cunning craftiness' such teachers 'lie in wait to deceive.' This is a circumstance not to be overlooked, that renders increased missionary labors indispensable."[41] Examples litter the narratives of missionary letter excerpts, cautioning against the perils of preachers who espouse false doctrines of immediate conversion. Jonathan Lesslie warned that "imposters, calling themselves ministers of the gospel, and propagators of the most dangerous errors, still abound. Infamous publications are industriously circulated, with a design to turn persons away from faith, and palsy the arm of Christian benevolence."[42] The Connecticut Missionary Society's publications connected unorthodox doctrine, ignorance, and immediate conversion with theological laxity, all the while asserting that this combination appealed to the vulnerable and the deluded. On a Wednesday evening in June 1815, Simeon Woodruff heard the Universalist preacher Mr. Bigelow give a sermon. Woodruff admitted that Bigelow had "*some* eloquence and *some* ingenuity + a *great deal* of vain confidence + self sufficiency." The trouble, Woodruff explained, was that "a considerable number embrace his pernicious error."[43]

Besides the competition from sectarian preachers, the Plan of Union missionaries also felt threatened by sectarian publications that either jeopardized their religious principles or attacked their authority. Missionary William Hanford complained that people living outside of New England gleaned information about Plan of Union missionaries from "Democratic Newspapers" that described the missionaries as unpatriotic and deceitful.[44] Abraham Scott worried that the Universalists gained converts by circulating "the works of the most able authors in favor of Universalism," which he believed many settlers admired and read to the exclusion of other "orthodox" texts.[45] *The Plain Truth*, *The Reformer*, *The Gospel Advocate*, and *The Christian Baptist*, according to Randolph Stone, all circulated in the Western Reserve, constituting a "considerable phalanx of infidelity," not to the "well-informed + well principled part of the community, but to the lower classes of society whose minds and hearts are equally uncultivated to the rising generation."[46] These people, Stone believed, were the most vulnerable to such writings because they were "just beginning to form a moral and religious character."[47] Likewise, Simeon Woodruff found that some people had gathered on the Sabbath in Burton to read Universalist writings, an act that he viewed as part of a larger theological battle. "The enemy," he wrote, "have taken the alarm + are making efforts." Woodruff did not fail to mention to the society, however, that the Universalist publication originated not in the Western Reserve but in Hartford, Connecticut.[48] John Seward also complained of the increase in "sin and error" and located the primary cause of the moral degeneration in "the influence of vile publications from the land of pilgrims + of steady habits."[49] While missionaries admitted the presence and power of these publications, they were careful to remind the Connecticut Missionary Society that for the most part these threatening works were imported to, not originating in, the Western Reserve.

To fight the increase in Baptist, Methodist, and Universalist publications, the missionaries asked the sponsoring society to send more religious books and tracts to frontier settlements. Missionary Luther Humphrey begged the trustees to send Joseph Emerson's *Evangelical Primer* "by the hundreds and the thousands," saying that the benefit to the Western Reserve settlers would "far out-weigh the cost to the society."[50] Missionary Harvey Coe reported in 1825 that "the enemy is unwearied in his exertions. The greatest efforts are made to gain proselytes to the most abominable errors, and to promote the circulation of the most pernicious publications."[51] The Connecticut Missionary Society responded energetically to the missionaries' requests and continued to send religious texts to the frontier well into the 1830s. The two most commonly supplied texts were Lyman Beecher's *Sermon on Divine Government* and Joseph Emerson's *Evangelical Primer*. In 1812, for example, the missionary society sent 909 copies of Emerson's primer and 436 copies of Beecher's text, as well as 486 miscellaneous religious tracts.[52]

Theologically, the greatest threat posed by the competition was the apparent ease with which Baptist, Methodist, and Universalist believers obtained grace. Rather than a lifelong process of spiritual labor, the emotional sacramental occasions produced a rapid and seemingly easy experience of grace. From the perspective of the Plan of Union missionaries, a true sign of a regenerate soul was a spiritual seriousness that came from hearing the truth of the gospel. This change could occur in a moment, but that renewal was part of a long process of spiritual attentiveness.

As troubling as the theology, however, were the bodily expressions reported during the religious services of Baptists, Methodists, and Universalists. The most reported issue regarding dissenting religious groups in the missionary letters was emotionalism. The dramatic, embodied response to a spiritual crisis, such as fainting, yelling, or jerking, was not a new phenomenon in the Western Reserve. Ezekiel Chapman wrote in 1803 that "at several religious meetings which I have attended in this place the shrieks and groans have been so great that it was necessary to suspend entirely religious exercises." He was shocked to see that "the distressed persons wring their hands—distort their limbs into many shapes and turn and twist themselves in many ways."[53] But while Plan of Union missionaries experimented with some revivalistic techniques—sometimes preaching without notes and placing a larger emphasis on a "heart-felt" conversion experience—they rhetorically marked boundaries between themselves and "sectarians." Plan of Union missionaries, for the most part, discredited embodied religious practices, using language that invalidated emotionalism as disorderly, ignorant, and noisy.

Plan of Union missionaries admitted that a certain amount of bodily response accompanied an experience of grace, but they looked for sobering signs such as "solemnity" and "seriousness" to authenticate a change of heart. In order to discredit their rival preachers, the Plan of Union missionaries portrayed the bodily responses to the preaching as "emotional," "sensual," and "enthusiastic." Many people, the missionaries believed, were fooled by their senses. In the town of Chardon, for example, Luther Humphrey failed to convince two women to leave the Baptists and return to the Congregational church. He explained to the missionary society that "they appear to follow their own feelings more than the word of God."[54] Although emotionalism was perceived by the Plan of Union missionaries as originating with sectarians, it seemed to spread quickly to the Presbyterian and Congregational congregations in the Western Reserve. The missionaries felt compelled to identify the type of emotionalism they encountered and in each instance to judge whether it signaled the beginning of a "glorious revival" or the progress of infidelity. Randolph Stone found New England emigrants living in the town of Lebanon practicing what he termed "bodily religion": "They seem to be unsusceptible of any impressions in religious things, that are not made upon the *senses*. Whatever is not *felt* is of no account to them."[55] Here resided a group of New Englanders who, according to Stone, modified their religious practices because of sectarian influences. Left to their own devices without missionary instruction, the group adopted the sensualism associated with immediate assurance of grace. Writing against the prevalence of emotive religious occasions, missionary Jonathan Lesslie lent credence to his worship services by asserting that "strict order has been maintained in our meetings. . . . Nothing enthusiastic appears in their exercise." Rather than exhibiting the quick and dramatic bodily response to conversion that was increasingly popular, his congregation was led to "most cordially" accept grace.[56] For the Plan of Union missionaries, theological authenticity remained tied closely to a slow, dignified salvific process.

The Connecticut Missionary Society's instructions to missionaries regarding revivals remained guarded even as its advice changed over time. While the society hoped for religious renewal on the frontier, it worried that the reports of enthusiasm and unruly behavior on sacramental occasions showed nineteenth-century revivals to be different in spirit from the "orthodox" revivals of eighteenth-century New England. Although reluctant to forbid or discredit these "unusual outpourings of the spirit," the missionary society asked missionaries who witnessed such events to describe and interpret the activities for Connecticut readers. The Plan of Union missionaries carefully recorded the location, number of people, and format of the revivals that they attended. The missionaries struggled to understand the emotionalism of the frontier and to assure their sponsors in the East that the religious awakenings fit within the theological context of New England piety. Missionary Thomas Robbins voiced these concerns in a letter to the society printed in the *Connecticut Evangelical Magazine*: "You once observed to me, you wished to have an account of this work, from one who had been an eyewitness, and who was acquainted with Connecticut ideas, modes of thinking and expression. . . . I conceive this work in many respects to resemble the great revival of religion in New England in 1740, '41 and '42. . . . The manner of the ministers' preaching is also much as it was then; Calvinist in sentiment, serious, earnest and pathetic."[57] Casting back to Jonathan Edwards's eighteenth-century Northampton revivals, Robbins placed the emotionalism within a historical context that lent theological credibility to what he saw.

Baptists, Methodists, and Universalists were often portrayed as uneducated and, in the minds of the Plan of Union missionaries, unqualified to provide religious guidance. Missionary historian James Rohrer argues that as well as vying for denominational dominance, the Plan of Union missionaries actively sought to protect recently converted souls from false doctrine. While they hoped to increase their ranks, the missionaries also worried about theological delusions, particularly a "premature sense of assurance" spread by enthusiastic but "ignorant" sectarians.[58] After yielding his pulpit to two Methodist preachers while on an itinerant tour, Plan of Union missionary Luther Humphrey noted that the two "pretended ministers" were "extremely ignorant of gospel truth + extremely illiterate as to common knowledge."[59] Humphrey exemplifies the crucial link between literacy and theology that grounded the Presbyterian and Congregational commitment to long-term spiritual labor.

The Plan of Union missionaries worried about the sectarian threat to building a moral society in the Western Reserve. They responded to these challenges by asserting the importance of town planning and upholding the patriarchal family through family prayer, Sabbath observance, and public worship. And while the missionaries commented in their letters on the cultural and regional backgrounds of sectarians, it was the bodily practices—the social manners, customs, and behaviors of Baptists, Methodists, and Universalists—that received the most attention. The missionaries found the strongest evidence of improper conduct in worship services and during revival meetings; Simeon Woodruff reported that "a pretty powerful religious excitement is attended with considerable noise and disorder." In this particular case he noted uncharacteristically that although the meeting was conducted primarily by Methodists, "it is believed however that there is a gracious work of the Holy Spirit."[60] Further, the missionaries complained that the worship services lacked structure. Specifically, the logic of sermons seemed skewed to the missionaries, and the congregants' behavior appeared chaotic. For example, Jonathan Lesslie claimed that "the Methodists carry their enthusiasm to the utmost extravagance. They lye in trances + see visions, + can distinguish the subjects of grace etc."[61] Missionary Randolph Stone attended a Methodist quarterly meeting in Chardon where he "beheld a scene of confusion, equally revolting to reason + religion, + I may say humanity."[62] In contrast, William Hanford highlighted the quiet and order of his services: "I hardly know what to say respecting the moral state of things in this quarter," he confided in 1814. "Assemblies for public worship where I preach are generally so still that the least noise would be noticed."[63] Moreover, the dissenters of the Western Reserve seemed to espouse the most radical doctrines and religious practices of their denominations. Upon visiting the town of Canfield, Stone commented on the contentiousness of Methodists, who "appeared to be opposed to everything but Methodism in its wildest form."[64] And lamenting the fact that "stupidity prevails," John Seward warned that "the disorganizing spirit, in many places is becoming popular."[65] Here Seward baldly equated sectarianism with disorderliness.

While Plan of Union missionaries focused on establishing church-centered settlements, Methodist missionaries traveled to find people where they lived, carrying a portable faith that did not require a fixed religious space. The antipathy of Plan of Union missionaries toward their counterparts reflects the fact that many other missionaries were much more effective than they at covering and claiming religious space on the frontier. On a Sabbath morning, for example, Simeon Woodruff preached a sermon in the town of Tallmadge. Later that day he went to a well-attended Methodist meeting and listened to a circuit rider preach. "It was painful to hear him," Woodruff wrote to the Connecticut Missionary Society.[66] Because the Methodist missionaries were organized into traveling circuits, they were able to preach within a moveable structure that was well suited to the frontier.

For these reasons, the Connecticut Missionary Society steadfastly insisted that the threat to the establishment of a moral society in the Western Reserve came from religious dissenters. In editorials in the *Connecticut Evangelical Magazine* and the *Narrative of Missions*, the society portrayed the sectarians as subversive, not only because their presence signaled regional and cultural diversity but also because their theologies seemed lazy and inane. More important, their worship styles appeared disorderly. In the minds of the trustees, religious dissent paralleled the uncultivated land, a wild expanse that needed to be "mapped," cultivated, and ordered. It is not surprising that the editor of the *Narrative of Missions* often used agricultural metaphors to make a point. In a preface to a list of the obstacles that confronted missionaries, the editor observed, "While the husbandman was changing the forest to a fruitful field, the servant of Christ began the work of the garden of God."[67] While the society acknowledged in its journal that the population was becoming more heterogeneous, the editor celebrated the missionary successes in sowing and harvesting, as it were, morality and order. And this was the task of the Plan of Union missionaries: "Here may be seen the cheering influences of religious institutions, in forming the manners, elevating the character, and improving the condition of a mixed and increasing population."[68]

"Scattered promiscuously over the face of the country": Town Planning and Moral Order

Of the town founders of New Connecticut, no one strove harder to replicate the New England ideal than thirty-nine-year-old David Hudson of Goshen, Connecticut. His desire to establish a godly community "based on moral and religious principles" and to settle in the Western Reserve was linked to his desire to atone for his former sins. Hudson published an account of his spiritual journey in the 1803 edition of the *Western Missionary Journal*. Although he was "born of religious parents, and received an early education in the principles of religion, according to the Calvinistic Presbyterian plan proffered in the state," Hudson marked his adolescence by a slow decline in piety with religious intervals in the company of Baptists, Quakers, and finally Deists.[69] For years he openly decried orthodoxy and followed the beliefs of Thomas Paine and David Hume; then he underwent a political and religious conversion upon realizing that the French Revolution failed to provide the national and moral rebirth he longed for. After months of agony he finally confessed his spiritual state to the Reverend Asahel Hooker and commenced a secret devotional life.

Hudson found solace in renewed religious convictions, yet kept his change of heart a secret because he feared the social implications of his new life: "I had lived a long time in the open profession of infidelity, and could not willingly meet the scoffs of all my neighbors and acquaintances, who I expected would call me a turncoat, a fool, or an enthusiast." Rather than face his neighbors and friends, Hudson decided to begin anew in the West. Comparing himself to a biblical prophet, he noted: "I, like Jonah of old, formed a design of fleeing from the presence of the Lord, and removing myself to the solitary wilds of the Connecticut western reserve, and there commenced a life of religion, where my former way of thinking was unknown."[70] Hudson's reasons for moving to the frontier settlements were not unique. While many settlers were inspired to move by the prospects of wealth and other material gains, most also hoped for a new start. But Hudson, even more than most, illustrates the connection between cultural assumptions about the western frontier and religious experience. The frontier represented a place to hide from public scrutiny and to avoid accountability for statements and actions. It also signified a place to atone for transgressions, enabling a radical restructuring of the body and the soul.

Spiritual renewal was not Hudson's only motive for moving to New Connecticut. He also hoped for financial gain. Before his conversion, Hudson and four other coproprietors had purchased "sight unseen" seven thousand acres of land in the Western Reserve, Hudson himself investing a considerable amount of capital. In the spring of 1799, armed with ample provisions and a copy of Jedidiah Morse's *American Geography*, Hudson set out with his eleven-year-old son, Ira, and a few hired hands on the grueling journey to locate and mark his property's boundaries. After two months of traveling, he arrived in the vicinity of his township and spent six days searching with "inaccurate" maps for the surveyor's boundary of township four, range ten. Like the God of Genesis, exhausted after six days of toil, Hudson slept on the seventh day, "with grateful pleasure in resting on my own land."[71] Hudson and his crew surveyed the town, cleared fields, and built makeshift cabins; he then returned to Connecticut to retrieve his wife and five other children as well as some neighbors whom he had convinced to settle in his town. Hudson sold the land for $2.50 per acre, half the price of lots closer to Cleveland. The settlement grew rapidly, and soon visual signs on the landscape proclaimed its direct link to its Puritan past. Within two years of his return to New Connecticut, David Hudson saw the founding of a Congregational church and the building of a school; the town also adopted his name.

The town of Hudson was organized around a town green, with a Congregational church on one side and houses radiating out from the center. Henry Leavitt Ellsworth visited Hudson in 1811 and described it as "quite settled." Unlike many of the Western Reserve towns that Ellsworth passed through on his tour of the region, in Hudson "the houses are many of them framed, and the tavern where we lodged is *painted* white, a novelty in this western country."[72] Hudson was shaped to resemble the physical and moral landscape of Puritan New England. The "Articles for the Regulation of Members" in the First Congregational Church of Hudson outlined the social and religious duties of its members. The fourth regulation, for example, explicated the role of family members in religious instruction and worship. This included Scripture reading, prayer, and singing "when it can be performed with propriety."[73] Article 5 promoted strict parental governance of children, while Article 7 condemned Sabbath violations such as "the collecting of hay or grain, . . . attending to any part of the business of making sugar or cheese, . . . visiting friends, except of cases of sickness, + the prosecution of journies on that day."[74] The adoption of these explicit regulations came after two recorded cases of disciplinary action against members. The first occurred when Samuel Bishop was charged in 1804 with "intoxication, quarrelling, falsifying the truth + profane expressions"; to these charges he pleaded not guilty. He withdrew his membership and inverted the blame by stating: "I pray that God may forgive your immoral + irreligious conduct."[75] The second incident arose when Steven Thompson voluntarily confessed that he had "used such language to his wife at various times without provocation from her, as justified her in believing that she was in danger while living with him."[76] Thompson retained his membership by professing repentance and begging the forgiveness of God and the "brethren + sisters of the church whose feelings his conduct has wounded."[77] These two incidents exemplify the moral climate that David Hudson and members of the Connecticut Missionary Society hoped to establish in every township in New Connecticut. But the town of Hudson proved the exception of the Western Reserve, rather than the rule.

Connecticut land surveyors dutifully drew Western Reserve town lines in accordance with a "grid"—a New England ideal. But while they indicated the town center on the map, settlers argued about the appropriate location for a center green and about which church, if any, should be honored with that prime spot. Religious concerns thus surfaced even over a seemingly "non-negotiable spot" on the mathematical survey. The connection between a town center and religious competition was not lost on missionary Giles Cowles, who worried about the consequences of these disputes in the Western Reserve towns of Hartford and Smithfield. In an 1810 letter to the missionary society he reported that the settlers "have fallen into unhappy division about fixing their centres, which render the prospect of their forming a society + supporting preaching very unfavorable at present."[78] Fixing a spatial center must precede the formation and support of society and religion. Cowles reflected the understanding among Plan of Union missionaries that, unlike the case for rival denominations, their preaching strength ultimately remained tied to a fixed point in space, the pulpit. The accurate layout of towns was thus part of the missionary endeavor to instill moral order. For the Plan of Union missionaries, space, time, national memory, and religious identity all proceed from the town center (figure 14).

The difficulty of re-creating the paradigmatic New England town resulted not only from improper surveys but also from settlement patterns.

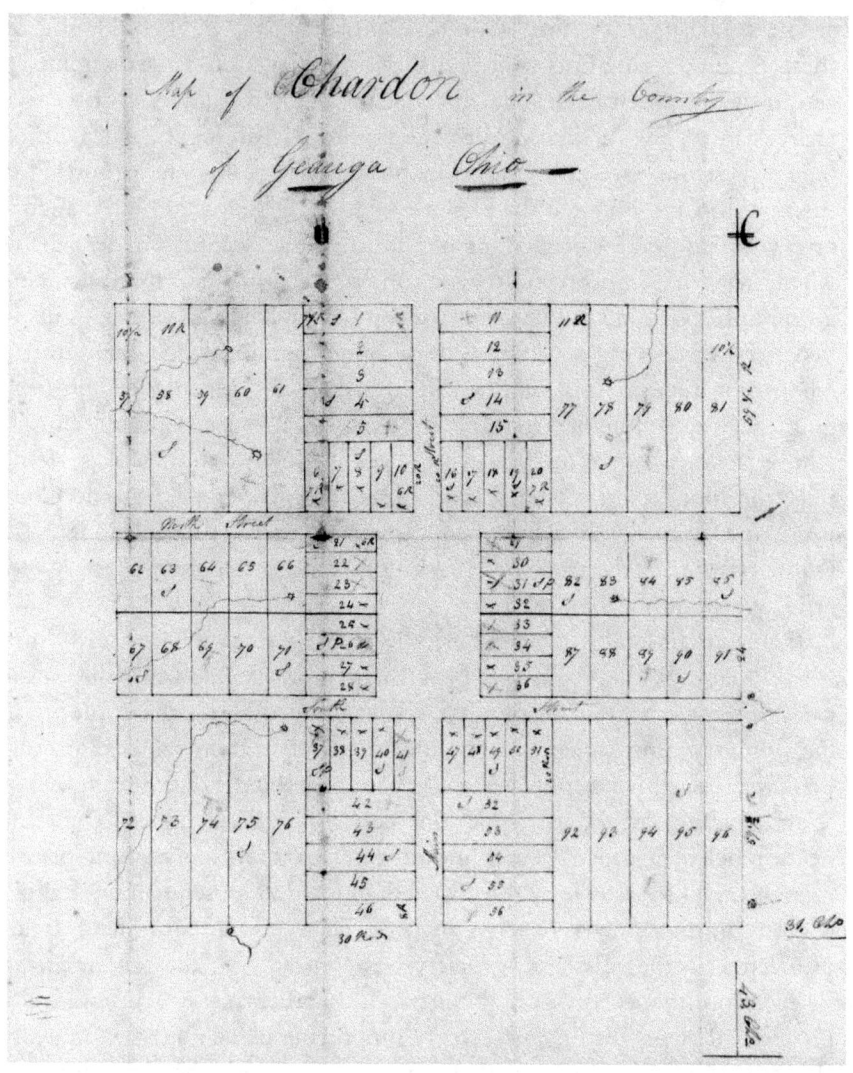

FIGURE 14. "Map of Chardon in the County of Geauga, Ohio." The carefully gridded New Connecticut towns that replicated idealized New England towns with central greens often were the sites of competition among missionaries of competing denominations. Courtesy of the Western Reserve Historical Society, Cleveland.

Where people chose to live and how they occupied that space often threatened the missionary efforts to gather the settlers together in a unified community. Of the 212 townships surveyed within the Western Reserve, a majority contained public open spaces at their centers. Ninety-six of those towns were settled primarily by New Englanders, and ten of the ninety-six exhibited physical contest by the presence of two central greens.[79] According to geographers Alexander T. Bobersky and David T. Stephens, the choice for these central greens could not have been made based on land quality but was the result of the survey system or an individual's desire for a specific site as the town center. Significantly, the easternmost segment of the Western Reserve, which was surveyed first and contained the largest proportion of New England settlers, had the most centralized public spaces in the region. While the idealized Puritan central green formed a perfect rectangle, few New England towns could boast such geographic symmetry, and correspondingly only twenty-one of the public squares in the Western Reserve fit that formula.[80] More commonly, Western Reserve central greens, like New England town greens, formed a quasi square or a shape "that defied exact geometric definition."[81] Surveyors relied on compass readings, mathematics, and natural landmarks to divide the nonconforming terrain. Seth I. Ensign's 1806 survey of Tallmadge's public square, for example, measures the site through a combination of grid and natural markers: "Beginning at the NE cor. of subdivision No. 2, Lot No. 11, at an ash post 14 lnks NW of an oak tree."[82] While the ideal and the grid survey demanded a geometric shape, its lack of conformity to the mold in the Western Reserve is perhaps its most persistent landscape feature. Nonetheless, John Seward notes that the eight Western Reserve churches organized by August 1812 were "all included in a parallelogram 25 miles long north + south + 20 miles broad."[83]

If Plan of Union missionaries appeared to be concerned with town centers, they were equally interested in town margins. Along the eastern and southern borders of the Western Reserve, towns were settled by a diverse regional and religious population that paid less attention to town squares than the missionaries believed they should have. Plan of Union missionaries noticed that these "border" towns often welcomed sectarian preachers, proving, as they believed, that spatial disorganization led to moral disorder. Missionary Randolph Stone found the town of Euclid particularly chaotic because of its regional and religious diversity. From Stone's viewpoint, there was little hope for Plan of Union missionaries in that town. The settlers ranged "in nearly equal numbers from the New England states, from those of Pennsylvania + New Jersey" and carried "their manners + customs + their religious predilections." This, Stone believed, created an insurmountable obstacle for him and future New England missionaries because of the settlers' strong attachment to their regional and religious identities and their reluctance "to yield anything in compliance."[84] Rather than taking up the population's diversity as a challenge to meet, he decided to direct his energy toward the more homogeneous settlements that he believed constituted propitious missionary ground. Missionary Erastus Ripley in 1817 traveled to Salem, the first town established in the Western Reserve, and reported to the society that Plan of Union missionaries rarely visited. There he found all the elements of a functioning society: sawmills, gristmills, a falling-mill, a double-cording machine, an ironwork, and many able-bodied men. Although the town, according to Ripley, could easily support a missionary, the inhabitants were divided by "smithites, Free Will Baptists, Universalists, Methodists, etc. They are so loose in sentiments and practice that missionaries have not labored much here for want of patronage."[85]

When missionary William Hanford traveled south of the Western Reserve border in the summer of 1814, he met "people from all parts of our country" and detected that many of the inhabitants held "very strong prejudices" against New Englanders.[86] Randolph Stone toured the region a few years later and determined that there were significant hurdles to effective missionizing. Stone indicated that the primary barriers were the dearth of New Englanders and the haphazard town planning and construction. He described this problem in terms of "the mixed character of the population, which is made up of emigrants from England, Scotland, Ireland, France, Germany + Holland, together with many from the back parts of Pennsylvania + Virginia + a *very few* from the New England States."[87] These settlers, like those in Euclid, "hold fast to their national manners, morals, religion, and habits of life" and, in Stone's opinion, were unlikely to adopt the position of the New England minority.[88] Furthermore, their distinct town organization would hinder any attempts by New England missionaries to establish religious order. The physical space, according to Stone, promoted immorality.

The settlement style in these communities, to Stone's dismay, inverted the New England town center by disregarding main roads that would have led to a physical and spiritual center. Stone reports that settlers were instead "scattered promiscuously over the face of the country with no little order + regularity as Autumn scatters the leaves of the trees."[89] Settlers "scattered promiscuously" presented spatial obstacles to the establishment of a moral society. The settlers chose locations based on natural resources rather than social access; Stone was astonished to find that they "build their houses wherever they can find a good spring of water, no matter where that is."[90] Stone's assessment reflects his sincere belief in the connection between town order and moral order: he could not envision overcoming the greater challenge posed by missionizing a delocalized region.[91]

In Richmond, by contrast, Stone found a town that met his approval. A dozen families from the same neighborhood in Massachusetts established the town; according to Stone, they "pitched their dwelling in the wilderness merely as fortune seekers. Here, insulated from the rush of the world by extensive forests on every side, they have thrown up their temporary log dwelling in sight of each other—felled the trees around them and made an opening somewhat larger than a common farm in New England." In this secluded setting, "deeply immersed in the toil of subduing the wild," while waiting for their future crops, "the Savior of sinners found and blessed them."[92] Even settlers who sought worldly fortune in the West might have been surprised by spiritual blessings—if their settlement was properly organized.

The missionaries' efforts to establish moral order through spatial planning reflect the conviction that a settled clergyman who operated from the town's center brought stability to a society. The Connecticut Missionary Society hoped that eventually all of the Western Reserve missionaries would assume such positions there and would be financially supported by their local congregations. But the increasing challenges made by Baptists, Methodists, and Universalists spurred the trustees to vote in favor of requiring Western Reserve missionaries to devote every other month to on-the-road missionary labor. The decision came at a time when many of the missionaries had settled in a town and were financed jointly by the Connecticut Missionary Society and their local congregations. Following the model of moral communities situated around a church, the missionaries viewed themselves as progressing toward the goal of becoming settled pastors. For example, in 1812, within a year of his arrival in the Western Reserve, John Seward accepted a call to pastor a church in Aurora. Simeon Woodruff settled in Tallmadge, William Hanford in Hudson, Luther Humphrey in Burton, Giles Cowles in Austinburg, and Randolph Stone in Morgan.[93]

The Connecticut Missionary Society's vote to increase the tours of Western Reserve missionaries was communicated to all of the missionaries through a letter to Giles Cowles. Cowles, a Yale graduate and a direct descendant of the Reverend Thomas Hooker, came to the Western Reserve after seventeen years as pastor in Bristol, Connecticut; he had resided in Austinburgh and been employed by the Connecticut Missionary Society for five years when the letter arrived. If the Connecticut Missionary Society thought it could quell any uproar from the ruling, though, it was mistaken. Cowles thought that the vote injured both the missionaries and the missionary endeavor. Primarily, Cowles worried that the home churches that supported the missionaries would suffer from their increased absences. Beyond that, he thought that the Connecticut Missionary Society requested too much of the missionaries' time in relation to the financial compensation they received. "It is more than is expected of other ministers of the Gospel in many ordinary situations, or even of missionaries to heathen countries."[94] Cowles reasoned that because the paltry $400 to $450 annual missionary salary was inadequate to support a family, missionaries needed extra time to supplement their income through farming. He also pointed out the probability of a reduction in time for study, a crucial component for an educated clergy. Finally, Cowles urged the trustees to consider the strain placed on missionary families: "We beg you to remember that we are formed of flesh and blood like yourselves. . . . Our families are as near and dear to us, as those of our brethren and friends in Connecticut, who live on paternal inheritance, surrounded with natural friends + connections, + know nothing of the privations and hardships of a new country, are to them."[95] To make such a heartless ruling, Cowles asserted, not only would be "sorely oppressive" but also would indicate, above all else, that the Connecticut Missionary Society had no conception of the circumstances of its missionaries. The society might not receive complaints from missionaries, but, Cowles assured the trustees, while "*few* feel *disposed* to censure, *all* unite in the opinion that you are ignorant of our real situation or you could never have passed such a resolution."[96]

While most missionaries did not respond directly to the home society, Luther Humphrey felt compelled to write and defend himself against what he believed constituted a personal attack. The trustees mentioned in their letter that some missionaries shirked their responsibility of writing complete accounts of their missionary labor. Humphrey was certain that the statement referred to him. While he agreed that the journal entries he submitted to the trustees were slim, he questioned the value of meticulously recording every mile ridden and every sermon preached. Rather than responding to the question of the justness or appropriateness of increasing missionary labor, he noted that missionaries, like their sponsoring societies, held a certain moral accountability. The missionary society's position required that it "ought to be vigilant + watch over their missionaries that they do nothing to injure the cause of Christ." But, Humphrey pointed out, "the missionaries also are in a very responsible situation. They are not only accountable to men as their employers, but also to the great head of the church for the manner in which they perform their duty."[97]

Humphrey's assertion of missionary moral agency emerged from a larger process of claiming authority and independence from the Connecticut Missionary Society, a process that began with Badger and Robbins. And although still financially dependent on the Connecticut Missionary Society, in 1814 the Plan of Union missionaries formed the Grand River Presbytery. Its Articles for Regulations empowered the missionaries to license and ordain ministers, annually review church activities, and decide on church applications for membership to the presbytery. The articles also upheld the Plan of Union by allowing each newly established church to choose a Presbyterian or Congregational mode of governance. Besides structural decisions, the presbytery also concerned itself with moral questions. For example, it took up the question of entertainment, morality, and discipline: "Is it sinful to attend balls? Ought professors of religion to be disciplined for attending balls? Ought professors of religion to be disciplined for allowing their children to attend balls? After free conversation of the subjects, the Presbytery decided the questions in the affirmative."[98] Although the missionary society welcomed the establishment of the Grand River Presbytery as a positive sign for the missionary endeavor, the Western Reserve's independent missionary structure provided an arena in which missionaries could exert decision-making power and could begin to define themselves apart from their sponsoring societies.[99]

But not all of the Plan of Union missionaries felt empowered by their participation in the Grand River Presbytery. Pennsylvania native and Presbyterian missionary Thomas Barr felt the oppressive weight of the New England clerical dominance and believed that Congregationalists dictated the tone of the presbytery. Barr recounts: "I only remained about five years on the Reserve, after the Grand River Presbytery was formed, but in this space and time, I began to discover that *name* things as you will, the inherent properties remain the same. Congregationalism, wrap it as you may, is Congregationalism."[100] Even within this "frontier-grown" Plan of Union institution, animosity still arose between Presbyterians and Congregationalists. Missionaries continued to complain of low pay and decreased time with their families at home. And, the Plan of Union missionaries agreed, one could not afford to neglect the family.

"One great step towards a state of barbarism": Family and Home Order

Built landscapes such as homes and their material furnishings also become contested moral sites on the frontier. As such, the missionary society viewed the family and household to be central to the creation and reproduction of a Christian life and nation. Accordingly, rules for moral conduct were learned and practiced first in the home and later in society. Not only did the Christian family serve as an instructional space for those within it, it also provided a solid example for those on the outside. The moral government of the family illustrated in Philip Doddridge's advice manual to fathers relies on an orderly household ruled by a just and benevolent father. New Englanders invested in the ideal of the patriarchal family as the bedrock of society, and the structure and physical components of their homes, as well as family conduct, became a site of religious and social negotiation. Examining architecture and material artifacts, as Colleen McDannell has argued, blurs false distinctions between sacred and profane and provides a glimpse into how religious people construct their lives.[101] An interpretation of the home landscape and spatial sexual segregation can lead to a better understanding of one of the physical constraints of imposing a Puritan family ideology on the frontier.

By the eighteenth century, housing conditions in New England improved from one-room unfinished dwellings to more-stable one- and two-room dwellings. A growing number of homes included an entertaining area, such as a parlor, as well as a separate room for cooking. This period saw an increasing refinement, as utility and shelter in home construction yielded to the demands of a spatial organization that accommodated leisure activities of entertaining, reading, sewing, and conversation. An elite minority built more-elaborate homes in the late eighteenth century, with highly segregated spaces and decorative details. By the 1790s a variety of homes could be found along the New England landscape that reflected the occupants' economic and social status. In Connecticut, the one-room home with a large central chimney evolved into the lean-to home, which allowed for more space and sometimes a second floor. Eventually homes began to be built with a main hall and two chimneys on each side. This architectural shift signaled the increasing gap opened between the public street space and the private interior home space. In middle-class homes the hall allowed for a transition between the outside world and the inside of the home.

A person of above-average means living in New Haven or Hartford, Connecticut, could consult a few architectural guides for aid in building a new home. Owen Biddle's *The Young Carpenter's Assistant* advertised itself as being well adapted to the building style of the United States. The architect John Haviland published his architectural drawings in the widely used *Builder's Assistant*. Asher Benjamin's *Country Builder's Assistant* and *American Builder's Companion* provided detailed graphs and measurements for both the architect and the carpenter. Benjamin's manuals provided instruction in basic geometry, a history of building, a guide to the five orders of architecture, and designs for ornamental as well as functional detailing on buildings. At the end of the text, he included blueprints for houses, meetinghouses, and courthouses.

Benjamin's *American Builder's Companion* includes blueprints for three town houses and two country-setting homes. The town houses—decreasing in size from four to three to two floors—have highly segregated spaces, and each room is accorded a function. The homes have kitchens, cellars, parlors, dining rooms, breakfast or counting rooms, gentleman's bedchambers, dressing rooms, libraries, halls, and pantries. The model homes "intended for the country" are two-story buildings, similarly designed and demarcated. At the end of his text Benjamin notes: "The first thing to be done in planning a home, is to know the wants of the person who is to occupy it."[102] Taking the personal taste of the inhabitant into consideration, the builder must then strive for architectural beauty and balance. Proper lighting and windows as well as structural openness will allow the eye to take in every part of the building at once. Well-appointed homes, Benjamin cautions the builder, must avoid the visual distastefulness of a chimney projecting more than twenty inches into a room or small windows that do not provide light or a view. But such houses must have been the exception rather than the architectural rule in New England.

The New Englanders who settled in the Western Reserve during the first decades of the nineteenth century probably did not leave behind well-constructed homes built by trained carpenters.[103] What is certain is that they came from a variety of living situations, some more refined than others. What the first emigrants held in common regardless of their status in the East was that they all built western homes from the natural resources available on their property. The typical dwelling was a log cabin of "axe architecture," taking its name from the main tool used in its construction. The cabins generally were sixteen by twenty-two feet, with a door in the front center of the structure. Small windows were sometimes cut out of the walls and placed high, and clothes were hung to remove drafts, as glass generally was unavailable during the early years of frontier settlement.[104] Joseph Badger describes his modest cabin as "a rough one, rough logs without a chink; and only floored half-over with split stuff, and partly roofed with boards."[105] Many of the homes included a fireplace and a chimney; some, however, had only an area cleared in the center of the floor and a hole in the roof for ventilation. As one chronicler remembers, "The back end of the room was partitioned off into two bedrooms, originally by blankets hung up around the beds—a rack overhead with numerous poles for drying pumpkins, and numerous pegs driven in the logs all around the room for hanging up clothing, seed corn, red peppers, dried beef, and other articles too numerous to mention."[106] The one-room cabin fulfilled the family's consumptive, productive, and reproductive needs.

This simple architecture represents a living situation dramatically different from that to which most New England families were accustomed.[107] By the late eighteenth century the New England home and family stood at the center of a network of complex social and religious structures. Home architecture not only reflected an individual's class status but also reflected and reproduced religious, sexual, and social mores in its construction, and particularly in its division of space.[108] At the precise moment when missionaries and settlers were relocating to the frontier, religious and social ideologies that outlined rules for male and female behavior were quickly being refined among the burgeoning middle class. Numerous scholars have demonstrated that industrialization in post–Revolutionary War America helped to formulate sexual ideologies, particularly associating white middle-class women with domesticity and piety.[109] In the midst of this transitional moment, it is also possible to decipher religious, sexual, and moral norms codified in architecture.

The home, according to social anthropologist Pierre Bourdieu, is the "principal locus" that fuses all thought and action whereby individuals organize social relationships. The physical structure of homes sets up divisions and hierarchies between things, persons, and daily practices that always reflect societal norms.[110] As the sexes became increasingly segregated in the late eighteenth century, a parallel development occurred in home architecture: men and women inhabited and controlled distinct areas of the home. This architectural stratification buttressed patriarchal authority by connecting spatial control to surveillance and gender.[111] For example, in more elaborate homes, the sexual spatial stratification would include a study for the man of the house and a dressing room for the woman of the house. These separate rooms ensured privacy—a fashionable commodity in antebellum white America—and bolstered a growing sexual ideology that linked middle-class men with the mind and middle-class women with the body.

The architectural move toward privatization and spatial sexual segregation is best reflected in the position of the parents' bedroom in the home. Keeping the matrimonial bed out of sight, and preferably out of earshot, represented the physical manifestation of a dominant ideology of male and female sexuality. For middle-class white women it was essential to uphold their virtue by creating at least the illusion of sexual purity. Even after women were married, their sexuality remained hidden. Male sexuality, on the other hand, was understood to be lustful and always verging on a loss of control. Rather than erasing male sexuality, the separate bedroom contained it.

The luxury of privacy and the degree of spatial sexual stratification always are linked closely to economic and social status. The majority of Connecticut emigrants to the Western Reserve, and certainly those connected to the missionary culture, had resided in homes in which the parental bedroom was separated from the rest of the house. The switch to the "axe architecture" of log cabins signified a spatial and ultimately moral reorganization of family, privacy, and sexuality. The open home space presented numerous problems for settlers, missionaries, and the missionary society. One angle from which to view these difficulties is to examine their effects on cultural rules for male and female behavior. The sexual ideology that upheld women as moral guardians of the home and family, and men as public, sexual beings, could not operate in the spatial arrangements of the frontier domicile.

The mixing of household items and practices in one space was disorienting for New Englanders who were accustomed to task-segregated areas in the home. For example, a table for most settlers would be used for eating, writing, food preparation, sewing, and any other task that required a level surface. Not only did this force men and women to interact and share space that they were accustomed to inhabiting alone or with members of their own sex, but it also required that they reevaluate household priorities. Writing letters at the table might have held a high status in a Connecticut home, but, in a Western Reserve home that was pressed for space, that activity could not be granted as high a status as food preparation and consumption. Small shifts such as this, based on shortages, undermined the family ideology that the Connecticut Missionary Society deemed essential for the maintenance of spatial and moral order.

The blurring of spatial segregation occurred at every level, both inside and outside the home. The nineteen-year-old Henry Leavitt Ellsworth of Windsor, Connecticut, traveled to New Connecticut in 1811 to inspect his deceased father's 41,350-acre estate.[112] During his ten-week round-trip journey with his brother-in-law, Ezekiel Williams, Ellsworth described in detail the land, climate, housing conditions, and people he saw along the way. Riding between Easton and Bethlehem, Pennsylvania, Ellsworth observed women, working alongside men in the fields, who, despite being barefoot and "as black and as hardy as the males," he perceived had beautiful features that would rival "Connecticut damsels" if "they were kept within doors and ornamented with a handsome dress."[113] The most obvious and dramatic example of spatial blurring was the practice of parents' sleeping in the same room as their children. Any pretense that women were not sexual beings eventually had to be abandoned. Ellsworth discovered to his dismay that even in public lodging houses all the guests slept in the same room, "man and wife, children, acquaintances, strangers, and servants."[114] While he found sleeping in close proximity to others difficult, it was not as troubling as "to dress and undress since this must be a public maneouvre. However, the female part of the family do all in their power to preserve delicacy and lessen the embarrassment of strangers by shutting up their eyes, putting their hands to their faces, or putting their 'side seams' while the male part of the family are getting into bed."[115] Besides sight, the mixing of social space filtered into the more subtle areas of sound and smell. Ellsworth's complaints regarding cramped sleeping arrangements also included unpleasant food smells and bugs. In one home he slept in, he noticed that over his head hung "a long board with cheeses on it—over that another with milk, butter, &&—close by the bedside lay piled up a large heap of onions."[116] Western Reserve chronicler Christopher Gore Crary also noted that in many makeshift homes the pumpkins hung from poles near beds.

While Ellsworth and Crary were uncomfortable with the close quarters, they did not expand on the moral implications of such arrangements. Dr. Zerah Hawley, however, believed that the "indelicacy of this practice" had a "demoralizing tendency" that, if continued, would likely cause the deterioration of Western Reserve society.[117] Hawley traveled for a year through the Western Reserve in 1822 gathering both physical and moral evidence to show that the Western Reserve was neither a Garden of Eden nor a second New England. In letters to his brother he expressed astonishment at the poor living conditions and immoral conduct of settlers. Describing the household of a family that had lived in the Western Reserve for seventeen years, he noted dilapidated furniture and makeshift utensils numbering only enough to accommodate the family.[118] Hawley found that the homes of "titled men" were equally distressing. He described these homes as log or block houses in which "the whole establishment consists of one room in which all the family, with their guests, eat , sleep, and perform all domestic operations."[119] Hawley learned that one family he visited was in the habit of "sleeping promiscuously in one room" where parents, children, strangers, neighbors, and anyone else regardless of age, sex or marital status lodged "without anything to screen them from view of each other." This habit alarmed him. In fact, he found it so morally dangerous that he characterized it as "one great step towards a state of barbarism, and . . . a rapid approach to the custom of our savage brethren of the wilderness, who sleep without ceremony around fires of their cabins."[120] Besides town layout, behavior on religious occasions, and home construction, even the sleeping quarters were visible to the moralizing gaze of missionaries and travelers alike. In New Connecticut no space was too sacred to violate or too intimate to escape description and moral appraisal.

The presentation of frontier settlements and people by the Plan of Union missionaries was filtered through their expectations. The missionaries struggled to fit themselves to a preconceived model of frontier piety; likewise, they described and defined frontier space from within a particular mental context that linked physical and moral order. Casting their memories back through biblical and national history, missionaries found meaning in the physical landscape. Not simply moral signs but moral lessons could be drawn from the way that space was organized. More important, shaping the physical space offered a concrete opportunity for missionaries and settlers to re-create an imagined past while moving closer to a millennial future. But the physical landscape also presented obstacles to that goal. Denominational rivals captured the attention of many settlers and sometimes seized the focal point of the landscape by placing their churches on the center green. Unorthodox bodily practices, such as charity kisses, were seeping into Plan of Union missionary gatherings. It remained unclear whether these practices occurred because of the congregation's location on the frontier, beyond the surveillance of eastern society, or because of an accommodation to the practices of other denominations. Further, the quest to shape the physical landscape suggested that New England patterns of physical space and moral habits could not be replicated on the frontier. The missionaries and their sponsoring society would need to find new models for establishing moral behavior.

Plan of Union missionaries continued to see signs of hope in the Western Reserve, and, if they looked closely enough, they could almost discern God's benevolent design. But other Western Reserve visitors perceived the landscape through different lenses. While the physical landscape still held sacred meaning, many travelers to the region realized that "fairy tale" reports, which exaggerated the landscape's physical and moral qualities, deceived the public with claims that the Western Reserve was a Garden of Eden or a second New England. The next chapter will address Western Reserve travel literature, a genre that contributed to the print culture that defined the region. The focus will be on accounts that illustrate the connections that travelers made between physical landscape and morality, thus extending the imaginative construction (and in some cases destruction) of "New Connecticut" beyond the Plan of Union missionary letters and publications. Not all of the texts refer directly to missionaries or religious beliefs and practices, but they all employ moral categories to evaluate frontier space. Even in narratives that seem distant from the concerns of the Connecticut Missionary Society and its missionaries, similar themes surface, calling attention to the pervasive desire to inscribe the Western Reserve landscape with moral meaning.

CHAPTER 4

Geography Made Easy
Geographies and Travel Literature

Writing to her cousin Elizabeth Woolsey in November 1810, the niece of Timothy Dwight complained that the arduous trip to the Western Reserve left her so exhausted that she had "lost all interest about the country I pass through."[1] Margaret Dwight traveled the southern route along the Pennsylvania road and over the Allegheny Mountains with a penny-pinching deacon who exposed her to less than desirable overnight accommodations, food, and frontier inhabitants.[2] But when she finally arrived at her destination in Warren, Ohio, she described the town and the house she would live in as "pleasanter" than she had expected. Weary from her seven-week trip, she was rejuvenated by the sight of family and friends and predicted that she would be "very happy & contented" living in New Connecticut.[3]

Dwight's journal ends just where the reader would like it to begin. A tired traveler's first glimpses of her final destination far exceed her expectations. But what happened the next day? Dwight's longtime acquaintance from Connecticut, Henry Leavitt Ellsworth, would remark in his own travel journal some seven months later that he found Dwight "pleased with her new situation and [she] lives perfectly contented, in the enjoyment of good health."[4] Dwight's account of her tedious and difficult journey from

Connecticut to northeastern Ohio resembles descriptions in most domestic travel journals of her time. Rough terrain, inclement weather, poor sleeping conditions, sickness, exhaustion, and general privation are common themes in these personal and published travel diaries and letters. Her happy ending, however, proved more the exception than the rule. Many other prospective settlers who arrived in the Western Reserve were frustrated because they, like David Hudson, could not locate their lots. They were isolated from any society they deemed acceptable, and they were disappointed to find that the land presented perils rather than the promises they expected. Margaret Dwight, like other emigrants, had read and heard a great deal about the region and, happily, found that the town and people of Warren suited her. Others were not so fortunate and cursed the promotional literature that persuaded them to buy lots and move their families to an unrealized "promised land." In the words of a six-year-old emigrant to the Western Reserve, "instead of finding a land flowing with milk and honey we found it flowing with all sorts of wild animals."[5]

In this chapter I examine how Western Reserve travel literature participated in a larger conversation about expectations associated with region. This vast literature includes promotional publications, emigrant guides, newspaper articles, official land agent documents, and, most important, personal and published letters and journals.[6] These texts were written for many reasons: to encourage potential investors, to entice settlers and tourists, and to provide an insider's view of the land and the people.[7] It is not my intention to survey all of the Western Reserve travel literature of the period.[8] Instead, I focus on three accounts that illustrate the connections that travelers made between physical landscape and morality, links that extend beyond Plan of Union missionary letters and publications. Although they participate in broader conversations about western emigration and exploration, the texts under examination here are significant because they seek to overturn the metaphorical conception of the Western Reserve as a Garden of Eden or a second New England. Much of the travel writing takes the tone of misadventure reminiscent of some of Joseph Badger's letters. The writers emphasize their discontent and typically conclude their narratives with the author returning to New England and warning readers against falling prey to false promotional literature.

Not all the texts refer directly to missionaries or religious beliefs and practices, but they all employ moral categories to evaluate frontier space and, for that reason, it is fitting to read them alongside missionary tracts and letters. In each case, travelers wrote selectively about their experiences to describe and to define the quality of land and life in the Western Reserve.

Their observations, I will suggest, follow a typology of physical and moral analysis that was promoted by geographer and Congregational clergyman Jedidiah Morse. Their writings also reflect the biblical values assigned to the region, even though most writers had little to say about religion. Anchoring their narratives in observations of flora and fauna, the writers are concerned not merely with the *discovery* of a new space but also with the *creation* of the place. As will become clear, Western Reserve travel writers were as much involved with calling this region into being as with representing it accurately. However much they complained about and endeavored to correct the distortions of the landscape and the people that issued from the pens of land surveyors, land agents, and missionaries, they could not escape the limits of their own perspectives, or cultural "cartographies." The physical and conceptual maps examined in previous chapters were as much a product of fantasy as they were a reflection of reality. But that did not make them any less influential. This chapter will illustrate how travel writers relied on these "maps" even as they attempted to "remap" the region. Western Reserve travel writers could describe how the region and the people fell short of expectations, but their mental maps organized their observations in a particular way, fitting all of the new information into an existing cultural grid. In other words, the mapping efforts examined in the first three chapters reappear in Western Reserve travel narratives in positive and negative descriptions of the physical and moral landscapes.

Travel narratives, as Mary Louise Pratt demonstrates, are a literary expression of exploration and cultural contact.[9] Pratt's work shows that seventeenth-century European travel narratives served as brokers between the European scientific community and the general European reading public. Embedded in travel literature is ethnographic information about indigenous people and their "manners and customs" that aids colonialism by representing the subjects of conquest. The process of writing about the "manners and customs" of indigenous people, Pratt argues, "normalizes" this observational category and fixes the people under study as strange "others." This style of travel literature became increasingly popular in nineteenth-century Europe and set the standard for viewing foreign people and places as objects of observation and representation. The trend, I argue, appears, too, in Western Reserve literature.

Generally, the Western Reserve travel writers assess the region's value in terms of its physical and moral resources. Unlike Pratt's study of naturalists' travel narratives, the authors of these travel narratives did not "discover" new lands and classify unusual plants and wildlife; rather, Western Reserve travel accounts addressed the habitability, "mapping" it for New Englanders. The travel writers generally did not collect scientific evidence but made use of empirical categories to assess the frontier; "accuracy" and "precision"—at least in dispelling false claims about the region—were the order of the day.[10] Written as first-person testimonials, their investigations relate details about the physical landscape in terms of its soil quality, weather patterns, natural resources, and road conditions; they also describe the moral landscape, including settlers' habits and dispositions, religious organizations and instruction, and the future social and moral outlook for the region. Above all, the Western Reserve travel narratives ask, how does this region compare to New England? To answer that question, travel writers depended on their own cultural cartographies, which relied in part on the work of Jedidiah Morse.

Geography Made Easy: *Mapping and Moralizing*

No one better represents the aims of moral geography during the early Republic than the Reverend Jedidiah Morse. A New England Congregational clergyman, described by one of his biographers as "a rigid, unlovable man," Morse fused geography and religion in his forty-two-year career as America's first geographer.[11] Though Morse claimed no formal training in cartography or geography, he recognized the importance of this scientific endeavor for nation building and set as his life's goal amassing all the current geographical literature pertaining to the United States. Morse's project began modestly enough but exploded into a never-ending series of revisions as he updated and republished his geographies almost every year from 1794 to 1819.[12] All the while Morse held a prominent pulpit in Charlestown, Massachusetts, from which he preached that the key to a godly republic resided in the maintenance of Congregational orthodoxy and New England culture.[13] Authoring his first text in 1784, Morse literally mapped the new nation through his geographical writings.

Morse wrote his first geographical text, *Geography Made Easy*, in 1784 while teaching in a New Haven girls school. Morse's friends read the book, which was written as an instructional tool for students, and convinced him to modify it for a general reading audience. Morse quickly discovered that the American reading public craved geographical information: his book sold more than three hundred copies in the first few weeks after publication.[14] The success made such an impression on Morse that he set out to write a more extensive geography by collecting materials from mapmakers, travelers, newspapers, and any other printed or spoken sources that could inform his work (figure 15).[15]

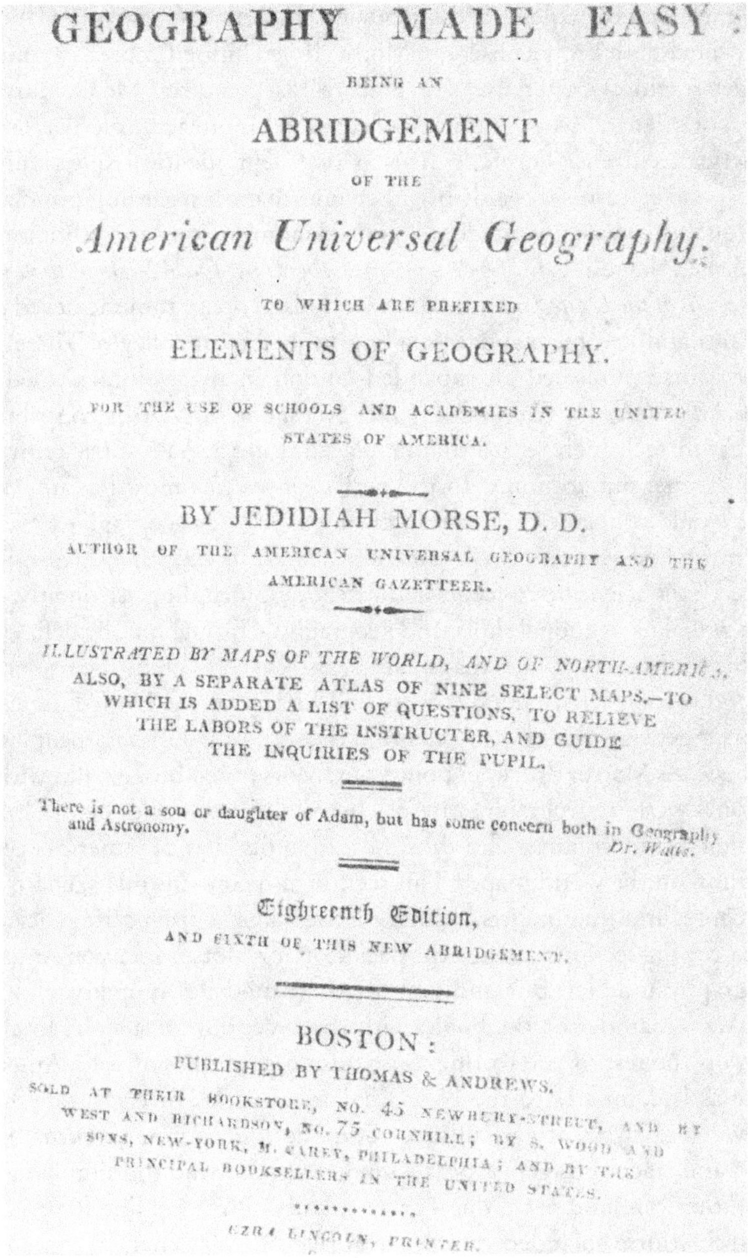
GEOGRAPHY MADE EASY:

BEING AN

ABRIDGEMENT

OF THE

American Universal Geography,

TO WHICH ARE PREFIXED

ELEMENTS OF GEOGRAPHY.

FOR THE USE OF SCHOOLS AND ACADEMIES IN THE UNITED STATES OF AMERICA.

BY JEDIDIAH MORSE, D. D.

AUTHOR OF THE AMERICAN UNIVERSAL GEOGRAPHY AND THE AMERICAN GAZETTEER.

ILLUSTRATED BY MAPS OF THE WORLD, AND OF NORTH-AMERICA,

ALSO, BY A SEPARATE ATLAS OF NINE SELECT MAPS.—TO WHICH IS ADDED A LIST OF QUESTIONS, TO RELIEVE THE LABORS OF THE INSTRUCTER, AND GUIDE THE INQUIRIES OF THE PUPIL.

There is not a son or daughter of Adam, but has some concern both in Geography and Astronomy.

Dr. Watts.

Eighteenth Edition,

AND SIXTH OF THIS NEW ABRIDGEMENT.

BOSTON:

PUBLISHED BY THOMAS & ANDREWS.

SOLD AT THEIR BOOKSTORE, NO. 45 NEWBURY-STREET, AND BY WEST AND RICHARDSON, NO. 75 CORNHILL; BY S. WOOD AND SONS, NEW-YORK, M. CAREY, PHILADELPHIA; AND BY THE PRINCIPAL BOOKSELLERS IN THE UNITED STATES.

EZRA LINCOLN, PRINTER.

FIGURE 15. Title page of Jedidiah Morse's *Geography Made Easy* (1816). Jedidiah Morse, Congregational clergyman and American geographer, fused moralizing and mapping in his geographies. This publication ran through twenty-five editions. Property of the author.

Morse was early described as "our first American geographer," but, as historian Ralph Brown observes, Morse viewed himself more as a compiler of geographical materials.[16] To prepare his new text, Morse consulted "men of science," whom he acknowledges in his preface, as well as leading American citizens. For four years Morse sent identical questionnaires across the eastern seaboard to gather information regarding population, soil quality, townships, trade, religious denominations and schools.[17] He published the results in *The American Geography; Or, A View of the Present Situation of the United States of America.* This 543-page tome achieved rapid acclaim and became standard reading in American colleges. Three years later Morse published an expanded edition in two volumes titled *The American Universal Geography.*[18] Ezra Stiles, one of Morse's contributors, held it in such high regard that he placed it in the Yale curriculum soon after its first publication.[19] In the next twenty years most literate Americans would read at least a portion of one of Morse's geographies.[20]

In the first section of *The American Universal Geography* Morse introduced basic scientific concepts and categories, including astronomy, geology, global navigational skills, and geography. Throughout, he defined scientific terms and provides maps, tables, and charts to guide the reader. The second section relates the discovery and history of the United States and offers a general overview of scientific theories on aboriginal peoples and animals. As Martin Brückner points out, Morse's text broke ranks with traditional western geographies by placing the United States before Europe in the table of contents and thus indicating his view of America's central position on the world map.[21] This section also contains maps, charts, and anecdotes from naturalists, military leaders, and citizens. Together these two opening sections provide the backdrop for Morse's focus on American geography and New England as the nation's model of morality.

The remainder of the book, with the exception of a short final section on the rest of the world, constitutes case studies of each American state as it compares to the New England model. For each state Morse provided analyses of agriculture, population, government, climate, history, and trade. His geography extended well beyond the simple facts of the American landscape, demography, and commerce; like Pratt's travel writers, Morse included moral categories such as "character, manners, etc." and "religion." These categories contain information about the appearance, habits, diversions, and moods of inhabitants. The subsections on manners and religion bring into focus the intersection between morality and geography.

Morse viewed American geography through an orthodox Calvinist lens. Although trained at Yale, he was not numbered among the "New Divinity" men. Morse remained skeptical of revival excesses, but he supported the New Divinity commitment to missions. He agreed that there was an urgent need to evangelize the frontier, and he held fast to the millenarian view that God's kingdom would eventually be established on Earth—and, in his view, probably in New England.

Morse's commitment to Calvinism and to New England morality was reflected boldly in his *American Geography*, in both its content and organization. For example, although he provided details about all the states established by the time of publication, he recognized only New England as a distinct, unified region. He based this assessment on his perception of the common cultural heritage of New Englanders and their shared personal dispositions. New England society in Morse's mind was well ordered precisely because the inhabitants held in common religion and habits. Further, New England's inhabitants, according to Morse, constituted a homogeneous ethnic group of English descent. They were "generally tall, stout, and well built." They were also well educated, enterprising, hardworking, frugal, benevolent, and cultured. Moreover, "many of the women in New England are handsome."[22] New England's perfection for Morse resided in three grand qualities: ethnic homogeneity, personal industry, and moral society. This trinity not only produced order in New England but set a standard by which all other states could be measured.[23]

It is not surprising that Morse located the epicenter of morality and order in his birth state, Connecticut. According to him, Connecticut's religion served as the cohesive element for its orderly society. He declared Connecticut's religion to be "the best in the world, perhaps, for a republican government."[24] As evidence for this claim, he added that "all religions that are consistent with the peace of society are tolerated in Connecticut" and noted that "there are very few religious sects in this state."[25] Alongside its religious harmony, Connecticut also boasted some of the most beautiful towns in the nation: in New Haven Morse found well-built homes, "handsome" and "commodious" churches, an "extremely beautiful" view, and a "convenient" and "delightful" public square. "New Haven," wrote Morse, "is not exceeded by any city in America."[26] Although he described physical landmarks, his principal goal was to show how these built constructions reflected morality. Echoing Timothy Dwight's assessment of the Connecticut River Valley, Morse observed that the town's physical structures signified its moral structures.

Morse had little to say about the Western Territories in 1798. He did caution readers about the Spanish Catholic presence west of the Mississippi River, asserting that "the God of nature never intended that some of the best part of his earth should be inhabited by subjects of the Monarch, 4000 miles from them."[27] Morse's anxiety about foreign influences on American soil related to his hope of expanding New England across the continent. In this respect Morse subscribed to the commonly held Protestant millenarian belief in God's sacred plan for America, which he integrated into his scientific publication, balancing in his geography a theological agenda and a national expansionist agenda. "Besides, it is well known," he reminded his readers, "that empire has been traveling from east to west."[28] This progressive westward movement, Morse believed, would eventually culminate in the eradication of all distinction, "when the languages, manners, customs, political and religious sentiments of the mixed mass of people who inhabit the United States become so assimilated, as that all nominal distinctions shall be lost in the general and honourable name of Americans."[29] Morse did not advocate here ecumenism or some variant of pluralism: rather he trumpeted that all should adopt the New England Way.[30]

Morse divided his time between a pastorate in Charlestown, Massachusetts, and the work of compiling geographic information. Not an adventure-seeking soul, he completed most of his cataloging and writing from his study.[31] Morse's attention to geography and to his substantial financial gains caused concern among some of his congregation: was he shirking his ministerial duties in favor of scientific undertakings and economic profit? For his part, Morse did not view his "scientific" work as competing with his theological work; on the contrary, he found the two endeavors highly compatible. "I find that my mind," he wrote, "after being engaged in Geographical pursuits, returns with ease and pleasure to my Theological studies."[32] Morse located morality in scientific categories and published his geographies as sermons—sermons that espoused national unity under the New England moral model.

Further, Morse had a direct connection to the Connecticut Missionary Society and shared its concerns regarding the moral future of the West. He strongly supported its missionary efforts and helped to send two Andover Theological Seminary students, John Schermerhorn and Samuel J. Mills, on a yearlong western tour to assess the viability of missionary labor in frontier settlements. And despite his virtual silence on the subject in earlier editions, Morse later found immense possibilities in the western physical landscape, particularly in Ohio, and wrote glowingly about its animal life, botany, and mineralogy. In the 1812 edition of *American Universal Geography* Morse noted that "springs of excellent water abound in every part of the territory" and "no country was originally better stocked with wild game of every kind than this."[33] He scrupulously detailed the flora and fauna but made little comment on the inhabitants or their manners, religion, and customs. It seems unlikely that he lacked information: after all, he read the *Connecticut Evangelical Magazine* and associated with clergy who were intimately connected with frontier home missions. Unlike the inhabitants of New England, however, whom he described in general, totalizing statements, the inhabitants of the Western Reserve resisted a unifying description. It was left to other travel writers to use the descriptive categories of Morse's geographies to evaluate frontier settlements and settlers.

Domestic Travel Narratives

Travel narratives always aim to make the strange familiar. Whether describing distant lands, exotic beasts, natural marvels, or foreign peoples, the travel writer endeavors to translate the fantastic through literary images that the reader can comprehend.[34] By the nineteenth century, European and American travel writers enjoyed a wide readership that longed for dramatic and detailed information about exotic people living in foreign lands. Travel literature in all of its forms—land sales publications, emigrant guides, newspaper articles, personal letters, and published diaries—collects ethnographic observations, which, as David Chidester notes, portray indigenous peoples and territories as "objects for conquest and subjects for representation."[35] Travel writing exploits and defines the exotic and, simultaneously, domesticates or "naturalizes" what is seen as foreign, making it comprehensible. In this way, travel writing is an act of cultural appropriation. Travel writers not only "view" but also define the difference between themselves and others. Thus the travel writer always portrays the "other" in relation to the "self."

A good travel writer adopts a comparative approach while maintaining some of the mystery and foreignness of the "other." As art historian Jaś Elsner argues, travel writing would lose its appeal if the foreign became completely domesticated: "Writer and reader alike must negotiate between the familiar and the remarkable in their attempts to grasp the foreign."[36]

Travel literature that results from cultural encounter operates to subjugate the foreign while defining the writer (and his or her culture) in comparison to others. But what about the travelers who moved in and wrote about their own culture? Did the same hold true for them? In the case of Western Reserve travel writers, their challenge was to describe the "foreign" that was supposed to resemble "home." New Connecticut was not simply an explanatory category for understanding the "strange" or "foreign"; it was mapped and promoted as a second New England. Additionally, as Western Reserve travel writers described the frontier settlements and settlers, they were not simply comparing their observations to themselves; they were gazing, in effect, at the "self" not the "other."

While Western travel writers in all corners of the globe render the strange familiar, Euro-American domestic travelers of the early nineteenth century made the familiar strange. Domestic travel writers, such as the home missionaries, toured their *own* country and observed people of their *own* culture. But the frontier, in their eyes, was a foreign country, and the settlers were alien people. Indeed, travel writers who toured the western territories participated in a discourse that threw frontier settlements into relief against an idyllic past and a "civilized" home, and "civilization" for Western Reserve travel writers often meant New England. Margaret Dwight wrote longingly about the home she left during her journey to the Western Reserve. When she arrived and met a cousin in Warren, she instantly appreciated all that she had left behind. "A cousin in this country, is not to be slighted I assure you," she wrote to her cousin Elizabeth. "I would give more for one in this country than for twenty in Connecticut."[37]

Home for Dwight meant New Haven; but for others, it signified a desired scriptural or national home.[38] Since the region had been linked so effectively to the biblical metaphors of Eden and Zion, as well as to the national metaphor of Puritan New England, travel writers strove to articulate the realities of the frontier in those terms. Readers could easily conjure an image of the remarkable bounty of the Garden of Eden or the orderly towns of a Puritan New England, so descriptions of the Western Reserve sought to reconcile reality with scriptural and national fantasies. When the reality fell short of fantasy, the travel writers continued to employ these metaphors as they attempted to "remap" the territory for their readers. In this setting, writers stressed the veracity of their eyewitness accounts; such narratives gave readers direct access to the Western Reserve. Dr. Zerah Hawley traveled to almost every town in the Western

Reserve over the course of two years; in his writings Hawley maintained that he did "not exaggerate in the description" of the unsavory practices he saw there. The information printed in his account, he assured his readers, did not come "from a report; but from my own knowledge."[39] The primacy Hawley placed on his firsthand knowledge was not simply the experience of traveling through the place but also the opportunity to see the region and its inhabitants for himself. Before arriving in the Western Reserve, travelers like Hawley often cataloged all the marvelous things that they had heard, read, thought, and hoped for about the land and the people. What they saw (or did not see) after they arrived lent credulity to their own accounts.

Comparing the Western Reserve to New England served to reassert New England's strength and importance. In promotional land sales literature and missionary publications, "New Connecticut" represented a second chance for worthy settlers to re-create an idealized Puritan New England; for weary travelers, the Western Reserve amplified, as it were, New England's superiority. This literature, then, is far from an example of "the empire writing back": Western Reserve travel writings do not represent the resistant voices of the colonized. Rather, such texts extended Euro-American influence and control on the frontier.[40] Not simply "eyewitnesses," the travel writers were active agents in describing, categorizing, and taming the territory.

Western Reserve travel writers connected landscape with morality. Gazing on an untilled field in New Connecticut, Hawley perceived that New Connecticut settlers lacked the industrious nature that he believed typified New Englanders. Hawley then set out to find examples of laziness to prove his point. His investigation led him to wonder about the power of the landscape itself, a setting that transformed industrious New England emigrants into lazy, deficient farmers. The significance of Hawley's work for our analysis lies in the landscape: he deduced "laziness" from a fallow field. The move from landscape to morality is typical of firsthand reports, reflecting on the imaginative context in which evidences of moral and immoral behavior could be beheld by viewing the landscape. Here Hawley wrote in terms that the Plan of Union missionaries could understand.

Landscape in Western Reserve travel writings is sometimes the object of interest and other times the backdrop for exploits. What is striking is how firmly embedded moral discourse remains in the descriptions. Cultural geographers tell us that landscapes are "non-verbal documents" laden with meanings: one can discern a culture's ideology by viewing the manner in which physical space is shaped. Roads, town layouts, cultivated fields, building construction and placement—all reflect the values held by the people who organize the land. Simple landscape descriptions jotted down in travel accounts, such as notes on an unimproved road or a neglected field, are not mere descriptions but representations of larger values for the writer and the reader. Signs in the built and cultivated landscape, represent a lack of human industry, in Hawley's eyes. Nature, in this case, is not viewed for its beauty or its productive potential; rather, it is examined for evidences of human activity. Landscapes, for travel writers in the Western Reserve, invariably gauged the level of human interaction with nature. Exploring the landscape as nonverbal document, the travel writer could proceed from viewing the landscape to moralizing.

While some Western Reserve travelers rejected the notion that the region was a second New England, their writings continued to link morality with the physical landscape. Judgment of the region was based not only on the natural resources and the built environment of the land but also on the descriptions of settlers who peopled the landscape. Their habits, manners, appearance, and customs provided clues as to the future state of the society. The traveler studied and recorded observations of the people as he or she would any other feature of the landscape. To describe the region's inhabitants, travel writers employed categories that emphasized cultural homogeneity, personal industry, and morality—qualities, it was believed by Morse and others, that characterized New Englanders. Just as fallow fields called to mind laziness, a destitute farmer also indicated a lack of industry. How, the writers wondered, could a farmer fail to thrive in a "Garden of Eden"? The poor manners of settlers—they stared at strangers and allowed families to share one room for sleeping—indicated immoral behavior. People as well as the soil, water, plants, animals, roads, and buildings were significant landmarks in the travel accounts.

Like Zerah Hawley, most travel writers pledged to give a realistic portrayal based on firsthand knowledge. But, as in maps and missionary letters, the omissions in such accounts are revealing. Some authors wrote almost exclusively about the landscape, while others devoted equal space to the inhabitants. Illustrative of such selective narration is Estwick Evans's *A Pedestrious Tour of Four Thousand Miles, through the Western States and Territories, during the Winter and Spring of 1818.* In it he promised to include information on religious, moral, and sentimental topics, but his description of the Western Reserve focused almost exclusively on the landscape.[41]

Evans, a New Hampshire lawyer dressed entirely in buffalo skins, set off on February 2, 1818, to become a "citizen of the world" and to discover "amidst the grandeur of the western wilds, more correct views of human nature and of the true interests of man."[42] Evans incorporated observations of Native Americans in his narrative, since one of the objectives of his tour was to "acquire the simplicity, native feelings, and virtues of savage life."[43] For the most part, however, he looked to the natural world to understand human nature. In fact, the account gives the impression that he was the only person traversing the region. In the Western Reserve, for example, he noted hunting grounds, domesticated cattle, and healthy wheat crops—signs of human industry all around him; yet no people work the landscape. The writer himself even seems disembodied as his narrative jumps repeatedly from material observation to moralizing.[44] After seeing a wild deer for the first time, he wrote two lengthy paragraphs about the cruel food chain that destines animals "too innocent for death" to wind up in our hungry mouths: "Man, although a compound being;—altho' possessing a moral as well as physical nature, is a great devourer."[45] And while he admitted that the destruction of animals was necessary for the security and health of humans, Evans urged the reader not to trifle with the life of an animal; such possessed no souls, and death extinguished them for eternity. Only a careful reader would notice that this moral excursus was occasioned by watching his dogs bring "one of these guileless animals to the earth," presumably to provide Evans with a meal.[46]

In the course of his travels through the Western Reserve Evans met Native Americans from whom he purchased deerskin shoes. His portrayal of them was strikingly similar to his descriptions of plants or animals that he saw during his travels. Typical of many nineteenth-century travel writers who sought to discover the wisdom and virtues of "Noble Savages," Evans viewed the people to be more a part of the natural landscape than of human society. They were neither frightening nor friendly; they were instead a curiosity on display: "Indian women, often accompany the men in their hunting expeditions; and one may frequently see them in the woods employed in dressing Deer and Elk skins, and in making shoes of them."[47] In reality, Evans communicated with the Native Americans (of an unidentified tribe); in the text, he depicted them as voiceless beings, mere "traces on the landscape," to borrow Mary Louise Pratt's terminology.[48] Interestingly, Evans is one of the few travel writers who reported seeing Native Americans in New Connecticut, yet he neglected to mention encountering any Euro-American settlers. Thus, while most travel writers located Native Americans outside of the Western Reserve's borders, at a safe distance from Euro-American settlement, Evans redrew the map of the region to place Native Americans at the center of his narrative and Euro-American settlers on the borders.

Unlike Evans, cartographer and travel writer John Melish populated his Western Reserve landscape with Euro-American settlers. His *Travels in the United States* informed future emigrants of the potential for settlement throughout the West (figure 16).[49] His travels took him to all parts of the new nation, and he published his observations in popular guidebooks.[50] Melish found little to praise in New Connecticut's predominantly muddy landscape and impassable roads. He blamed marshy rivers for the prevalence of fever in Portage and Cuyahoga Counties. For him, however, the woods redeemed the landscape: they were thick with hickory, white oak, beech, maple, and chestnut. He also discovered several salt springs, freshwater streams, and "beds of freestone" containing coal and iron. The loam and clay soil he found to be fit for cultivating and cattle grazing, but, he confessed, "very little of it can be called the best."[51] Despite this less than rave review, Melish maintained that New Connecticut would be an advisable place to settle. Unlike Evans, who traveled a vast empty landscape in seeming solitude, Melish described inhabitants who have "generally the frugal, industrious habits of the New England states, and are civil in their manners, and moral in their deportment."[52] He included the names and birthplaces of these people and other personal information he could remember. "A Mr. Bond, from Massachusetts, whom I met with at Cleveland, agreed to be my travelling companion." "Judge Don's family were busy manufacturing homespun, and appeared to be quite healthy." "I saw a settler by the way, who told me he was from Connecticut. . . . He likes the country very well and finds it healthy." "We met two men on horseback. . . . One of them was from Massachusetts, and said he liked this country much better than his native state, chiefly on account of the mild winters."[53]

Besides related emigrant testimonials, Melish himself found evidences of New England character in the settlers. In Chagrin, Melish stopped at a "Yankee" farm to feed his horse. "In the house, the females were busy carding and spinning wool." Mr. Bradley, he remarked cryptically, had "quite the Connecticut appearance."[54] Melish remained vague about what precisely constituted New England character or a Connecticut appearance; nevertheless, as Western Reserve historian Robert Wheeler notes, "he seems to relish the residents' Yankee attributes, celebrating their ingenuity

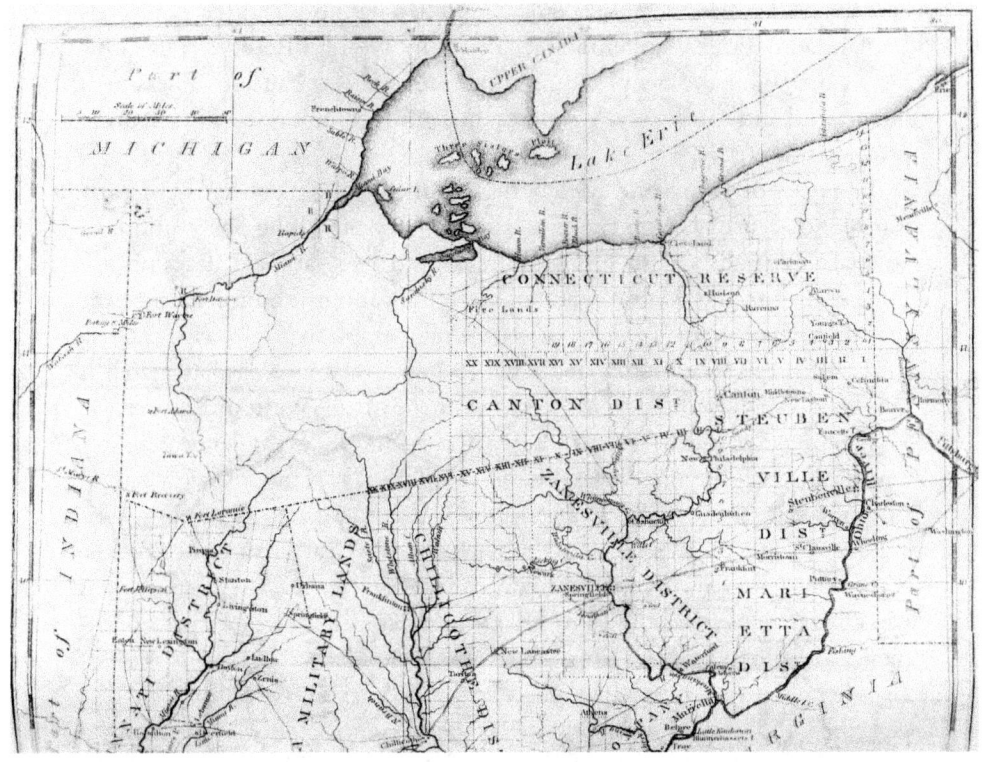

FIGURE 16. Western Reserve portion of map of Ohio in John Melish, *Travels in the United States* (1812). Travel writer John Melish criticized much of the Western Reserve's landscape but praised the inhabitants' moral character and habits. Courtesy of the Western Reserve Historical Society, Cleveland.

and their commitment to education and religion."⁵⁵ Through Melish's eyes the reader sees a mediocre landscape filled with busy, industrious New England emigrants who happily reside in the Western Reserve. The glowing report about the people counterbalances Melish's cautious assessment of the land and the natural resources; he thus recommended the region to prospective settlers.⁵⁶

The texts of Evans and Melish suggest the general parameters of early nineteenth-century Ohio travel literature. They blend the observations of amateur naturalists with ethnographical and geographical descriptions. Further, Evans and Melish made observations about the moral landscape that they encountered. Absent of scriptural metaphors to describe the territory, the reports, though, never fail to make reference to that which is familiar—New England—in their assessment of the Western Reserve.

The image of the Western Reserve as a second New England or a Garden of Eden functioned as a literary landmark for anyone who passed through that region.⁵⁷ As has been shown, the members of the Connecticut Land Company extolled its remarkable physical virtues, noting the exceptional flora and fauna that covered the landscape. The Connecticut Missionary Society focused on the moral possibilities of new space occupied and formed by New England settlers. The Plan of Union missionaries who navigated between these two groups searched for the paradise described and desired by their New England sponsors, but acknowledged that life on the frontier often fell short of their desires. In the midst of the glowing reports, another informational source about the Western Reserve emerged. The travel narrative, written through the eyes of prospective settlers, in some instances matched the exaggerated descriptions of the region and in other cases provided a corrective to the "fairy tale reports" published in missionary journals and other printed venues.⁵⁸

Fairy-Tale Reports: Western Reserve Travel Literature

Jedidiah Morse's praise of the western physical landscape was consistent with the western promotional literature written about the Western Reserve. But alongside such positive reports a competing literary tradition emerged to challenge their sanguine accounts of "New Connecticut." A few publications, notable for the virulence with which they attacked the myth of a paradisiacal western frontier, appeared during the second wave of Western Reserve settlement, which lasted from 1812 to 1830.⁵⁹ John

Stillman Wright, Dr. Zerah Hawley, and Henry Trumbull composed travel accounts to debunk the published claims that the western lands and society were equal or superior to eastern lands. Each author wrote from a particular perspective, uncovering misrepresentations about the moral and physical landscape in Ohio's frontier settlements; Wright and Hawley wrote specifically about Connecticut's Western Reserve. Besides their common interest in Ohio's frontier settlements, their writings unite around the impulse to explore the themes about New England expressed in Morse's geographies: homogeneity, industry, and morality. To dismantle the myth that the region was a garden paradise, Wright and Hawley attempted to prove that the settlements lacked these three crucial elements.

In *Letters from the West; or a Caution to Emigrants: Being Facts and Observations Respecting the States of Ohio, Indiana, Illinois and Some Parts of New-York, Pennsylvania and Kentucky,* John Stillman Wright explained what led him to travel west. Like other communities in New England, Wright's neighborhood became "infected" with "Ohio mania," and he "did not escape the contagion."[60] A self-described "plain practical farmer," Wright spent six months in Ohio during the winter of 1818–1819 to judge "the merits of a country so highly extolled."[61] He had read "glowing descriptions" of Ohio in both private letters and public print; these led him to sell his farm, to abandon his family, and to see the region for himself. His motivation for viewing the landscape, he told the reader, was strictly personal. "I went not like the land speculator—to purchase immense tracts of land with a view to future profit by the monopoly;—not like the traveller for amusement, who loves to astonish his friends at home, with 'something of the marvelous;'—not like the scientific enthusiast—to invade the secret recesses of nature. . . . But, I went as a plain practical farmer."[62] He intended to assess the soil quality, the waterways, the climate, the price of produce, the prospect for future markets, the necessity of foreign items, as well as "the manners, customs, and moral character of the inhabitants and the state and prospect of their literary and religious institutions."[63] This was, in sum, the information that a farmer would need in order to make an informed decision about moving to the frontier to farm.

Wright returned from his travels unimpressed by what he had seen. The majority of the land in Ohio remained uncultivated; the buildings were generally log cabins, not framed barns or houses; and few provisions were available for purchase. What was available was sold at triple the price in

New England. The lands and homes that met his approval were invariably owned by land speculators and "capitalists." Those like himself, who worked the land, lived in poverty. He described the farmers as "mostly, of indolent slovenly habits" who "appear to be a meager, sickly spiritless and unenterprising race."[64] Even New Englanders, who arrived in Ohio with good habits, soon sank to a disgraceful level of living. Wright arrived at such conclusions, not surprisingly, by observing the landscape. Cornfields had not been harvested, and roads remained unimproved. The majority of settlers seemed content to live in one-room log cabins. He rarely saw a school or a church in the frontier settlements. Such were the physical signs of moral failure.

More troubling than lazy inhabitants, the land held perils even for the most industrious farmer. Wild weeds named "blue joint" and "nimble Will" choked tender English grasses.[65] Wright spotted poisonous roots that killed cattle, and milk spoiled mysteriously inside the cow and sickened those who drank it. The waters, he claimed, were almost "universally impregnated with lime," a cause of dysentery to all and death to some.[66] The water tasted so repugnant that it was fit only for distilling in whiskey, which, according to Wright, was the drink of choice on the frontier.[67] The list of natural hazards in his account was endless. "Another of the evils of this 'garden of the world,' is what is termed *sick wheat*." This pernicious plant appeared to be a healthy stalk of wheat but "is said to be a certain death to any creature that eats it."[68] Copperheads and rattlesnakes abounded in Ohio and tended to "annoy the happy inhabitants of this terrestrial paradise."[69] Wright occasionally saw a promising tract of land for cultivation or raising cattle. But, as noted, he found that the property had been purchased already by land speculators or, as he called them, "land jobbers" who would sell to him only at an inflated price. This land of murderous weeds and unscrupulous land speculators looked more like a biblical wilderness than like an Eden.

But the one section of Ohio that escaped Wright's negative assessment was the Western Reserve, with its "handsome and well-cultivated farms." The water, soil, and timber were among the best he had seen during his six-month journey. Wright found that the "industrious enterprizing" inhabitants, being "principally from Connecticut," owned "elegant painted houses," placed "lofty spires" on the village churches, and boasted "decently clothed and well-behaved children." The people charmed him. Wright described the inhabitants as having "easy manners, refined conversation and open, cheerful countenances."[70] In contrast to other settlements in Ohio, in the Western Reserve "the traveller is almost led to believe himself transported to a land inhabited by a different order of beings."[71]

Wright's praise for the Western Reserve seems strange when examined against contemporary travel accounts and missionary letters. Where others saw little to recommend the land or the people, Wright discovered lovely homes and charming settlers. Further, for Wright, the region's merits extended beyond the physical landscape to include Morse's moral categories. Practically quoting Morse, he wrote that the Western Reserve society was homogeneous, and its men were industrious and enterprising. And while Wright failed to comment explicitly on morality and religious practice, he nevertheless implied his approval of both elements in the Western Reserve. In reference to natural resources, he noted that the potable water that he found in the Western Reserve did not have to be distilled to whiskey. The built landscape included well-constructed churches, showing that settlers paid attention to religious duties. The people boasted well-behaved children who in themselves demonstrated the understanding that a stable society begins in a morally ordered household with proper child-drearing. Wright's rhetorical strategy, although complimentary to the Western Reserve, ultimately reinforced his position that in both the land and the people New England surpassed the western frontier settlements. Why, Wright asked, would a farmer choose to settle in a region where settlers strove, yet ultimately failed, to replicate their native land?

Three years later Doctor Zerah Hawley published *A Journal of a Tour Through Connecticut, Massachusetts, New York, the North Part of Pennsylvania and Ohio, Including a Years Residence in the Part of the State of Ohio, Styled, New Connecticut, or Western Reserve, in Which is Given, A Description of the Country, Climate, Soil, Productions, Animals, Buildings, Manners of People, State of Society, Population &c. From an Actual and Careful Observation.*[72] Hawley picked up on the metaphorical construction of the Western Reserve as an Edenic paradise but quickly dispensed with the metaphor through empirical observation of the land and the settlers. He pointed out that his writings, unlike reports penned by eager land speculators or hasty visitors, provided an "eye-witness" account based on a year of extensive travel throughout the region.

Written in the form of travel letters addressed to his brother, Hawley's account was intended to prevent "the evil effects that may arise from the high sounding recommendations, (in most cases totally unfounded in fact), of land speculation."[73] The Western Reserve was not the replication of New England land and culture that Hawley had expected. He described instead, poor soil, an unpredictable climate, impoverished people, and a disorderly society. Hawley considered it his duty "to undeceive the community, respecting a portion of the Western country, which has been represented as an earthly paradise, where every thing necessary, every thing convenient, and almost every thing which is considered a luxury, might be had almost without care labour or exertion."[74] His deep conviction regarding the danger of deceptive promotional literature emboldened him to write vividly in tone and content about the causes of his disillusionment with the "earthly paradise." In a style and tone reminiscent of Jedidiah Morse, Hawley presented information based on his careful observation of the Western Reserve and linked the natural and the moral worlds.

Hawley's narrative is largely a dissertation on unrealized expectations. He expected luxuriant vegetation, but found destitute pastures. He anticipated herds of healthy cattle, but beheld only thin, diseased animals, worn out by the severe cold. The paradise of plenty turned out to be a barren wasteland. Yet Hawley also described dense forests of beech, ash, chestnut, oak, sycamore, sugar-maple, black walnut, and wild cherry trees. The sky was filled with hawks, crows, and ravens. In trees he spotted woodpeckers; in the ponds he recognized different species of ducks. Elk, deer, wolves, foxes, skunks, squirrels, opossums, hedgehogs, and an occasional black bear roamed the landscape, while sturgeon, catfish, whitefish, and bass swam in streams, rivers, and Lake Erie.[75] Hawley, it seems, dismissed these obvious signs of nature's bounty because they remained in a natural, feral state. Uncultivated fields, undomesticated animals, and forests too dense to traverse resembled more a howling wilderness than a Garden of Eden.

Unpredictable weather patterns made Hawley's daily life in New Connecticut a misery: "I never knew so variable and unsettled weather in any part of New-England or the Middle States, as I have known in the northern part of Ohio."[76] In December the erratic weather changed from hour to hour, making it difficult to plan for work or travel. The clay roads remained muddy for months on account of the torrential rains, and deep wagon wheel marks froze when the temperatures dropped, keeping roads nearly impassable all winter.[77] Violent winds from Lake Erie uprooted trees, and bitterly cold days threatened to kill early buds on peach trees. Hawley depicted a cold, stormy, and sometimes frightening environment, a display that suggests nature's crushing power and human vulnerability. The hostile environment provided the perfect backdrop for his low opinion of the region. The Western Reserve was no garden paradise but a setting that harbored a recalcitrant natural world.

The sparse settlement and impoverished population did not escape Hawley's critical eye. The towns did not impress him; only a few of them received his praise. He characterized the majority of the Western Reserve as "thinly settled, many townships remaining in the same situation, or nearly so, as they were when possessed by the savages of the forest."[78] He estimated that there were 150 inhabitants in each township, about 6 people per square mile; still, "in some townships . . . there is four-sixths of a person to a square mile."[79] Hawley was unprepared for the empty towns and was stunned by the poverty that he encountered, imagining that people as well as plants and animals flourished in the land of plenty. "From all accounts I had heard, I had no reason to expect, and to discover so few marks of wealth, and so frequent and great appearances of poverty and distress."[80] That was, in fact, what he encountered. The majority of the inhabitants were living in a deplorable state, half starved and half naked. Even those settlers who had some money were unable to acquire basic items such as shoe leather, since, according to Hawley, nothing was available for sale. "Many children were literally barefoot."[81] This description differs considerably from Wright's, who tells of well-dressed children and their charming parents, living comfortably in lovely homes. Still, while Hawley and Wright see different settlers in the landscape, their descriptive categories, harking back to Morse's geography, remain the same.

Hawley's primary intention was to assess the land quality and potential; his account, however, includes much more information. He devoted as much attention to the manners, habits, morals, and religious practices of the inhabitants as to the weather conditions, soil quality, and natural resources. For the state of society in the Western Reserve, as it was described to prospective settlers in promotional literature, was, to Hawley's mind, the greatest deception of all: "They are told that society is good: 'As good,' says those who are interested in the assertion, as in any of the country towns in the New-England states."[82] Against this claim Hawley detailed accounts of the people's manners and habits, including clothing, conversation, demeanor, literacy, and work habits. He observed, for example, that the Western Reserve women wore homespun dresses of unremarkable style, designed more for comfort than beauty. They rarely wore bonnets; and when they did, the bonnets were of an old-fashioned cut with dreary colors, and only occasionally did a ribbon or lace enliven the hat. Men also dressed in homespun cloth, looking presentable on special occasions but "miserably deficient" in their everyday wardrobe. Most wore a sheepskin covering over their "pantaloons" or a leather apron tied behind their backs with straps. Older women wore their gray hair plaited "very much in the manner of a Chinese gentleman."[83]

In regard to manners, Hawley gave a few telling examples. When entering a room, women rarely knocked, and men generally did not remove their hats.[84] Both sexes stared impolitely, asked blunt questions, and gossiped incessantly. But these uncouth practices paled in comparison to the blatant laziness of the settlers. During all of his travels, Hawley maintained, he never saw "a person in haste";[85] "in many towns here," he remarked further, "industry is not so much the order of the day."[86] Hawley found farmers who preferred to hire themselves out by day; choosing to purchase their food rather than grow it. Instead of preparing for the coming summer by chopping winter wood, Hawley stated, the Western Reserve settlers "spend half the day in idle chit-chat."[87] Industry, a hallmark of New England character, was not practiced among the Western Reserve settlers that Hawley encountered.

These manners and habits, though distasteful, would not, on their own, lead to immorality. But the "indelicate" custom of parents, children and guests "sleeping promiscuously in one room," had, of course, "a very demoralizing tendency."[88] This was practiced not just among the poorest families but also among the "richest and most respectable," even in homes that could accommodate the sexes separately. Hawley contended that this custom "may be considered one great step toward a state of barbarism, and is a rapid approach to the custom of our savage brethren of the wilderness, who sleep without ceremony around the fires of their cabins."[89] This quick descent into "barbarism" calls to mind the Connecticut Missionary Society's warnings about the importance of establishing straight moral habits, like straight roads, that would extend through the generations. Without concrete moral boundaries, even the most righteous New England emigrant might succumb to the indecent power of the wilderness environment. Landscape and morality were here intertwined: not only was the land of a lesser quality than that of New England, but the settlers were themselves of poorer character, lacking manners, proper habits, an industrious nature, and morality.

Hawley's most stinging criticism focused on the paucity of proper religious leaders and instructors. His remarks centered on Presbyterian and Episcopalian clergymen, for "the other preachers are illiterate Baptist Elders, and still more illiterate Itinerant Methodists."[90] He reported that clergymen (presumably Plan of Union missionaries) settled in a few towns for four to six months, but spent the remaining months missionizing, leaving congregants vulnerable to the preaching of "the most uninformed and fanatical Methodist preachers" whose "sermons are without plan or system, beginning with ignorance and ending with nonsense, interlarded with something nearly approaching to blasphemy in many cases."[91] These preachers would "bawl forth one of their incoherent rhapsodies in two or three townships in the same day."[92] Hawley concluded that the Western Reserve needed missionaries as desperately as in the "Islands of the Seas" because many frontier families lived without the "word of God" and were "groping in almost heathenish darkness."[93] All of these things considered, Hawley deemed the "future prospects" for religion in New Connecticut unpromising.[94]

Barefoot children, women who resembled Chinese gentlemen, settlers sleeping like savages, lazy men, ignorant preachers, and families groping in heathenish darkness—all inhabited the "New Connecticut" that Hawley encountered. For him, the Western Reserve was a wilderness, not Eden. Hawley's account emphasized the perils of the region, whereas the Connecticut Missionary Society reports praised its possibilities. Hawley, however, did not indict the missionary societies but blamed panicked land speculators and settlers for spreading misinformation about the Western Reserve: "The former [speculators] speak highly of the climate, in order to induce people to purchase their lands, and the latter [settlers] do the same to induce people to come and settle among them in order to increase their number, and that they may sell their produce to immigrants, each caring little, whether the truth is known, till people move into the highly extolled country."[95] The two groups, he believed, were joined in the common goal of enticing unknowing New Englanders to settle in the Western Reserve. If the aim of travel literature is to make the strange familiar, then Hawley inverted this technique: using all the customary landmarks of the ideal New England society—homogeneity, industry, and morality—Hawley began his narrative with the metaphor of the Garden of Eden, only to dismantle it. The people and landscape of the Western Reserve failed miserably to fit each of the categories. Hawley envisaged a garden paradise but found a wilderness. Although he attempted to "remap" the region, he stayed within the conceptual lines drawn by the spatial and moral mappers who had come before him.

But not all of the publications that aimed to overturn false descriptions of the frontier were so serious-minded. In the same year that Wright produced his account, Henry Trumbull penned *Western Emigration. Journal of Doctor Jeremiah Smipleton's* [sic] *Tour to Ohio. Containing An account of the numerous difficulties, Hair-breadth Escapes, Mortifications and Privations, which the Doctor and his family experienced on their Journey from Maine, to the "Land of Promise," and during a residence of three years in that highly extolled country* (figure 17). Trumbull, however, adopted a satirical approach, addressing potential emigrants who have been "deceived by the fairy tale reports and the specious colorings of land speculators."[96] He cleverly structured his text to parallel the misadventures of Don Quixote. The frontier settlements are associated with the futility of chasing false hopes.[97] Trumbull's account of "Doctor Jeremiah Simpleton" chronicled his three-year stay in the "Land of Promise," during which time he started out "with as big a belly, as fine a nag, as well attir'd, and with as fleshy a purse as you now possess—but ah! a three year's residence in your 'Garden of Eden' has deprived me of them all."[98]

Trumbull described the Western Reserve as an uninhabitable region of infertile soil, squalid shelters, terrifying storms, and wild animals that could not be caught for food. The narrative tells of a Maine farmer, Jeremiah Simpleton, who is persuaded by a "land jobber" to leave his modest home "for four times the number of acres of land in Ohio—represented to me to be equal to the Garden of Eden."[99] But what Simpleton and his family found in this Eden was swampy lands unsuitable for cultivation and settlement. Simpleton was unable to catch the many beasts that inhabited the areas, and dined instead on flying squirrel. He did not hunt bears and buffalo but feared they would make a meal out of his family. Half-starved and half-naked, the Simpleton family nearly perished after their first few days in the promised land.

A further affliction was the lack of society. Simpleton and his family were so isolated from human contact that he had to fill all the local civic offices, including "Colonel," "Justice of the Peace," "Doctor," and "School Master." His nearest neighbors were a Dutch couple, the husband of which represents a "Sancho Panza" figure: he is a "blunder-head, beetle-head, cabbage-head, double-headed Dutchman."[100] In view of the lack of

FIGURE 17 (*opposite page*). "Western Emigration," broadside, 1810s(?), also front page of H. Trumbull, *Western Emigration. Journal of Doctor Jeremiah Smipleton's* [sic] *Tour to Ohio* (Boston: S. Sewall, 1819). This illustration represents the comical cautionary tale of immigrants whose desires for the Promised Land left them destitute. Courtesy of the Western Reserve Historical Society, Cleveland.

WESTERN EMIGRATION.

JOURNAL

OF

DOCTOR JEREMIAH SIMPLETON's

TOUR TO OHIO.

CONTAINING

An account of the numerous difficulties, Hair-breadth Escapes, Mortifications and Privations, which the Doctor and his family experienced on their Journey from Maine, to the 'Land of Promise,' and during a residence of three years in that highly extolled country.

BY H. TRUMBULL.

Nulli Fides Frontis.

BOSTON—PRINTED BY N. SEWELL.

Conversation between Dr. Simpleton and Mr. Scruple, on the impropriety and folly of emigrating from the good States of Rhode Island, Massachusetts, &c. to the Western Wilderness.

society, Simpleton repeatedly compared his plight to the sufferings of the biblical Job; he came to believe that he would "rather be a hog-reeve in good New England, than hold any office in the back woods country."[101] And though Simpleton clearly felt deceived by land promoters, he was more discouraged by the immoral "state of society" than by the unmanageable physical landscape.

The clever appropriation of the Don Quixote epic moves beyond correcting misinformation about the physical landscape to underscoring anxieties about "foreigners" on the frontier. By equating the "Dutch-man" with Sancho Panza, Trumbull points to Morse's New England ideal of "industry" and "good society": this "foreign" character was imbued with the undesirable attributes of laziness, slovenliness, and cowardliness. In so doing, the character reflected many of the anxieties of the day, especially a pervasive association of "foreigners" with disorderly society. Unlike other writers, Trumbull did not present New Englanders misbehaving far from society's watchful gaze, but focused on foreigners acting outside of the New England moral categories.

Although Simpleton did not directly address religion, he narrated his travails in biblical terms. In the most dismal moment of crushing defeat, he compared his adversities to those of Job and expressed compassion for Cain if, as an outcast in the land of Nod, he experienced half of the difficulties that befell Simpleton on the frontier. He cited Solomon's warning against vanity to explain his ill-fated desire for public office and social station in Ohio. After holding all the civic offices of a nonexistent town, Simpleton loosely quoted Scripture to characterize his predicament: "If the Bible contains but a single *truth*, it is that which declares us, that 'man is born unto trouble, as the sparks fly upward!'"[102] And Simpleton encountered only troubles in the "land of plenty." Ravaging storms, unending suffering, punishment for vanity, the misery of living as an outcast from society—all led Simpleton to the conclusion that he was a target of God's wrath rather than an inheritor of God's blessings.

A Correct View: *New Connecticut as the Promised Land*

By the third decade of settlement, Western Reserve travel accounts improved dramatically. Travelers and emigrants who toured the region were more likely to describe its promise than its perils. Thomas Kelly, an Irish emigrant from "Manx," the Isle of Man, who settled with his family in Concord Township in 1827, praised the region in a letter to a "friend." The letter, originally published in the *Manx Sun*, encouraged the friend to immigrate to Ohio, and if possible, to New Connecticut. Compared to his native land, the Western Reserve was a paradise; there Kelly found "no begging, no men in rags, no striving about work, there is plenty for all—all is liberty, union and love."[103] The land, according to Kelly, practically grew crops on its own. Echoing the early reports about the abundance of the land, he gushed that it "bears crops without any labor."[104] He testified further that potatoes and pumpkins grew without manure, and vegetables that he could not even name appeared to self-propagate. He reconceived the perception that the New Connecticut inhabitants were lazy—he portrayed them as fortunate. In the Western Reserve a person needed to do so little to survive that "you may call it lazy, it would make you wonder."[105] From Kelly's vantage point, New Connecticut truly was a garden paradise.

David Griffiths Jr., a Welsh clergyman who toured the region between 1832 and 1843, also found much to praise. In his *Two Years' Residence in the New Settlements of Ohio, North America: with Directions for Immigrants*, Griffiths compared the Western Reserve's magnificent natural resources to those of his homeland.[106] Like Kelly, he esteemed the land and the society as good, if not better, than his native land. Griffiths wrote to provide practical advice for people who wanted to settle there; in the course of explaining how to find a job and how to build a cabin, he emphasized that the country is not as "wild" as it appeared. In one telling example, he described a visit to some parishioners in their home in the woods. Bugs, thick brushwood, mud, a difficult road, and mounting anxiety hampered his progress. When he arrived at the solitary log cabin, which he estimated to be at least two miles from the closest neighbors, he was surprised to discover that they were "both civilized and Christianized beings; they are well informed, and well behaved."[107] Despite the "wildness of their situation," they remained morally sound in the middle of the woods.[108] It is worthwhile to notice that although Griffiths came to opposite conclusions from those of Wright, Hawley, and Trumbull, he nevertheless connected morality with the landscape. In this case the couple's morality overcame the wilderness environment.

The moral and physical features of the frontier landscape continued to capture the attention of many travelers throughout the settlement period and beyond. Their published writings discouraged some and inspired others to follow in their footsteps and to see the land for themselves. In the summer of 1812 two travelers crossed the Allegheny Mountains and stepped into the Western Reserve to survey the moral and physical landscape. John F. Schermerhorn and Samuel J. Mills toured the western frontier settlements from New England to New Orleans to provide the Connecticut Missionary Society and the Massachusetts Missionary Society with *A Correct View of that Part of the United States which Lies West of the Allegany Mountains: with Regard to Religion and Morals*.[109] Although their account included information about the physical landscape, the primary purpose of their tour was to map the moral landscape. In fact, landscape was secondary to evangelistic potential, as Schermerhorn explained in the report's endnotes: "The topographical remarks on the country are introduced to give the Trustees an idea in what parts of the country population, in all probability, will most rapidly increase; and of course where missionary services will be most wanted."[110] Both men were employed as missionaries and as information gatherers to "enquire particularly into the religious and moral state of that part of the country."[111]

The account was divided geographically into states and regions, with general comments about the physical landscape and natural resources as well as occasional anecdotes about inhabitants. It also contained brief mention of population, transportation, and other information that pertained to missionary labor. But the bulk of the text was devoted to describing the progress of Plan of Union missionaries in these places. Schermerhorn, who signed his name to the portion of the narrative that included New Connecticut, provided "Statistical Tables" to chart the number of inhabitants, ministers, churches, and vacancies among different denominations in each county. For the most part he counted Presbyterians (including Congregationalists in this group), Baptists, and Methodists. Other religious groups, such as the Quakers in Jefferson County and the Halcyons in Marrieta, were mentioned occasionally throughout the narrative but did not merit a place on his chart.[112]

In Schermerhorn's eyes the Presbyterians were the unrivaled dominant denomination in New Connecticut. There he tallied ten preachers, seventeen churches supplied part-time with preachers, and ten vacant congregations eagerly waiting for leaders. The Methodists, according to his chart, had only one circuit, and the Baptists were "very few."[113] Not surprisingly, he found that in the Western Reserve most of the inhabitants hailed from Connecticut and Massachusetts, and he described them as "well informed and with some exceptions their manners are less vicious than in the new countries generally."[114] Missionaries in New Connecticut were well respected. Schermerhorn claimed that some influential men who were recently "Infidels" had been "brought to acknowledge Christ." The prospects for the region looked good because "many churches had been formed," and "many more were ready to be organized."[115] While a great number of the settlements west of the Alleghenies possessed a moral landscape as deplorable as the physical landscape, the New Connecticut territory remained pristine, a place in which to continue Plan of Union missionary labor. On the whole, the region, in his opinion, provided hope for future missionary success. This was good news for the Connecticut Missionary Society, and the trustees gave a large portion of their resources to the evangelism of this region for the next two decades.

In 1812, two years after Margaret Dwight wrote her travel journal and just a few months after Schermerhorn jotted down his findings in the region, six-year-old Emily Nash began her personal daily diary. That fall she had moved with her family from Windsor, Massachusetts, to Troy Township in New Connecticut. Nash's journal provided a glimpse into the mind of a hopeful girl who was painfully aware of the difficulties her family faced during the first few months of settlement. Explaining their plight, she repeated a set of phrases she had heard before from adults: "Instead of finding the land flowing with milk and honey we found it flowing with all sorts of wild animals such as bairs, wolves, wild cats and snakes of every kind and every sise."[116] The power of the biblical metaphor for New Connecticut was strong enough to surface even in a child's diary. Nash wrote that it was only after her father constructed a makeshift cabin that the family "began to feel that we were at home in Ohio with wild beasts and wild men."[117] Being "at home" in New Connecticut for Nash, and so many other Euro-American settlers, meant fulfilling a desire steeped in biblical imagery. Such desire, of course, could never be fully realized, but it could be partially satisfied; biblical metaphors granted even children a language to express the expectations and disappointments that attended travel to a strange and distant place.

Nash scribbled these lines in her journal before many of the travel narratives discussed above were written. How, one might ask, did a six-year-old learn to conceive of the Western Reserve in these terms? She did not reveal that she heard her parents describe New Connecticut as a promised land, nor did she mention that she listened to a sermon, read a newspaper article, or saw a broadside that depicted the region as a Garden of Eden. In one sense, speculating about where she picked up this image is unimportant and would tell us very little. What is significant is that the metaphor of New Connecticut as a promised land was available and ready to be appropriated and challenged even by a child.

Whether or not Emily Nash ever came in contact with a Plan of Union missionary, the missionaries and their sponsoring society helped to invent the spatial and moral construction of New Connecticut that many of the Western Reserve travel writers subverted. In essence, the travel writers attempted to "remap" the physical and moral landscape. To do this they disputed exaggerated claims about the landscape and objected to misrepresentations about the state of the society in New Connecticut, focusing specifically on the inhabitants' crude "habits and manners." To emphasize the disparity between imagination and reality, the travel writers compared the region and the settlers to "home," a New England ideal; in every respect the Western Reserve fell short of expectations. More important, through such comparison, they both exploited powerful biblical images and reshaped perceptions of the Western Reserve, and in the process they reaffirmed that New England was the moral and physical center of the map. It was "home."

Twenty-nine years after the first Plan of Union missionary, Joseph Badger, entered the Western Reserve, and just a few years after Western Reserve travel writers attempted to "remap" the region, another missionary, John J. Shipherd, arrived in the region hoping to advance God's kingdom on the frontier. Like Badger and so many other Western Reserve missionaries, Shipherd believed that the Puritan-covenanted community was an exemplar of moral and social order. But unlike missionaries who earlier sought to foster multiple congregations on the frontier, Shipherd fixed his attention on building one covenanted community, the Oberlin Colony. Shipherd and the founders of the Oberlin Colony fused theology and landscape to realize their goal of a pious frontier colony. The community members believed that shaping the physical landscape was equal in importance to writing and signing articles of faith. I now turn to the Oberlin Colony as an example of missionary labor to shape successfully a moral and spatial "Puritan" community on the frontier. This effort to re-create Puritan New England ironically brought an end to Connecticut's Plan of Union mission to the Western Reserve.

CHAPTER 5

A Beacon in the Wilderness
Moral Inscriptions on the Landscape

The Russia Township of the 1830s was mostly uncleared wilderness. A swampy area located in the nineteenth range of Connecticut's Western Reserve, eight miles from Elyria, Lorain County's seat, it remained unorganized until 1825.[1] In 1830, John Jay Shipherd—a Presbyterian graduate of Middlebury College who had become a missionary after hearing the Presbyterian revivalist Charles Grandison Finney preach—accepted a call from the American Home Missionary Society to be a missionary pastor in Elyria. Shipherd, like the Plan of Union missionaries before him, believed that the West would be the proving ground for building a revived Christian nation. But unlike the more Calvinistic Plan of Union missionaries, Shipherd embraced the popular revivalist Charles G. Finney's Arminian beliefs that individuals could effect their own salvation and that society could be made perfect. Shipherd, in other words, was concerned less with discerning God's benevolent design on the frontier landscape than with constructing a Christian community with his own hands.

After deciding to remove to New Connecticut, Shipherd explained his evangelical desire in a letter to his parents. Sounding remarkably similar to the words penned by Plan of Union missionaries, Shipherd's missive joined scriptural language with landscape metaphors to write himself into the salvific history of the region, the nation, and the world. "It strikes me, that the Glory of God, the prosperity of our American Zion, the peace of our Republic, and the good of the world, all conspire to press the servants of Christ into that part of his vineyard."[2] On the frontier, however, Shipherd did not achieve the immediate results he had hoped for. Less than a year after he ventured West, he confessed his discouragement in a letter to his father: "Our moral conditions are deplorable. There are two Presbyterian ministers besides myself laboring in this country + these two have for months been unable to labor."[3] The moral landscape was not what he had expected. A year later Shipherd had reached the point of despair: despite a few hopeful converts, he explained, "I however feel that my sphere of usefulness is now much circumscribed." To compound his problems, "the emigrants to our place of the last year are, mostly, so hostile to God that they have not, many of them, even for once, entered his house."[4] He had set out to evangelize the world, but was unable to overcome the resistance in his own neighborhood.

Not surprisingly, the idealistic Shipherd soon began to question his missionary vocation. His letters home reveal a young man vacillating between hopeful conviction and growing desperation. Although he found little cause for optimism in his daily missionary work, Shipherd felt inspired as he dreamed about the future. A month before he sent the discouraging news to his father, he wrote to his brother about the frontier's religious needs, which, in his opinion, were considerable. He believed that the Western Reserve churches were "dead and greatly in need of a revival."[5] By "revival" Shipherd meant not individual religious renewal but that "a general + thorough reformation must take place, or infidelity will wave its infernal flag over desolation."[6] Unfortunately, according to Shipherd, "there is not among us a reformer to break up the stupid soul ruining customs of churches and minister."[7] It might seem odd that a Presbyterian missionary employed by the American Home Missionary Society would depict churches and clergy as maintaining "stupid soul ruining customs," but Shipherd was a Finney disciple, and as such he was deeply suspicious of institutional religious practices. True piety, in Shipherd's mind, depended solely on a person's conscious decision to choose salvation. Rituals, doctrines, and traditions served only to obscure this goal. Unlike the previous Plan of Union missionaries who struggled to establish new churches, Shipherd concerned himself with reviving these now "dead" congregations.

After laboring unsuccessfully in Elyria for two years, Shipherd became increasingly convinced that his role in the creation of God's kingdom would be that of a needed reformer, and that his life's work would be to construct a Christian colony in the wilderness. He imagined a closed community of regenerate souls, working together to evangelize the world, both through moral example and through the education of missionaries. With the help of his friend Philo Penfield Stewart, Shipherd planned the Oberlin Colony and Institute.[8]

The Oberlin Colony and Institute draws together many of the themes discussed throughout this book. Like the Plan of Union missionaries before him, Shipherd struggled to reconcile his preconceptions of frontier labor with the realities of missionary life. He believed wholeheartedly in the redemptive possibilities of shaping the physical landscape. He also understood that the landscape itself could shape moral habits: therefore, he hoped to construct the physical space to reflect and promote moral values. Shipherd's desire to begin anew, to cut down trees and to lay roads, recalls the efforts of earlier missionaries to shape the physical and moral landscape. The wilderness, they believed, provided unique opportunities for spiritual growth. The Oberlin Colony also tapped into the nostalgic desire to reconstruct a lost biblical or Puritan home. As did missionaries and settlers before him, Shipherd thought of himself and the other colonists as pilgrims in a new land. And finally, Shipherd was steadfast in his belief that world redemption would begin on the American frontier, and the labor of missionaries would bring this moment to pass. Shipherd, like many before him, "mapped" the town in his mind and then set out to shape the physical and moral landscape.

The Oberlin Colony and Institute

Shipherd's vision for the colony focused on erasing economic and social distinctions so that "the church may be restored to gospel simplicity."[9] To this end, he required all prospective colonists to sign a covenant that included a mission statement and regulations. Gospel simplicity, according to Shipherd, required highly detailed moral reform. "Lamenting the degeneracy of the Church," the colony had as its purpose "to glorify God and to do good to men." But glorifying God demanded that the colonists first pay close attention to themselves—both soul and body—before doing "good to men." Shipherd believed that the colonists could best achieve gospel simplicity through strict moral habits. To this end, he required everyone to "simplify food, dress &c., to be industrious and economical, + give all their current and annual expence for the spread of the gospel."[10]

The twelve regulations attached to the Oberlin Covenant outlined the specific ways in which Oberlin colonists would "strive to maintain deep-toned and elevated personal piety."[11] These regulations point to a connection that Shipherd drew between elevated personal piety and regulated bodily practices. To maintain "deep-toned piety" the colonists were required to practice "industry, economy, and Christian self-denial" as well as dietary restrictions ("only plain and wholesome food"), dress prohibitions renouncing "all of the world's expensive and unwholesome fashions," and mutual aid and education.[12] Colonists scrutinized all aspects of their lives in order to purify body and soul. Becoming wholly new people living in a sanctified space, they imagined themselves to be exemplars of true Christian virtue by strictly regulating their physical bodies and moral habits. Striking a balance between inward piety and outward appearances, the Oberlin colonists signed the covenant and prayed to bring on a new Christian era. This orderly life was also represented in the colony's landscape.

The Oberlin colonists were appalled by the laxity in piety that they saw among professing Christians. They joined together as a covenanted community with a sincere desire to revitalize Christianity and to evangelize the world starting in Lorain County, Ohio. Rather than aiming to "awaken" their nearby neighbors, the Oberlin colonists set their sights farther away: they maintained a "peculiar interest" in the spiritual well-being of the Mississippi Valley and beyond.[13] Unlike the Plan of Union missionaries, the colonists believed that they could create a pious western community *and* a school to train missionaries: their graduates would be better at combating western moral evils than missionaries from the East were.

Their confidence in the integrity of the colony and the institute was palpable in the community's rejection of "unregenerate souls." Not only did they maintain strict moral boundaries through a shared covenant, they also marked geographical boundaries by refusing to sell property to religious outsiders. From the start, this exclusionary practice alarmed the neighbors of the colony. In 1834 Philo Stewart remarked that "our inducing so many Christian families to locate together is made use of by those not friendly to the object." He suggested to Shipherd that to avoid harassment, they "dispose of some of the colonial lands to persons of a certain character who are not pious," and then the college would not be "surrounded by a corrupt and irreligious population."[14] Stewart thought that persons of social standing who were not pious would provide a moral buffer along the colony's borders. Four years later, however, the colonists officially resolved "that it is inconsistent with our covenant obligating to encourage any settlers among us who are immoral or unfriendly to our Institution, or to dispose of our lands to those whom we have no reason to believe seek the furtherance of our great object."[15] The colonists both promoted a theologically unified community and maintained their identity in the face of a hostile outside environment. The urgency and importance of their endeavor only increased in the face of outside opposition. The colonists practiced, in a sense, what the Plan of Union missionaries preached: the establishment of moral boundaries by mapping firm geographical boundaries.

Soon the boundaries extended to include new members, the students in the colony's institute. Shipherd had all along conceived of the Oberlin Institute as an outgrowth of the covenanted community. The students, like the colonists, adopted a rigorous lifestyle that connected their theological beliefs and desires with their everyday actions. The institute, therefore, was inseparable from the colony. Shipherd, in fact, viewed this relationship as a sign of the institute's strength. The Oberlin Institute, for example, advertised itself as "embosomed in the Oberlin Colony which consists of pious eastern families" who moved to the frontier for the "purpose of glorifying God."[16] From the inception of the Oberlin Institute, Shipherd held high hopes for it, believing that it would not only educate western students but also eventually provide an equal if not superior education for eastern students. Others, however, were not initially sanguine about the institute's prospects. Philo Stewart worried that if "education shall fall short of the pledge that was given, bad consequences must follow."[17] Stewart's plan was that the institute should operate first as a preparatory school for Western Reserve College, which served Plan of Union missionaries and settlers, before it would be allowed to evolve to a college.

Shipherd disagreed with Stewart's more cautious approach and worked tirelessly to raise funds and promote the institute. He attracted students by providing scholarships through an innovative work-study program, employing the new educational opinions regarding the efficacy of manual labor schools. This idea made sense to Shipherd not just for economic reasons but for its moral soundness as well. The manual labor system required students to work for the institute; their pay would then be deducted from their tuition costs. Such a system was coextensive with Shipherd's view that hard physical work went hand in hand with moral labor. Manual labor, in his eyes, constituted a distinct type of theological practice that was consistent with gospel simplicity; "I mean *practical theology*. They [the students] are to connect workshops + a farm with the Institution, + to simplify diet and dress. . . . And all this saves money, + what is more promotes muscular, mental + moral vigor."[18] Shipherd's commitment to "muscular, mental + moral vigor" echoed the early lessons of the Plan of Union missionaries: physical labor both promoted and authenticated spiritual labor, and moral lessons could be gained through physical exertion. So, too, Jedidiah Morse's moral categories of homogeneity, industry, and morality hovered over the entire Oberlin experiment: the covenantal community, its manual labor system, and its strict rules about behavior, diet, and dress, put on display Morse's "moral geography."

The physical layout of the colony and institute became an important aspect of the endeavor. The founders, not surprisingly, modeled the town on the paradigmatic Puritan New England town. Similar to the New Haven map discussed earlier, a central green connected the colony with the institute. Eventually, a Congregational church would stand on one side of the green, but the earliest map shows that a revival tent occupied the central location, signaling the colony's commitment to the revival preaching of Charles Grandison Finney. Within a couple of years, the town layout would look very much like it does today: the Congregational church was fixed on one side, the president's house sat on the southwest corner, and the Oberlin Institute rested on the opposite side; homes and town bordered the area. According to Oberlin College's third president, James H. Fairchild, at first "everything was new and rough"; two years after the institute's founding, the trustees took up the question of how to address this "roughness" and what architectural style and spatial organization would best exemplify the moral goals of the colony and the institute.[19] The landscape and the buildings needed to reflect the theological commitment to gospel simplicity.

Did gospel simplicity require architectural simplicity? Benefactor Arthur Tappan, for whom the town green—Tappan Square—was named, thought not and offered some architectural suggestions in a letter sent to Shipherd. He was concerned particularly with "the *style* of buildings and laying out your college ground."[20] He cautioned Shipherd not to be swayed by the popular notion that "chasteness in architecture and adjoining grounds has a refining influence on the character."[21] On the contrary, constructing beautiful buildings and landscapes, Tappan believed, constituted "a religious duty to imitate our heavenly benefactor in this as in all his other perfections."[22]

Colonist T. S. Ingersoll held the opposite view. In his 1836 letter to the trustees, Ingersoll pleaded that the buildings and grounds be set up appropriately "for the accommodation of those whom God has called to take the charge of others whom he in his providence has called to prepare to preach the everlasting gospel."[23] For Ingersoll, the students enrolled at the Oberlin Institute were not only doing "God's work," they were living in "God's buildings," studying and teaching at "God's Institute" and landscaping "God's property."[24] Ingersoll reasoned that the trustees had to choose the types of buildings carefully because they constituted the physical representation of divine intention. He suspected, however, that funds raised for the "Lord's work" were being used for "those things that are highly esteemed among men," such as commodious living quarters or unnecessary furnishings. Ingersoll, for example, toured the campus and found fault with President Asa Mahan's house: he objected to the costly chimneypieces, doors, and windows, which in his mind seemed only "to please the tastes of a vitiated world."[25] Ingersoll argued for a "plain, neat, simple stile of building which commends itself to every man's enlightened good sense." This style would be appropriate for the Oberlin Institute, because according to Ingersoll, although it "will not only be highly esteemed by the world, neither is it an abomination in the sight of God."[26] Ingersoll challenged the board of trustees to consider the seriousness of their decision about the design—whether human or divine—that they would use for buildings. Asking which style they planned to use, he queried, "From whence will they draw their models—from the word of God—or from the word of Benjamine or some other human Architect?"[27] God's buildings, Ingersoll warned, should be constructed according to God's blueprint, and that model did not include fancy chimneypieces. Like Shipherd, Ingersoll believed in the moral purpose of the manual labor system and contended that only plain-style architecture was consistent with Oberlin's theological goals. In the end it was Ingersoll, not Tappan, who won the day: architecture, like dress and diet, provided visual representations of theological beliefs and moral practices.

Despite the plain-style architecture, strict moral habits, and carefully planned landscape, Oberlin was not "highly esteemed" by many of its closest neighbors, including a good portion of the clergy associated with the Plan of Union. This antipathy is puzzling, because in many ways

Shipherd and the Oberlin colonists strove to achieve goals that were consistent with the Connecticut Missionary Society's intentions. The project to set up a Puritan-modeled community both spiritually through a covenant and physically through the constructed landscape, realized what many of the missionaries had worked for in other towns during the first three decades of Western Reserve settlement. Nowhere on the Western Reserve was there a more homogeneous population or greater agreement regarding the re-creation of New England. Moreover, the colonists believed that their efforts in the wilderness would bring sacred history one step closer to its redemptive conclusion. The Oberlin Colony, therefore, appeared to embody a perfectly re-created Puritan town on the frontier (figure 18).

But this was not the New England religious community that the majority of the Plan of Union missionaries had imagined. The Oberlin colonists' theological leanings and interest in radical moral reform triggered suspicion and antagonism from the local clergy. There were a few specific reasons for this tension. First, most of the Oberlin colonists were deeply affected by Charles Grandison Finney's revivals in New York and New England; they accepted his new measures as an integral component of reviving churches and establishing Christ's kingdom on earth.[28] The emotionalism of frontier revivals had always been a difficult question for the Plan of Union missionaries, who carefully monitored the fervor and feared all "false" sense of grace. And Finney's revivals went beyond "emotionalism": he preached that individuals could attain assurance of grace and work toward perfection. Second, the principal aim of colonists was to set a pious example for the newly established Plan of Union churches on the Western Reserve; local evangelism was secondary. In essence, they labored to maintain a sanctified insular community, and Oberlin missionaries were dispatched to regions further west. Like the Connecticut Missionary Society, the Oberlin colonists understood their position as the sacred "home base," not as an unredeemed frontier. Similarly, the Oberlin Institute, conceived initially as a preparatory school, quickly evolved into a college that was geared toward training missionaries. Unlike the Plan of Union Western Reserve College in Hudson, the Oberlin Institute did not simply provide an education for westerners who could not afford to attend college in the East; it also boldly insisted that eastern students could obtain an excellent education, as well as first-rate missionary training at Oberlin.[29] Rather than seeking to import New England moral values to frontier settlements, the Oberlin colonists believed that they had imprinted these

FIGURE 18. "A plan of Oberlin Colony, 1835." The founders of the Oberlin Colony sought to shape the physical and moral landscape to reflect the theological ideals of the colonists. The town survey as well as the building architecture reflected a nostalgic desire to re-create Puritan New England through a central town green and "gospel simplicity." Courtesy of Oberlin College Archives, Oberlin, Ohio.

values so thoroughly onto the physical and moral landscape that easterners should travel west to find a community that was more "New England" than their own.

Shipherd and the Oberlin colonists worked tirelessly to construct a covenantal community that represented gospel simplicity in all of its forms. By paying attention to moral habits and the physical landscape, the colony came close to realizing an imaginary biblical or Puritan past in frontier Ohio. The dual aim of instituting moral and spatial order is the theme that weaves through all of their discussions and attempts to establish a pure place from which to herald a providential future. For colonists, imagining the future evangelization of the world required not only becoming moral exemplars but also training missionaries to spread the word. Unfortunately, training missionaries to evangelize "all corners of the globe" became a point of conflict with the Plan of Union missionaries, who were still working to redeem sections of New Connecticut.

Building Up Society: Missionary Institutions

The founding of the Oberlin Colony occurred as Plan of Union missionaries were becoming settled ministers in New Connecticut. The third decade of Western Reserve settlement witnessed unity and internal structure among missionaries through large national organizations. Yet divisions over theological beliefs and practices ultimately led to the breakup of the Western Reserve Plan of Union. The tensions between Presbyterians and Congregationalists were exacerbated by the presence and increasing national visibility of the Oberlin Colony and Institute. Before the breakup in 1837, the Western Reserve missionaries worked hard to maximize their labor through increasingly efficient organizations, but the specter of disunion and disharmony accompanied all of their efforts.

As the Oberlin colonists were carving a new moral space in the physical landscape, the Plan of Union missionaries were busy institutionalizing their labor by setting up three presbyteries to oversee most of the Western Reserve congregations.[30] Besides administrative responsibilities, the presbyteries took charge of supervising missionaries sent by the Connecticut Missionary Society: directing their labors, assessing their readiness for ordination, watching their character, and disciplining and dismissing them when appropriate. In 1825 the Western Reserve Synod was founded to supervise the thirty-two active ministers who served eighty-four churches. To reach all of the congregations, the clergy were divided into three classes; further, the churches were organized into three circuits covering Geauga, Medina, and Huron Counties. This arrangement allowed missionaries to cover more ground and reach more settlers. While missionary visits included preaching, prayer, and fasting, the main objectives, according to synod clerk William Hanford, was "to promote a spirit of purity, watchfulness and prayer, among Christians, to persuade them to make vigorous efforts for the prosperity of Zion."[31] The Plan of Union missionaries were unable to meet all the needs of struggling New Connecticut churches, but they assured the Connecticut Missionary Society that, in most cases, they were able to lend considerable spiritual support. This optimistic appraisal, however, was not consistent with the dismal state of affairs that Shipherd would describe only a few years later in Elyria.

The creation of the Western Reserve Synod represented an important landmark for the Plan of Union missionaries because it signaled religious stability and the missionaries' growing independence from the Connecticut Missionary Society. Missionary Randolph Stone expressed the optimism of most missionaries in a series of letters sent to the Connecticut Missionary Society during 1825: "Even a warm imagination," Stone gushed, "would hardly 20 years ago, have anticipated such a result from the efforts of a single missionary society." Stone suggested that the future of the Western Reserve looked bright, and he believed that the "present expectations [will] be as much surpassed by future results."[32] Stone was impressed by two main features of the synod's timely establishment. First, he stressed the importance of the synod's presence in the Western Reserve; this he attributed to the success of missionary labor. Second, he believed that missionary efforts would be more efficient because of the synod's organization. Rather than duplicating missionary visits, or neglecting some areas altogether, the Western Reserve Synod built an infrastructure for missionary routes that connected preachers to struggling churches.

This period also signaled a national shift in American home missionary goals and procedures. Organizations such as the Connecticut Missionary Society began to realize the advantages of national missionary programs above those of local societies. This interest in promoting larger entities arose in tandem with the growth of national benevolent institutions, such as the American Bible Society, and the American Tract Society.[33] The most prominent group, the American Home Missionary Society, which sent John Shipherd to Elyria, absorbed many smaller local missionary efforts.

Over the next twenty years, the American Home Missionary Society grew into a powerful national group controlled primarily by Presbyterians and Congregationalists. The Connecticut Missionary Society continued to exist, but it was slowly incorporated into the American Home Missionary Society, an institution that operated more effectively than the Hartford-based organization. To the end, however, the Connecticut Missionary Society maintained a particular interest in the Western Reserve.

Throughout the 1820s and 1830s, the Connecticut Missionary Society continued its "long-distance" management of Plan of Union missionaries. The constant correspondence between missionaries working in New Connecticut and the trustees in Hartford attests to the strength of this relationship. Although many missionaries accepted settled pastorates in Western Reserve churches, the majority continued to be financed, at least partially, by the eastern society. As Western Reserve clergy made considerable gains in claiming authority by establishing local ecclesiastical organizations such as the Western Reserve Synod, they nevertheless remained accountable to the benevolence and interests of the sponsoring society.

As the population of the Western Reserve increased and more churches were established, the Plan of Union missionaries expressed doubts about the ability of the Connecticut Missionary Society to meet the region's needs. The earlier plan to survey the moral landscape and to cut moral inroads no longer seemed appropriate in a more settled society. The early mapping efforts, so apt for frontier missionizing, did not transfer easily for "building up" societies. The working model had to change to a missionary "system." Even after so many years, the missionaries still had doubts about the effectiveness of eastern-trained missionaries in New Connecticut. This concern, voiced by Calvin Chapin in his 1806 moral survey of New Connecticut (see chapter 2), arose again as the settled clergy first organized into local presbyteries and then resurfaced when the missionaries began to work under the Western Reserve Synod. In 1822 missionary John Seward decided that the question of missionary labor had to be addressed, since the majority of New Connecticut clergy were accepting settled pastorates. According to Seward, the main problem that the home society needed to resolve was the unsatisfactory nature of dividing missionary work with a settled pastorate. This system, Seward explained to the society, did not allow the laborers to commit fully to either job. The New Connecticut clergy struggled to balance half-time appointments as pastors and missionaries, which left them little time for their families or for study. More important, some of the ministers, including Seward, questioned whether the half-time positions and circuit riding organized by the Western Reserve Synod ultimately led to the establishment of lasting religious institutions. "The union of pastor and missionary is not the way to *build* up societies," Seward complained to the Connecticut Missionary Society. "It may lay the foundation when the country is very new and the population sparse, but it is not calculated to *build up* after the country becomes older and the population more numerous."[34] Missionary Giles Cowles agreed, but pinpointed the problem as "a want of system among missionaries." Cowles noted that although the plan had its merits, in reality missionaries failed to cooperate in providing enough preaching "to destitute parts of the Reserve." But Cowles believed the missionaries were not entirely to blame for this problem. The members of vacant congregations also had neglected to make "suitable efforts to provide for themselves the preaching of the gospel."[35] Cowles maintained that these problems could be overcome by further systematizing missionary labors and, to that end, he formed a synod missionary board and appointed John Seward as president and William Hanford as secretary. This group answered all future queries regarding Plan of Union missionary labor.

The most pressing question discussed was the merits of local theological training. It was obvious to the Plan of Union missionaries (as it had been to Joseph Badger and Thomas Robbins) and to many settlers that missionizing the frontier required a certain type of person who could rise to the physical challenges and understand the western character of religious piety. It was also clear, however, that true piety for the Plan of Union missionaries did not rise out of the West but had to be carried by eastern missionaries and often strenuously defended against the infidelity that, according to the missionaries, seemed to prosper in frontier settlements. The unique challenges of preaching in western settlements, and the role of eastern-trained clergy, continued to be hotly debated issues for the Plan of Union missionaries.

Evaluating missionary labor remained closely linked in the minds of the Plan of Union missionaries to missionary training. John Seward typified many such missionaries when he told the Connecticut Missionary Society that "this country will never be supplied with ministers until they are raised up among us."[36] The problem, of course, was funding and time. The Plan of Union missionaries considered the advantages of eastern versus western theological education at the same time that they began to accept settled pastorates in the Western Reserve. By the spring of 1822, members of Portage and Grand River Presbyteries resolved to establish a literary and theological institute on the Western Reserve "for the purpose of educating young men as pastors for our destitute churches."[37] Missionaries and laity closely monitored the establishment of the school. When the first cornerstone was laid in Hudson in 1826, the three Western Reserve presbyteries each appointed four representatives to serve on the board of trustees.[38] Included among these prominent men were settlers David Hudson and Elizur Wright, as well as missionaries John Seward, Simeon Woodruff, and Harvey Coe. The college trustees modeled the curriculum on that of Yale College, with an emphasis on the classics, higher mathematics, natural sciences, and theology. An endowment and a faculty trained in the Northeast eventually were secured.

The founders of the college believed that educating ministers in the West solved two related problems. First, it provided struggling western churches with much-needed clergy. Simeon Woodruff noted in a letter to the Connecticut Missionary Society that in his Huron Presbytery, eleven churches were "exposed to numerous evils, and not a single spiritual shepherd to take the oversight of them."[39] Thus the college became a training ground for western men who would assume leadership in the local Plan of Union churches.[40] Second, and equally important, the local college allowed students to stay close to their homes rather than being forced to travel east for an education.

Although it was located in the West—or perhaps because it was in New Connecticut—the college's founders did not hope to create an innovative curriculum that addressed the particularities of frontier life and education. Instead, they modeled their curriculum on theological training at eastern schools. The Western Reserve College, therefore, constituted the logical outcome of the Plan of Union settlement agenda of establishing towns, churches, and school. This approach differed dramatically from that taken to establish the other theological school only a few years later and some thirty-odd miles away. The founders of the Oberlin Institute disregarded the Plan of Union missionaries' scheme for a missionary training school and moved further west to build a new religious community and school on the frontier.

While the establishment of Western Reserve College was a moment of harmony for the Plan of Union missionaries, the settlers, and the sponsoring society, most of the missionary letters to Hartford showed growing disunion among those parties. More than any other issue, the conflicts over monetary compensation for missionary labor were brought before the missionary board. The majority of letters written between missionaries and the Connecticut Missionary Society during this time included discussions about proper missionary compensation. The letters are reminiscent—not in tone, but in content—of those issued from the angry pen of Joseph Badger twenty years earlier. In 1827, for example, William Hanford, acting as a financial liaison between the missionaries and the Connecticut Missionary Society, reported to the home society that "Brother Lesslie has spent 20 weeks as a missionary, + expects the whole of his compensation from the missionary society of Connecticut."[41] The missionary society, more often than not, questioned the validity of the amounts that the missionaries requested. Hanford acted as a middleman between the missionaries and the society, clearing up misunderstandings and rectifying errors. After a few years of this work, Hanford felt compelled to respond truthfully to the board of trustees' suspicion that "evils" existed in the local missionary organization—evils of a pecuniary kind. Hanford stated bluntly, "Evils do exist," but he was uncertain of "a suitable & adequate remedy."[42] The problem, he believed, stemmed from a "diversity of views" among the missionaries about continuing to solicit financial aid from the missionary society. Some, according to Hanford, "are opposed to system, & rules in conducting their missionary operations"; these clergymen drew on the treasury "to the full extent of their ability."[43] Others believed that "every man should work in his proper place" and thus requested as little financial assistance as possible.[44] From his description of the "diversity of views," it is evident that Hanford made judgments about his colleagues' behavior; nonetheless, he found himself in the awkward position of calling into question "the propriety of a brother's account." The main problem, according to Hanford, was that the requested funds often surpassed the salaried amount, due to "special necessity." Unfortunately, it became difficult to assess the extent of a missionary's "special necessity." In Hanford's mind the only solution to this problem was to place the job of evaluating missionary labor in the hands of another local organization or to entrust "the business to judicious men on the ground, who have no pecuniary interest involved."[45]

Hanford's vague response did not satisfy the Connecticut Missionary Society, and in the next communication it requested "specific & exact answers" about each missionary's need. Hanford reluctantly obliged, stating, "I suppose the Trustees regard the advancement of the Redeemer's kingdom rather than the continuance of particular missionaries as the object on which their attention is to be fixed."[46] As he assessed the Western Reserve missionaries and their needs, he concluded that "the circumstances & habits of a number of us are so changed that it is not proper that we should longer derive any part of our support from the funds of your society."[47] To that end, Hanford recommended that the Connecticut Missionary Society dispense with the services of all the missionaries in Portage County: Simeon Woodruff (because of his large congregation); Giles Cowles "as an itinerant missionary" because of his advanced age; and a number of others who for various reasons Hanford believed should no longer request funding.[48] After thirty years of funding missionary labors in New Connecticut, it seemed to Hanford that the time had come for the society to end its support of missionaries who were now settled clergy.

Despite the financial squabbles, the efforts of the Western Reserve missionaries to operate independently, and Hanford's suggestion that the society curtail missionary funds, the tie with the Connecticut Missionary Society was not severed. Surprisingly, the society continued to dispatch missionaries to the Western Reserve into the 1830s, operating through a superintendent board appointed through the Western Reserve Synod in 1834.[49] Later it transformed itself into a missionary foundation, whose purpose was to raise funds to support the missionary endeavor. The Connecticut Missionary Society Auxiliary gave the annual income to the American Home Missionary Society.

After years of infighting between Congregational and Presbyterian missionaries, differences concerning theological beliefs and religious practices came to a head with the establishment of the Oberlin Colony and Institute in 1833. While the debates regarding the colony's and the institute's purposes were drawn along denominational lines, the schism that led to claims of orthodoxy and heresy divided both Presbyterians and Congregationalists between those who accepted the new theology and revival techniques and those who did not. In September of 1836 a number of Congregationalists, most of whom were affiliated with Oberlin, split from the Plan of Union and formed the Western Reserve Congregationalist Association, thus officially signaling internal discord. A year later, the Presbyterian General Assembly, alarmed by the growth in Congregational power and what it deemed unorthodox practices in Plan of Union churches, discountenanced the Plan of Union as unconstitutional and excised four synods, including the Western Reserve Synod. While this decision did not dismantle the churches, for all practical purposes it ended the Plan of Union mission to the Western Reserve.

In one sense, the 1837 end of the Plan of Union for missionizing New Connecticut is perfectly fitting. The denominational merger had been put into place thirty-six years earlier for the sole purpose of evangelizing the frontier. Presbyterians and Congregationalists worked together to consolidate manpower in a spiritual battle against infidelity and competing denominations. By 1837 New Connecticut was no longer a frontier, and most of the battles had already been won or lost. The Plan of Union had for the most part succeeded because Presbyterians and Congregationalists shared theological views and agreed to allow congregations to choose their organizational structure. The theologically radical views of the Oberlin Congregationalists disturbed that balance.

But in another sense, it is ironic that the Oberlin Colony and Institute was the catalyst for the Plan of Union dissolution. Presbyterians and Congregationalists had worked tirelessly for more than thirty-five years to carve a New Connecticut—both physically and morally—into the landscape of the Western Reserve. The Oberlin Colony came the closest of all settlements to achieving that goal. It is easy to discern in the founding, covenanting, and landscaping of the colony the particular attention that the colonists paid to moral and spatial order.

The mental mapping of New Connecticut and the Oberlin Colony are perfectly consistent with the theological distinction between the Plan of Union missionaries and the early founders of the Oberlin Colony. Disinterested benevolence, the spiritual goal of most of the Plan of Union missionaries, taught that individuals could sacrifice themselves for the greater glory of God, but no one could ultimately attain spiritual perfection in this world. Charles Grandison Finney's theology, which inspired the Oberlin founders, taught that moral perfection allowed for holiness in this world. Perfection, according to Finney's preaching, was possible. These theological positions are related to the physical and moral mapping undertaken by the missionaries and the colonists. Grounded in their theological beliefs, the Plan of Union missionaries understood that God's benevolent design for the frontier was only partially transferable through mapping and missionizing. Physical and moral maps, for the Plan of Union missionaries, set up ideal communities but remained just maps—models of perfection. For the Oberlin colonists, the map for the physical and moral landscape, once drawn in the mind, was not only possible to replicate but, indeed, necessary to duplicate immediately, at that precise time, through those particular bodies, and in that specific space. The perfection that for the Oberlin colonists was possible in the physical and moral landscape evidenced immoral pride and theological delusion to most of the Plan of Union missionaries.

Ecclesiastical Outlaws

The fundamental theological difference between striving for perfection and achieving perfection would not be a main feature in the stories narrated by historians of the Plan of Union mission to the Western Reserve. For years after the excision of the Western Reserve Synod and the nominal dissolution of the Plan of Union, historians and adherents squabbled over the cause of the rift between Presbyterians and Congregationalists. Those who believed that the Plan of Union missionaries lost an opportunity to evangelize the frontier and build a Christian nation looked for an event or person on which to place blame. While many people expressed their opinions, unquestionably the loudest voice came from William S. Kennedy. In 1856 Kennedy penned *The Plan of Union: or A History of the Presbyterian and Congregational Churches of the Western Reserve* to chronicle the Plan of Union mission to the Western Reserve and to provide biographical sketches of prominent missionaries.[50] Kennedy wrote his history not as the story of the Connecticut Missionary Society's endeavors but as a tribute to the Plan of Union missionaries' struggles to unify the region religiously. Employing all of the familiar landscape language that pointed to the redemptive possibilities of New Connecticut, Kennedy eulogized the efforts of this group of missionaries, which in his mind resulted in a missed opportunity. The 262-page text is divided into two sections and features charts and detailed lists. In the first half of the book, Kennedy presented sketches of New Connecticut missionaries, and in the second half he traced ecclesiastical organizations, educational institutions, and benevolent operations. The crux of his argument was that the Plan of Union disbanded because of the radical Congregationalists' disregard for ecclesiastical harmony. In his mind, nothing brought about the schism more quickly than the establishment of the Oberlin Colony and Institute.

To make this claim, Kennedy highlighted Presbyterian participation in missionizing the frontier settlements. He argued that the Presbyterians were the most successful of the Plan of Union missionaries. Similar to most Western Reserve historians, Kennedy stated that the Western Reserve "was mainly colonized by New Englanders," but added that the population "embraced enough of the more southern element, generally called the Pennsylvania or Virginia type of society."[51] Significantly, he noted that as early as 1800, two ministers preached on the Western Reserve, the Pennsylvanian-born Presbyterian William Wick and the Massachusetts-born

Congregationalist Joseph Badger, who worked harmoniously with Presbyterians. According to Kennedy, Wick arrived a few months earlier than Badger did and formed the first Presbyterian church. These two clergymen represented the "true fathers of the Church of the Reserve," and worked happily together free from all "clannish and partisan sentiments and feelings."[52] Kennedy's narrative described a united enterprise between Presbyterians and Congregationalists perfectly suited to the western frontier.

Kennedy wrote glowingly about both Presbyterian and Congregational missionaries, and he was careful not to emphasize the Connecticut Missionary Society but to focus on individuals committed to the Plan of Union. His account of missionaries' lives relied on biographical memoirs, personal interviews, and Connecticut Missionary Society correspondences. He organized all of this material around his interest in establishing joint Presbyterian and Congregational origins for the Western Reserve settlement. Perhaps one of the few missionary historians ever to do so, Kennedy applauded Joseph Badger's ability to "cultivate Presbyterial acquaintances" and consistently support the aims of the Plan of Union.[53] The missionary biographies, twenty-one in all, highlighted the men who showed evidence of desiring unity between the two groups. Kennedy reserved particular admiration for those missionaries who openly confessed their theological position, but believed that the Plan of Union superseded denominational divisions. For example, he noted that John Seward remained a Congregationalist, "yet he entered heartily and sincerely into the Plan of Union."[54] William Hanford and Luther Humphrey also received similar praise.

Following the tradition in the writing of Puritan sacred history, the felicitous beginning soon decayed as individuals turned away from the promise of the Plan of Union. Kennedy did not shy away from placing the blame for the dissolution on individuals, specifically the "ultra- Congregationalists" who established the Oberlin Colony and Institute. In Kennedy's rueful chronicling, the Presbyterians worked hard and made accommodations to promote ecclesiastical harmony, but they were ultimately betrayed by Congregational sectarianism. The Western Reserve Synod incorporated some people who supported "what has since been called New School Theology," including some Oberlin men, but these people left a "bad odor amongst strict Calvinists."[55] Although the majority of the synod's members disavowed these tendencies, Kennedy believed that outsiders associated Plan of Union Presbyterians with radical Congregationalists, and he thought that that misconception led to the General Assembly's 1837 excision.

Kennedy was especially bitter about the establishment of the Oberlin Institute "to represent their peculiar views of theology, education and social philosophy."[56] He felt it was unfortunate to divide limited resources between two colleges, and he questioned the quality of an Oberlin education. Rather than acknowledging its connection to New England, Kennedy believed that Oberlin exemplified "crude, western society." It was "a perfectly indigenous product of the Reserve," which remained "popular with the masses, particularly the radical portion" who desired above all a "cheap education."[57]

Kennedy's text arose from years of discussion among ministers in the Western Reserve Synod regarding whether the Plan of Union still addressed the needs of its congregations. Kennedy probably wrote in response to John Keep's defense of Congregationalism, published ten years earlier. In *Congregationalism, and Church-Action: with the Principles of Christian Union, etc.*, Keep argued that the Plan of Union from its inception was conceived of as a means to missionize the frontier, not as an organizing principle for settled churches.[58] While Kennedy believed that the union provided mutual benefits for Congregationalists and Presbyterians, Keep, a Congregational pastor in Trumbull County, felt that the Plan of Union had "crushed" Western Reserve Congregationalism. The Congregational clergy, "a large number of Ministers, fresh and warm from New England, and Congregational in their training, have undergone rapid and ominous changes in the Presbyterian crucible."[59] Rather than providing for harmonious cooperation, the Plan of Union, in Keep's mind, silenced New Connecticut Congregationalists.

Keep's text reads like a handbook for Congregational doctrine and government, with specific reference to the Western Reserve. Throughout the book, Keep addressed moral questions and linked Congregational theology with social action. For example, a good portion of the text is devoted to defending the Oberlin movement against Presbyterian claims of heresy and questioning the term *schism*. In a chapter titled "Oberlin Brethren no Intruders," Keep reminded his readers that the brethren were Congregational and that "most of the Churches on the Reserve were originally organized as Congregationalists, composed chiefly of settlers from New England, and cherishing strong attachment to the church polity of their father land."[60] After outlining their position on sanctification, Keep noted that the theological sentiments taught at Oberlin were similar to the teachings of New England Congregationalists and New School Presbyterians.[61] Despite Oberlin's reputable faculty, general public approval, and almost five hundred students, "the Presbyteries refuse to extend to them Christian and ministerial fellowship on the plea that they are a new and distinct sect, and teach error. Who then," queried Keep, "are the schismatics?"[62] While Keep clearly favored the Oberlin faculty and students as "eminent for their moral and religious worth, intellectual endowments and literary acquirements," he explained that his greatest concern was for "the cries of the poor and of humanity," and "the wants of the teeming population of the West." The Oberlin brethren, Keep claimed, did not deserve to be regarded as "ecclesiastical outlaws"; rather, they should be considered the guardians of piety who cared about the missionary endeavor on the frontier.[63]

Many years later a Congregational clergyman and historian, Delavan Leonard, would recast the story as one of fierce competition in which the Congregationalists triumphed. Rather than accusing the Congregationalists or the Presbyterians of betraying a unified missionary endeavor, Leonard found fault with the Plan of Union. The "mischievous Plan of Union," according to Leonard, did not serve its benevolent purpose on the frontier. The outcome of the merger between Presbyterians and Congregationalists "for our Israel," Leonard believed, "was mainly evil."[64] Tracing the Congregationalist lineage back to "Plymouth Rock," Leonard claimed that the Plan of Union constituted "the 'first disobedience' of the remarkably wise and good New England Puritans," that "was attended by the loss of our Eden in the older Northern States."[65] Leonard placed the blame for this "exceedingly ill-advised, scheme for Christian union and cooperation" on the "Connecticut saints" whom he believed lost faith in New Englanders' ability to govern themselves in politics as well as religion.[66] While the Plan of Union's ostensible purpose was to missionize the West, Leonard claimed that the ruling Congregational elite instituted this program to exact stricter control over congregations. "In other words," Leonard explained, "the Congregationalists who helped to father the plan were themselves semi-Presbyterian."[67] Rather than recollecting a pure New England religious past, complete with lofty aims, Leonard found the Plan of Union's corrupting force in the Presbyterian leanings of its progenitors.

For Leonard, the Oberlin Colony and Institute represented a turning point in Congregational history on the Western Reserve. "Oberlin had no love for the Plan of Union, and stood for Congregationalism pure and simple."[68] Specifically, Leonard admired Oberlin's resistance to the Plan of Union despite disapproval from most local Presbyterian and Congregational clergy. Sometimes the disapproval verged on harassment. For example, Leonard noted that the Huron Presbytery refused to examine theological students trained at Oberlin and prevented faculty from preaching in its churches. The antipathy grew after Charles G. Finney accepted a professorship and promoted "perfectionism," which pushed New School theology to its limits. Although he admitted that Finney's new measures and theological innovations came from a New Light Presbyterian background, from Leonard's vantage point Oberlin had "from the first and all along been true to Congregational principles. Liberty, equality, fraternity, there has been no sinning against these."[69]

Seventy-two years later, historian Stewart Holbrook wrote a tribute chapter to Oberlin College in his classic text, *The Yankee Exodus*. Hagiographic in tone, Holbrook's work nonetheless described Shipherd and Stewart as "two obscure Congregational preachers and fanatics" who dreamed Oberlin into becoming a religious and educational landmark on the frontier.[70] It was not Holbrook's aim to take sides in a denominational debate, but he unknowingly wrote the Oberlin Colony and Institute as the winners of a protracted theological battle by indicating that Oberlin became "a bright beacon in the immense night of the great forest of the Northwest Territory."[71] Others would claim that the Oberlin Colony and Institute would remain a fringe religious and social experiment that could exist only on its own, in the wilderness.

The scholarship dealing with the Connecticut Missionary Society's mission to the Western Reserve generally views the society's absorption by the American Home Missionary Society as the organization's logical end. National organizations like the American Home Missionary Society were better equipped to handle the long-distance management of frontier missionaries and settlers. But in missionary letters and the polemical histories written by Kennedy, Keep, and Leonard, it is evident that problems with the Plan of Union arose between missionaries and settlers well before the Connecticut trustees decided to officially terminate its operations in the Western Reserve. Ironically, the dissolution of the Plan of Union, and the subsequent end of the Connecticut Missionary Society's mission to the Western Reserve, did not come about because of the missionaries' failure to create a New Connecticut on the frontier. The Plan of Union ended because of the success of a few missionaries and settlers in re-creating their vision of a paradigmatic Puritan community by founding the Oberlin Colony and Institute.

Moral and Spatial Order

The chronicling of the creation of the Oberlin Colony and Institute presents an encapsulation of the many connections between religion, landscape, and rhetoric that have surfaced repeatedly throughout this study. In the founding, covenanting, and landscaping of the colony we can easily discern the connection between spatial and moral order. Kennedy, Keep, and Leonard, as well as many other scholars who wrote the colony's and the college's histories, were particularly interested in defining Oberlin's relationship to the discord among Presbyterians and Congregationalists, as well as in claiming its status as promoting true piety or true infidelity. This became complicated as the two denominations split internally along Old School and New School lines. Charles G. Finney, Asa Mahan, and Henry Cowles all had Presbyterian affiliations, but their theological and social views placed them on the fringes of the denomination. Therefore, defining Oberlin as truly Congregationalist or purely Presbyterian represented a stake in claiming the limits of orthodoxy or heresy for each group.

The language that connected morality with the physical landscape employed by the New Connecticut missionaries, land surveyors, settlers, travelers, and interested agencies never disappeared, but the urgency for that particular region eventually faded. Although the Western Reserve would continue to be called a second New England to the present day, the sense that the spatial and moral landscapes were at stake ceased to exist as the area was transformed from a frontier into a settled region. New Connecticut and the garden paradise would remain elusive, fixed in the mind's eye but just beyond the reach of experience. Presbyterians and Congregationalists who would missionize in later years under the auspices of different sponsors continually fixed their gaze on the moral perils and redemptive possibilities of landscapes further west.

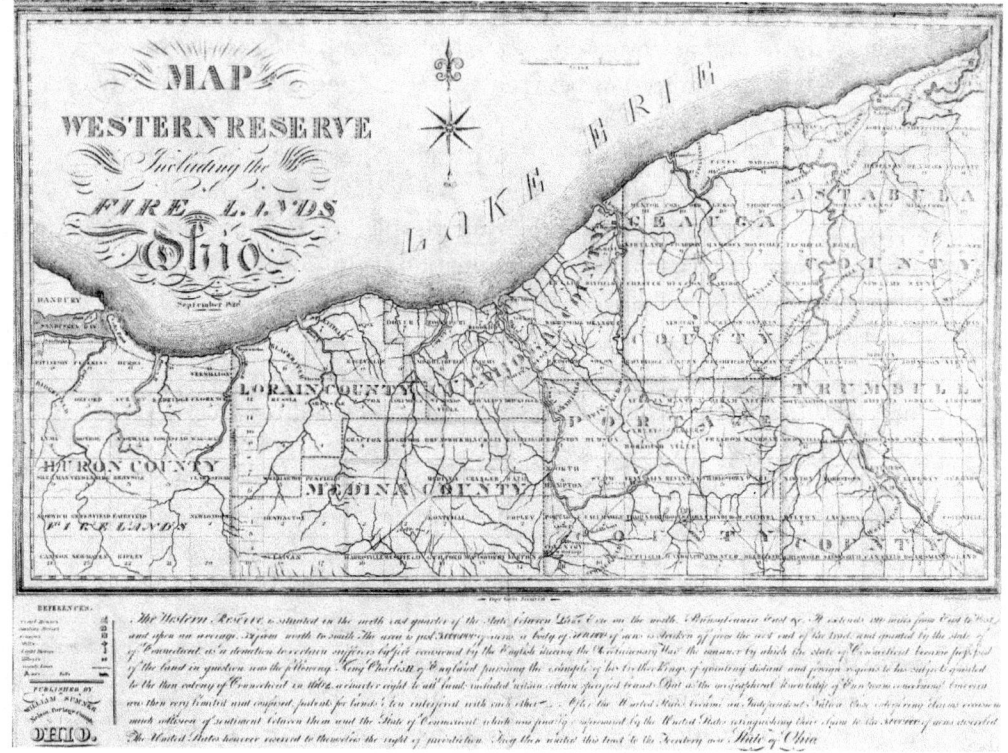

FIGURE 19. "Map of the Western Reserve, including the Fire Lands in Ohio," September 1826. By 1826 the entire Western Reserve had been surveyed and mapped. Courtesy of the Western Reserve Historical Society, Cleveland.

CONCLUSION

Moral Geography

Reminiscing to the Ohio Historical Association in 1873, President James A. Garfield described his pleasant childhood in northeastern Ohio in glowing terms. He attributed his education and moral upbringing to the successful transfer of New England manners and customs to the Western Reserve. Garfield observed "New England" character in the region's physical aspects such as landscape and architecture; but ultimately for Garfield, as for many of his contemporaries, the abstraction of New England manners and customs remained grounded in religion. Although by the time of his boyhood the Western Reserve was populated by numerous competing religious groups, Garfield overlooked this diversity by claiming a single religious heritage that extended back decades to the Protestant missionaries sent by the Connecticut Missionary Society. In one summary sentence he characterized a common nostalgia for the region and directed future scholarship by stating: "On this Western Reserve are townships more thoroughly New England in character and spirit than most of the towns of New England today."[1]

What made the Western Reserve "thoroughly New England" were the moral values that Garfield ascribed to a physical landscape. After an examination of different incidents in the Plan of Union mission to the Western

Reserve, the convergence between moral discourse and the physical landscape has become familiar, so Garfield's claim does not seem outrageous. What is curious about this statement is that historians have uncritically accepted Garfield's point as evidence for the successful transfer of New England habits and morals to the Western Reserve. Putting aside the troubling questions concerning Garfield's ability to make such a judgment and which religious groups and people this triumphalist statement denies, it is clear that this connection between morality and the physical landscape resonates deeply for Western Reserve residents and scholars alike. While Garfield's claim does not represent the contests examined in this study, he does bring us full circle to the question of the relationship between spatial and moral order.

In recent years, missionary studies as a field of inquiry has received an increasing amount of scholarly interest, particularly regarding roles that "foreign" missionaries played in national expansion and colonial contact. Studies such as David Chidester's *Savage Systems* demonstrate how Christian evangelization not only aided colonial expansion but also created epistemological categories for describing and defining the "other." How then might a study on "home" missions add a significant dimension to our understanding of the complex relationships among religious identity, national expansion, and colonialism? In this study I have focused on the aim of a group of missionaries to organize both spatially and morally one small region of the nineteenth-century American frontier. I have chosen this entry into the Plan of Union missionary endeavor in New Connecticut because the missionaries reveal these two concerns in their private and public letters. They themselves, as well as their sponsoring society, drew the close connection between spatial and moral order. But they were not the only nineteenth-century Americans preoccupied with that relationship. Land surveyors, travelers, settlers, geographers, and other missionary groups also saw moral values inscribed in the landscape. While these groups arrived at different conclusions regarding the success, failure, or even importance of assigning biblical and national values to the Western Reserve to create an imaginary home called New Connecticut, they nonetheless all participated in the process of shaping the moral and physical landscape.

But it is not enough simply to notice that missionaries use spatial language, or that there seem to be connections between the moral and spatial organization of the American frontier. In the end, the question presents itself: what is the importance of using a spatial analysis to interpret a home missionary endeavor? To understand home missions on the American frontier, and to interpret American religious history with more breadth, we all must pay more attention to space. Through a spatial approach I "read" landscapes, town surveys, and architecture, as well as more-traditional sources such as missionary letters and journals, to explore a wider collection of evidence and thereby gain a fuller understanding of the promotion of and resistance to home missions. I also take seriously the nostalgic desire to recreate a biblical or Puritan "home" to help the missionaries, settlers, and interested parties form religious identity in a frontier context. The frontier provided a salvific landscape, not only for themselves but also, as they fiercely contended, for the world. Building such a home allowed New Connecticut missionaries and settlers to step into sacred history and to write the penultimate redemptive chapter. The missionaries' work was not simply (or often) to convert souls, but to define religious identity by articulating the relationship between spatial and moral values on the frontier.

All five chapters of this study have been organized around the theme of the relationship between moral and spatial order. To make sense of the documents and people related to missionizing New Connecticut I have asked a series of questions of all of the texts. How did individuals imagine the Western Reserve prior to their arrival? How did they adjust their preconceptions to their frontier experiences? How did land surveyors, missionaries, and settlers organize the landscape physically and morally? What landmarks enabled people to mark time and space? In what specific ways was the landscape perceived to evidence or promote moral values? These questions refer to a particular time and place and describe specific perspectives; however, they also address larger issues of imagination and power, the ordering of physical and moral space, and the promotion of moral values over any defined region. They also prompt the question of the relationship between religious identity and place. In the frontier context, Protestant missionaries hoped to build a particular kind of "home" that both reinforced their own religious identity and distinguished them from the "irreligious" others who also populated the landscape. While insisting on the homogeneous nature of their religious community, the missionaries and their sponsoring society's urgent need to inscribe morality on the physical landscape make sense only when considered in the context of encounter with others. Creating an imaginary home called New Connecticut that was steeped in both biblical and national memory allowed all the characters not only to step into sacred history but also to construct a providential future from the ground up. And in the process of mental and physical mapping, they ultimately defined who they were in relation to their spatial and moral world.

Notes

Introduction

1. I have chosen to refer to the Missionary Society of Connecticut as the Connecticut Missionary Society for the sake of brevity. The group has commonly been referred to under both titles, although the primary sources generally use the former. Those who wish to read the documents may consult the twenty-reel microfilm collection Missionary Society of Connecticut Papers, 1795–1948. I have followed the original spelling and punctuation when citing or quoting from these primary sources, and in most cases I have refrained from using "[sic]."

2. Timothy Dwight, *An Address to the Emigrants from Connecticut, and From New England Generally, in the New Settlements in the United States* (Hartford: Peter B. Gleason & Co., 1817), 17.

3. John Winthrop, "Modell of Christian Charity," in Michael McGiffert, ed., *Puritanism and the American Experience*, 32 (Reading: Addison-Wesley, 1969).

4. Here I am referring to the Puritan belief in the radical decline in piety among second- and third-generation Puritans, not the historical question of whether this decline was significant. For studies of the Puritans' understanding of a decline in piety, seen primarily through sermons, see Perry Miller, *The New England Mind: From Colony to Province* (Cambridge: Harvard University Press, 1953, 1962), 27–39 (page citations are to the reprint edition); Sacvan Bercovitch, *The American Jeremiad* (Madison: University of Wisconsin Press, 1978); Robert Middlekauff, *The Mathers: Three Generations of Puritan Intellectuals, 1596–1728* (New York: Oxford University Press, 1971), 113–38. For an insightful response to the question of Puritan declension, see Ann Braude, "Women's History Is American Religious History," in Thomas A. Tweed, ed., *Retelling U.S. Religious History* (Berkeley: University of California Press, 1997), 87–107.

5. The Western Reserve, also known as "New Connecticut," an approximately 120-mile tract of land in what is now northeastern Ohio, constituted the remainder of land after Connecticut ceded western property to the United States government in 1780. This area was mapped by the Connecticut Land Company and missionized by the Connecticut Missionary Society. Missionaries dispatched to the Western Reserve by the Connecticut Missionary Society worked under the 1801 Plan of Union, an agreement that joined Congregational and Presbyterian efforts to send missionaries to frontier settlements. For general information on the history of the Western Reserve, see Harlan Hatcher, *The Western Reserve: The Story of New Connecticut in Ohio* (Indianapolis: Bobbs-Merrill, 1949; rev. ed., Cleveland: World Publishing, 1966; reprint, Kent, Ohio: Kent State University Press, 1991);

Harry F. Lupold and Gladys Haddad, eds., *Ohio's Western Reserve: A Regional Reader* (Kent, Ohio: Kent State University Press, 1988); Alfred Mathews, *Ohio and Her Western Reserve* (New York: Appleton, 1902); William Stowell Mills, *The Story of the Western Reserve of Connecticut* (New York: Brown and Wilson, 1900). For works on Connecticut's relationship to the Western Reserve, see Brian Harte, "Land in the Old Northwest: A Study of Speculation, Sales, and Settlements on the Connecticut Western Reserve," *Ohio History* 101 (1992): 114–39; David French, "Puritan Conservatism and the Frontier: The Elizur Wright Family on the Connecticut Western Reserve," *Old Northwest* 1 (1975): 85–95; Kenneth V. Lottick, "Cultural Transplantation in the Connecticut Reserve," *Historical and Philosophical Society of Ohio Bulletin* 17 (1959): 154–66; Richard Lyle Power, "A Crusade to Extend Yankee Culture, 1820–1865," *New England Quarterly* 13, no. 4 (1940): 638–53; Claude L. Shepard, "The Connecticut Land Company: A Study in the Beginnings of Colonization of the Western Reserve," *Western Reserve Historical Society* Tract no. 96 (Cleveland: Western Reserve Historical Society, 1916). For Protestant home missions to the Western Reserve, see James R. Rohrer, *Keepers of the Covenant: Frontier Missions and the Decline of Congregationalism, 1774–1818* (New York: Oxford University Press, 1995); John R. Pankratz, "The Written Word and the Errand into Ohio, 1788–1830" (Ph.D. diss., Cornell University, 1988). For a discussion of the Plan of Union and the Western Reserve, see Ronald H. Noricks, "Jealousies and Contentions: The Plan of Union and the Western Reserve, 1801–1837," *Journal of Presbyterian History* 60 (1982): 130–43; William Warren Sweet, *Religion on the Frontier, 1783–1850* (New York: Cooper Square Press, 1964), 13–42; William S. Kennedy, *The Plan of Union; or, a History of the Presbyterian and Congregational Churches of the Western Reserve* (Hudson, Ohio: Pentagon Stream Press, 1856); Reverend Delavan L. Leonard, *A Century of Congregationalism in Ohio* (Oberlin: Pierce & Randolph, 1896).

6. John Seward to Connecticut Missionary Society, October 19, 1812, John Seward Letters, Connecticut Missionary Society Papers.

7. My understanding of "mapping" as utilized by religious groups and religious people is influenced by Thomas A. Tweed's conception of mapping as "the ways that groups orient themselves in a natural landscape and social terrain, transforming both in the process." Thomas A. Tweed, *Our Lady of the Exile: Diasporic Religion at a Cuban Catholic Shrine in Miami* (New York: Oxford University Press, 1997), 136.

8. See, for example, James Axtell, *The Invasion Within: The Contest of Cultures in Colonial North America* (New York: Oxford University Press, 1985), esp. 152–78.

9. As Laurie Maffly-Kipp notes, even denominations theologically predisposed to individualism, such as the nineteenth-century Methodists and Baptists, "acknowledged that the forces of human sinfulness required the constraints of Christian community." Laurie F. Maffly-Kipp, *Religion and Society in Frontier California* (New Haven: Yale University Press, 1994), 21.

10. See for example, Henri Lefebvre, *The Production of Space*, trans. Donald Nicholson-Smith (Oxford: Blackwell, 1991); Edward W. Soja, *Postmodern Geographies: The Reassertion of Space in Critical Social Theory* (London/New York: Verso, 1989); Jürgen Habermas, *The Structural Transformation of the Public Sphere: An Inquiry Into the Category of Bourgeois Society*, trans. Thomas Burger (Cambridge: MIT Press, 1989); Michel Foucault, "Of Other Spaces," *Diacritics* 16 (Spring 1986): 22–27; Michel de Certeau, *The Practice of Everyday Life*, trans. Steven Rendall (Berkeley: University of California Press, 1984); Yi-Fu Tuan,

Introduction

Space and Place: The Perspective of Experience (Minneapolis: University of Minnesota Press, 1977); D. W. Meinig, "Symbolic Landscapes: Models of American Community," in D. W. Meinig, ed., *The Interpretation of Ordinary Landscapes: Geographical Essays* (New York: Oxford University Press, 1979); David Harvey, *The Condition of Postmodernity: An Enquiry Into the Origins of Cultural Change* (Cambridge: Blackwell, 1990); J. B. Harley, "Maps, Knowledge, and Power," in Denis E. Cosgrove and Stephen Daniels, eds., *The Iconography of Landscape: Essays on Symbolic Representation, Design, and Use of Past Environments* (Cambridge: Cambridge University Press, 1986), 277–313; J. B. Harley, "Deconstructing the Map," *Cartographica* 26 (1989): 1–20.

11. Mircea Eliade, *The Sacred and the Profane: The Nature of Religion*, trans. Willard R. Trask (New York: Harcourt Brace Jovanovich, 1959), 20–65.

12. Jonathan Z. Smith, *Map Is Not Territory: Studies in the History of Religions* (Chicago: University of Chicago Press, 1993), 88–103. Other religious studies scholars and historians have addressed the issue of space, including Rhys Isaac, *The Transformation of Virginia, 1740–1790* (Chapel Hill: University of North Carolina Press, 1982); William Cronon, *Changes in the Land: Indians, Colonists, and the Ecology of New England* (New York: Hill and Wang, 1983); Sidney Mead, *The Lively Experiment: The Shaping of Christianity in America* (New York: Harper and Row, 1963), 1–15.

13. David Chidester and Edward T. Linenthal, eds., *American Sacred Space* (Bloomington: Indiana University Press, 1995), 9–16.

14. Edwin Gaustad, *Historical Atlas of Religion in America* (New York: Harper and Row, 1962); Wilbur Zelinsky, "An Approach to the Religious Geography of the United States: Patterns of Church Membership in 1952," *Annals of the Association of American Geographers* 51 (June 1961): 139–67. For a geographer's view of the connections between religion and space, see Chris C. Park, *Sacred Worlds: An Introduction to Geography and Religion* (London: Routledge, 1994), or Rehav Rubin, "Ideology and Landscape in Early Printed Maps of Jerusalem," in Alan R. Baker and Gideon Biger, eds., *Ideology and Landscape in Historical Perspective* (Cambridge: Cambridge University Press, 1992), 15–30. For discussions of and studies on religion and region, see Samuel S. Hill, "Religion and Region in America," *Annals of the American Academy of Political and Social Science* 480 (July 1985): 132–41; Jerald C. Brauer, "Regionalism and Religion in America," *Church History* 54 (1985): 366–78; Donald G. Mathews, *Religion in the Old South* (Chicago: University of Chicago Press, 1977); Margaret Washington Creel, *"A Peculiar People": Slave Religion and Community Culture Among the Gullahs* (New York: New York University Press, 1988); James L. Peacock and Ruel W. Tyson Jr., eds., *Pilgrims of Paradox: Calvinism and Experience Among the Primitive Baptists of the Blue Ridge* (Washington: Smithsonian Institution Press, 1989); Marta Weigle, *Brothers of Light, Brothers of Blood: The Penitentes of the Southwest* (Santa Fe: Ancient City Press, 1976).

15. For a sensitive account of the evocative power of place, see Belden C. Lane, *Landscapes of the Sacred: Geography and Narrative in American Spirituality* (New York: Paulist Press, 1988). The home occupies a central site in many of the scholarly investigations of the relationship between religion and space. See, for example, Colleen McDannell, *The Christian Home in Victorian America, 1840–1900* (Bloomington: Indiana University Press, 1986); Richard L. Bushman, "Religion and Taste," chapter 10 in *The Refinement of America: Persons, Houses, Cities* (New York: Vintage, 1993), 313–52.

16. R. Laurence Moore used the spatial imagery of "insiders" and "outsiders" to challenge the dominant Protestant narrative found in American religious history and to demonstrate that rhetorical power moves in two ways. R. Laurence Moore, *Religious Outsiders and The Making of Americans* (New York: Oxford University Press, 1986). David Chidester, *Salvation and Suicide: An Interpretation of Jim Jones, the Peoples Temple, and Jonestown* (Bloomington: Indiana University Press, 1991), 79–104. In chapter 3, "Orientation in Space," Chidester analyzes the relationship between cosmic, geographic, and body spaces and Jim Jones's worldview. Catherine Keller uses spatial theory in her discussion of a counter-apocalyptic utopia that arises from her reading of the Book of Revelation. Catherine Keller, *Apocalypse Now and Then: A Feminist Guide to the End of the World* (Boston: Beacon, 1996), 140–80.

17. For example, see Colleen McDannell, *Material Christianity: Religion and Popular Culture in America* (New Haven: Yale University Press, 1995); Leigh Eric Schmidt, *Consumer Rites: The Buying and Selling of American Holidays* (Princeton: Princeton University Press, 1995); Ramón Gutiérrez, "El Santuario de Chimayo: A Syncretic Shrine in New Mexico," in Ramón Gutiérrez and Genevieve Fabre, eds., *Feasts and Celebrations in North American Ethnic Communities*, 71–86 (Albuquerque: University of New Mexico, 1995); see chapter 5, "Kitchen Judaism," in Jenna Weisman Joselit, *The Wonders of America: Reinventing Jewish Culture, 1880–1950*, 171–218 (New York: Hill and Wang, 1994). The most helpful article I have read regarding how to read and analyze American religious artifacts is Colleen McDannell, "Interpreting Things: Material Culture Studies and American Religion," *Religion* 21 (1991): 371–87.

18. Robert Orsi, in his article "The Center out There, in Here, and Everywhere Else: The Nature of Pilgrimage to the Shrine of Saint Jude, 1929–1965," *Journal of Social History* 25 (1991): 213–32, provides a helpful corrective to the spatial assumptions about pilgrimage through an example of pilgrimage that is an embodied spatial practice yet does not require human travel.

19. For example, see the essays in David D. Hall, ed., *Lived Religion in America: Toward a History of Practice* (Princeton: Princeton University Press, 1997).

20. See Tweed, *Our Lady of the Exile*, especially the Postscript (134–42), in which he argues for the relevance of place as an organizing theme for understanding U.S. religious history. The subthemes of "mapping," "meeting," and "migration" highlight the desires and negotiations involved in moving through religiously significant spaces. For understanding non-economic modes of exchange, see Pierre Bourdieu, *Outline of a Theory of Practice*, trans. Richard Nice (Cambridge: Cambridge University Press, 1977). For examples from the field of American religious history, see Mechal Sobel, *The World They Made Together: Black and White Values in Eighteenth-Century Virginia* (Princeton: Princeton University Press, 1987); Joel W. Martin, *Sacred Revolt: The Muskogees' Struggle for a New World* (Boston: Beacon, 1991); William Westphall, "Voices from the Attic," in Thomas A. Tweed, ed., *Retelling U.S. Religious History*, 181–99 (Berkeley: University of California Press, 1997); Ramón Gutiérrez, *When Jesus Came the Corn Mothers Went Away: Marriage, Sexuality, and Power in New Mexico, 1500–1846* (Stanford, Calif.: Stanford University Press, 1991).

21. For an insightful and expansive study of the connections between culture and the environment, see Simon Schama, *Landscape and Memory* (New York: Knopf, 1995). Schama argues that historians have created a false dichotomy between nature and culture,

1. The Benevolent Design: Mapping the Landscape

which has led many people to believe that some landscapes are pristine, free from the taint of culture. By examining myth, literature, art, and memory, he demonstrates the interconnections between nature and culture.

22. For a brief literature overview, see Robert A. Wheeler, "The Literature of the Western Reserve," *Ohio History* 100 (1991): 101–28. For specific examples, see Lottick, "Cultural Transplantation in the Connecticut Reserve"; French, "Puritan Conservatism and the Frontier"; Stewart H. Holbrook, *The Yankee Exodus: An Account of Migration from New England* (Seattle: University of Washington Press, 1968), 25–47; Power, "A Crusade to Extend Yankee Culture."

23. Frederick Jackson Turner, *The Significance of the Frontier in American History* (Madison: State Historical Society of Wisconsin, 1894).

24. For example, see Oliver Wendell Elsbree, *The Rise of the Missionary Spirit in America, 1790–1815* (Williamsport, Pa., 1928); Colin B. Goodykoontz, *Home Missions on the American Frontier* (Caldwell, Idaho: Caxton Printers, 1939); T. Scott Miyakawa, *Protestants and Pioneers: Individualism and Conformity on the American Frontier* (Chicago: University of Chicago Press, 1964); William Warren Sweet, *Religion in the Development of American Culture, 1765–1840* (New York: Scribner, 1952); Rohrer, *Keepers of the Covenant*.

25. Maffly-Kipp, *Religion and Society in Frontier California*; Pankratz, "The Written Word and the Errand to Ohio, 1788–1830."

26. For missions to Native Americans, see Henry Warner Bowden, *American Indians and Christian Missions: Studies in Cultural Conflict* (Chicago: University of Chicago Press, 1981); Bernard W. Sheehan, *Savagism and Civility: Indians and Englishmen in Colonial Virginia* (Cambridge: Cambridge University Press, 1980); Robert F. Berkhofer, *Salvation and the Savage: An Analysis of Protestant Missions and the American Indian Response, 1787–1862* (Lexington: University of Kentucky Press, 1965). My understanding of foreign missions is informed by William R. Hutchison, *Errand to the World: American Protestant Thought and Foreign Missions* (Chicago: University of Chicago Press, 1987); Jane Hunter, *The Gospel of Gentility: American Women Missionaries in Turn-of-the-Century China* (New Haven: Yale University Press, 1984); Patricia R. Hill, *The World Their Household: The American Woman's Foreign Mission Movement and Cultural Transformation, 1870–1920* (Ann Arbor: University of Michigan Press, 1985); David Chidester, *Savage Systems: Colonialism and Comparative Religion in Southern Africa* Studies in Religion and Culture (Charlottesville: University Press of Virginia, 1996); Paul William Harris, *Nothing but Christ: Rufus Anderson and the Ideology of Protestant Foreign Missions* (New York: Oxford University Press, 1999); Amanda Porterfield, *Mary Lyon and the Mount Holyoke Missionaries* (New York: Oxford University Press, 1997).

1. The Benevolent Design: Mapping the Landscape

1. Silas Allen to Moses Cleaveland, April 30, 1797, Moses Cleaveland Papers, 1754–1806.

2. J. B. Harley, "Maps, Knowledge, and Power," in Denis E. Cosgrove and Stephen Daniels, eds., *The Iconography of Landscape: Essays on Symbolic Representation, Design, and Use of Past Environments* (Cambridge: Cambridge University Press, 1986). Harley states: "The cartographic processes by which power is enforced, reproduced, and stereotyped con-

sist of both deliberate and 'practical' acts of surveillance and less conscious cognitive adjustments by map-makers and map-users to dominant values and beliefs" (303).

3. *Connecticut Evangelical Magazine* 5 (March 1805): 323–24.

4. Abel Flint, *A System of Geography and Trigonometry: Together With a Treatise on Surveying: Teaching Various Ways of Taking the Survey of a Field; Also to Protract the Same and Find the Area. Likewise, Rectangular Surveying; or, An Accurate Method of Calculating the Area of Any Field Arithmetically, Without the Necessity of Plotting it* (Hartford: Printed for Oliver D. Cooke, by Lincoln and Gleason, 1804).

5. Connecticut Missionary Society, *A Third Address from the Trustees of the Missionary Society of Connecticut, to the People of the State, and a Narrative on the Subject of Missions. To Which is Subjoined a Statement of the Funds of the Society, to the End of the Year 1812* (Hartford, Conn.: Hudson and Goodwin, 1813), 4. Hereafter referred to as *Narrative of Missions*. The missionary society published these accounts annually between 1801 and 1830. Because the titles vary, I refer to all of these documents as *Narrative of Missions*, using the publication date to distinguish them. As in this example, the publication date is the year following the date given in the title.

6. Miriam Peskowitz, "Tropes of Travel," *Semeia* 75 (1996): 183.

7. Simon Ryan, "Inscribing the Emptiness: Cartography, Exploration, and the Construction of Australia," in Chris Tiffin and Alan Lawson, eds., *De-Scribing Empire: Post-Colonialism and Textuality* (London: Routledge, 1994), 127.

8. The Connecticut Land Company bought the land for $1.2 million, payable over five years at a 6 percent interest rate. Connecticut reserved 500,000 acres in the westernmost parts of New Connecticut, known as the "Firelands," to compensate Connecticut citizens who lost homes and farms during the American Revolutionary War. R. Douglas Hurt, *The Ohio Frontier: The Crucible of the Old Northwest, 1720–1830* (Bloomington: Indiana University Press, 1996), 165.

9. *Connecticut Courant*, October 12, 1803.

10. Harlan Hatcher, *The Western Reserve: The Story of New Connecticut in Ohio* (Indianapolis: Bobbs-Merrill, 1949; rev. ed., Cleveland: World Publishing, 1966; reprint, Kent, Ohio: Kent State University Press, 1991), 15.

11. Articles of the Association Connecticut Land Company, September 5, 1797, Connecticut Land Company Records.

12. A newspaper later misspelled "Cleaveland," and the error was adopted as the current correct spelling of Cleveland, Ohio. It took a while before people settled in Cleveland. For example, by 1810 only fifty-seven people resided there.

13. Moses Cleaveland was the chief surveyor and general agent for the Connecticut Land Company. The surveyors were Amos Spafford, John Milton Holley, Richard M. Stoddard, and Moses Warren. Other members of the party included Theodore Shephard, physician; Joshua Stow, commissary; Joseph Tinker, boatman; James Hamilton, cook. Hatcher, *The Western Reserve*, 19.

14. John Milton Holley, The John Milton Holley Journal, July 7, 1796, John Milton Holley Papers.

15. Cotton Mather, *Magnalia Christi Americana; Or, The Ecclesiastical History of New England; From its First Planting, in the Year 1620, Unto the Year of Our Lord 1698: In Seven Books*. 1st American ed., from London ed. of 1702 (Hartford: Silas Andrus, 1820; reprint, New York: Russell and Russell, 1967), 89.

1. The Benevolent Design: Mapping the Landscape

16. Harley, "Maps, Knowledge, and Power," 289–90.

17. Mather, *Magnalia Christi Americana*, 87.

18. John Mitchell, "A Map of the British and French Dominions in America, with the Roads, Distances, Limits, and Extent of the Settlements." 1755. An original is housed in the Collections Division, Library of Congress.

19. Thomas H. Smith, *The Mapping of Ohio* (Kent, Ohio: Kent State University Press, 1977), 13.

20. Lewis Evans, "General Map of the Middle British Colonies in North America." The original map was published in Philadelphia in 1755 in Evans's *Geographical, Historical, Political, Philosophical and Mechanical Essays*. It was republished a year later, with corrections, in Thomas Pownall, *A Topographical Description of Such Parts of North America as are Contained in the (Annexed) Map of the Middle British Colonies &c in North America* (London: Printed for J. Almon, 1776). An original is housed in the Newberry Library, Chicago.

21. Smith, *The Mapping of Ohio*, 14.

22. White Woman's Town was established around 1750 and named for Mary Harris, a Deerfield, Massachusetts, woman who on February 29, 1704, at the age of ten was captured by French Indians and married into the tribe. See William M. Darlington, ed., *Christopher Gist's Journals with Historical, Geographical and Ethnological Notes and Biographies of his Contemporaries* (Pittsburgh: J. R. Weldin & Co., 1893), 41.

23. Smith, *The Mapping of Ohio*, 141.

24. Although this map was not published, scholars believe that Connecticut Land Company surveyors may have referred to it, because both the map and the accompanying journal were discovered among Moses Cleaveland's papers when his daughter donated them to the Western Reserve Historical Society in 1868.

25. The Treaty of Greenville demarcated the line between Indian territory and United States territory and was signed after the Battle of Fallen Timbers.

26. John G. Heckewelder, book 1, vol. 9, Heckewelder Papers.

27. J. B. Harley, "Maps, Knowledge, and Power," 278. Harley examines maps in the context of political power. He states that maps may be viewed as a language, as iconology (meaning that one may discern levels of meaning), and as a social product (meaning the power to create maps is the power to exert authority).

28. Ryan, "Inscribing the Emptiness," 116.

29. See, for example, Robert F. Berkhofer, *The White Man's Indian: Images of the American Indian from Columbus to the Present* (New York: Knopf, 1978); Stephen Greenblatt, *Marvelous Possessions: The Wonder of the New World* (Chicago: University of Chicago Press, 1991), 52–85.

30. Jean Nicolas Rotz, "Map of North America and West Indies." 1542. An original is housed in the Department of Manuscripts, British Library, London. A reproduction is printed in Seymour I. Schwartz and Ralph E. Ehrenberg, *The Mapping of America* (New York: Abrams, 1980).

31. Speed's map was reproduced numerous times, and reproductions may be found in most map libraries and collections. The reproduction I refer to is found in a pocket-sized travel book that contains a history of the world beginning with God in the heavens, descriptions of countries, and maps. John Speed, *A Prospect for the Most Famous Parts of the World* (London: M. F. for William Humble, 1646). This text is located in the Beinecke Rare Book and Manuscript Library, Yale University, New Haven, Connecticut.

32. Geoff King, *Mapping Reality: An Exploration of Cultural Cartographies* (New York: St. Martin's, 1996).

33. By "Native cartographies" I mean the Native Americans' land divisions and organizations. While these "maps" were not drawn like European maps, Native Americans did clearly mark and organize space.

34. Francis Jennings contends that the Puritans believed they landed on "virgin" soil, and American historians have likewise promoted the myth that the Europeans conquered an uninhabited land. Francis Jennings, *The Invasion of America: Indians, Colonialism, and the Cant of Conquest* (New York: Norton, 1975).

35. King, *Mapping Reality*, 141.

36. The Masesagoes resided near Conneaut Creek, on the northeastern boundary of the Western Reserve. They negotiated on behalf of themselves and "friends" who lived within the region's boundaries. Cleaveland informed them that they would not be disturbed and would be treated as "brothers." July 7, 1796, Moses Cleaveland Papers, 1754–1806.

37. The towns were Berlin, Bloomfield, Bristol, Brookfield, Chatham, Chester, Colebrook, Danbury, Fairfield, Farmington, Franklin, Greenwich, Guilford, Hartford, Hartland, Huntington, Litchfield, Lyme, Middlebury, Monroes, Montville, New Haven, New London, Norwalk, Saybrook, Sharon, Southington, Thompson, Trumbull, Vernon, Warren, Windham, Windsor. This list is taken from Stewart H. Holbrook, *The Yankee Exodus: An Account of Migration from New England* (Seattle: University of Washington Press, 1968), 37.

38. Board of Trustees of the Connecticut Missionary Society, *Annual Report of the Connecticut Missionary Society* (Hartford: Hudson and Goodwin, June 14, 1805).

39. General Association of Connecticut, *A Narrative of the Missions to the New Settlements, According to the Appointment of the General Association of the State of Connecticut; Together with an Account of the Receipts and Expenditures of the Money Contributed by the People of Connecticut in May 1793, for the Support of the Missionaries, According to an Act of the General Assembly of the State* (New Haven: T. & S. Green, 1794), 20.

40. General Association of Connecticut, *The Constitution of the Missionary Society of Connecticut: With an Address from the Board of Trustees, to the People of the State, and a Narrative on the Subject of Missions. To Which is Subjoined a Statement on the Funds of the Society* (Hartford: Hudson and Goodwin, 1800).

41. The Western Reserve constituted the remainder of land after Connecticut ceded its western property to the United States government in 1780.

42. William Warren Sweet, *The Presbyterians, 1783–1840: A Collection of Source Materials*, vol. 1 of *Religion on the American Frontier* (New York: Harper and Bros., 1936), 38–41. William Warren Sweet, *The Congregationalists: A Collection of Source Materials*, vol. 3 of *Religion on the American Frontier* (Chicago: University of Chicago Press, 1939), 15–16.

43. Matthew 28:19–20.

44. William R. Hutchison, *Errand to the World: American Protestant Thought and Foreign Missions* (Chicago: University of Chicago Press, 1987), 27–30.

45. The seal of the Massachusetts Bay Colony shows a Native American with outstretched hands, pleading, "Come over and help us."

46. James R. Rohrer, *Keepers of the Covenant: Frontier Missions and the Decline of Congregationalism, 1774–1818* (New York: Oxford University Press, 1995), 63.

1. The Benevolent Design: Mapping the Landscape 193

47. Jon Butler estimates that 10,000 new churches were established between 1780 and 1820. Jon Butler, *Awash in a Sea of Faith: Christianizing the American People* (Cambridge: Harvard University Press, 1990), 270.

48. David Grayson Allen demonstrates that Puritans held on to English regional distinctions seen through architecture and agricultural practices even after the social and economic reasons dissipated for these particular formulations in New England. Furthermore, although most Puritan towns replicated English towns as either an open-field village, an incorporated borough, or an enclosed farm, Allen finds diversity even within those three categories David Grayson Allen, *In English Ways: The Movement of Societies and the Transferral of English Local Law and Custom to Massachusetts Bay in the Seventeenth Century* (New York: Norton, 1982), 8–12; Joseph S. Wood, "Village and Community in Early Colonial New England," *Journal of Historical Geography* 8, no. 4 (October 1982): 333–46.

49. J. B. Jackson, *Discovering the Vernacular Landscape* (New Haven: Yale University Press, 1984), 60.

50. Harley, "Maps, Knowledge, and Power," 303.

51. Allen, *In English Ways*, 8–12; Wood, "Village and Community in Early Colonial New England," 333–46; Joseph S. Wood, *The New England Village, Creating the North American Landscape* (Baltimore: Johns Hopkins University Press, 1997), 66–69.

52. This effort continued throughout the nineteenth century as missionaries ventured further west across the continent. Laurie Maffly-Kipp demonstrates that California missionaries worked to replicate New England by transporting to California pieces of eastern sacred materials, such as church bells, pews, and sections of meetinghouses in an effort to resacralize the frontier landscape. Maffly-Kipp, *Religion and Society in Frontier California* (New Haven: Yale University Press, 1994), 82.

53. Jackson, *Discovering the Vernacular Landscape*, 60. James Wadsworth, "A Plan of the Town of New Haven," 1748. The original is housed in the Sterling Library, Rare Map Room, Yale University, New Haven, Connecticut.

54. Anthony N. B. Gravan argues unconvincingly that New Haven was based on the ideal Mediterranean town plans of fifteenth-century Roman architect Vitruvius, published in *The Ten Books of Architecture*. Although Vitruvius's treatise was not published in England until 1692, Graven believes that his ideas were available in England and transferred to American land planning, specifically to New Haven. Anthony N. B. Gravan, *Architecture and Town Planning in Colonial Connecticut* (New Haven: Yale University Press, 1951), 46–48. David Grayson Allen contends that New Haven's "nine squares" may have been inspired by scriptural accounts of ideal cities that situated a temple in the middle of a square settlement (Numbers 2:1–31; Numbers 35:5; Ezekiel 42, 46, 48). Allen, *In English Ways*, 30.

55. John William Reps, *Town Planning in Frontier America* (Columbia: University of Missouri Press, 1980), 109.

56. D. W. Meinig, *The Shaping of America: A Geographical Perspective on 500 Years of History*, vol. 1, *Atlantic America, 1492–1800* (New Haven: Yale University Press, 1986), 104. As Meinig points out, "There were neither manor houses nor tenant cottages in New England."

57. Michel Foucault, "Of Other Spaces," *Diacritics* 16 (Spring 1986): 22.

58. Ibid., 25.

59. Significantly, Hartford, Connecticut, planned in 1640, follows the same grid plan organized around the town green.

60. D. W. Meinig, "The Beholding Eye: Ten Versions of the Same Scene," in D. W. Meinig, ed., *The Interpretation of Ordinary Landscapes: Geographical Essays*, 33–47 (New York: Oxford University Press, 1979).

61. Rhys Isaac, *The Transformation of Virginia, 1740–1790* (Chapel Hill: University of North Carolina Press, 1982), 168–77.

62. William Cronon, *Changes in the Land: Indians, Colonists, and the Ecology of New England* (New York: Hill and Wang, 1983), 69–81.

63. Maffly-Kipp, *Religion and Society in Frontier California*, 84.

64. Henry Champion to Abraham Skinner, February 1, 1804, Abraham Skinner Papers, Connecticut Missionary Society Papers.

65. Although Champion's explicit statement calls for families, his implicit meaning may have equated family settlers with New Englanders.

66. George W. Knepper, "Migration to the Western Reserve," in Harry F. Lupold and Gladys Haddad, eds., *Ohio's Western Reserve: A Regional Reader*, 31 (Kent, Ohio: Kent State University Press, 1988).

67. *Connecticut Evangelical Magazine* 3 (January 1810): 22.

68. Joseph Badger, Letter, *Connecticut Evangelical Magazine* 2 (September 1801): 118.

69. Jonathan Lesslie to Connecticut Missionary Society, April 19, 1810, Jonathan Lesslie Letters, Connecticut Missionary Society Papers.

70. Connecticut Missionary Society, *Narrative of Missions* (1803), 4.

71. *Connecticut Evangelical Magazine* 2 (September 1801): 13.

72. Abraham Scott to Connecticut Missionary Society, October 16, 1807, Abraham Scott Letters, Connecticut Missionary Society Papers.

73. A specific example of this struggle was delineated in a political controversy over the appropriation of funds from the sale of the Western Reserve lands. From 1793 to 1795, Connecticut politicians in the General Assembly debated the question of the fund's appropriate recipients. Despite scathing accusations from citizens who hoped to topple the clerical and political balance, legislators passed a bill to establish a perpetual fund that granted the income to support Connecticut clergy and schools. This action sparked more debates that ended in the establishment of the School Fund Act of 1795, which appropriated funds to public schools. The shift from support of the churches to support of schools proved a direct challenge to the political power of the Congregational clergy. This powerful group, referred to by historians as the Standing Order, correctly interpreted the growing opposition in Connecticut as religious, social, and political. What began as a question of the appropriate distribution of funds expanded into a threat to a Connecticut "way of life" as defined by the more-traditional Congregational clergy. This incident formed the defensive foundation from which the Standing Order sought to protect its political and religious power in Connecticut and later on the frontier. See James R. Beasley, "Emerging Republicanism and the Standing Order: The Appropriation Act Controversy in Connecticut, 1793 to 1795," *William and Mary Quarterly*, 3d ser., 29 (1972): 590–93.

74. The traffic in religious activity was due in part to the location of the Western Reserve. To the northeast was the burned-over district of Oneida County, New York. To the south was Bourbon County, Kentucky, of the famous Cane Ridge revivals. Methodists,

1. The Benevolent Design: Mapping the Landscape

Baptists, Campbellites, Shakers, and Universalists preached throughout the Western Reserve. Besides religious competitors, political rivals such as "Jacobeans," "republicans," "Jeffersonians," and other non-Federalists circulated throughout frontier communities.

75. Simeon Woodruff to Connecticut Missionary Society, September 24, 1819, Simeon Woodruff Letters, Connecticut Missionary Society Papers.

76. Connecticut Missionary Society, *Narrative of Missions* (1815), 7.

77. Connecticut Missionary Society, *Narrative of Missions* (1802), 13–14.

78. Ibid., 5.

79. Numerous scholars write about the Garden of Eden metaphor and the American frontier. For example, see Leo Marx, *The Machine in the Garden: Technology and the Pastoral Ideal of America* (New York: Oxford University Press, 1964), 39–46; Roderick Nash, *Wilderness and the American Mind* (New Haven: Yale University Press, 1967), 15–43; Annette Kolodny, *The Land Before Her: Fantasy and Experience on the American Frontier, 1630–1860* (Chapel Hill: University of North Carolina Press, 1984), 9–13. For a specifically Puritan bifurcated vision of the frontier as "howling wilderness" or Garden of Eden, see Belden C. Lane, *Landscapes of the Sacred: Geography and Narrative in American Spirituality* (New York: Paulist Press, 1988), 114–23; Peter Carroll, *Puritanism in the Wilderness: The Intellectual Significance of the New England Frontier, 1629–1700* (New York: Columbia University Press, 1969); Alan Heimert, "Puritanism, the Wilderness, and the Frontier," *New England Quarterly* 26 (1953): 361–82; Catherine L. Albanese, *Nature Religion in America: From the Algonkian Indians to the New Age* (Chicago: University of Chicago Press, 1990), 34–46.

80. *Connecticut Evangelical Magazine* 5 (March 1805): 323.

81. Connecticut Missionary Society, *Narrative of Missions* (1815), 14.

82. Jonathan Lesslie to Connecticut Missionary Society, December 12, 1817, Jonathan Lesslie Letters, Connecticut Missionary Society Papers.

83. John Seward to Connecticut Missionary Society, October 19, 1812, John Seward Letters, Connecticut Missionary Society Papers.

84. Board of Trustees of the Connecticut Missionary Society, *Annual Report of the Missionary Society of Connecticut Trustees* (Hartford: Hudson and Goodwin, June 12, 1820).

85. *Connecticut Evangelical Magazine* 4 (January 1811): 26–27.

86. Ibid., 27.

87. Ibid., 23.

88. Connecticut Missionary Society, *Narrative of Missions* (1814), 16–17.

89. *Connecticut Evangelical Magazine* 5 (March 1805): 322.

90. Connecticut Missionary Society, *Narrative of Missions* (1812), 32.

91. Ibid., 32. Emphasis added to the quote.

92. Ibid., 33.

93. Timothy Dwight, *An Address to the Emigrants from Connecticut, and From New England Generally, in the New Settlements in the United States* (Hartford: Peter B. Gleason & Co., 1817), 3.

94. Ibid., 3.

95. Ibid., 32.

96. Connecticut Missionary Society, *An Address From the Trustees of the Missionary Society of Connecticut, to the Inhabitants of the New Settlements, in the Northern and Western Parts of the United States* (Hartford: Hudson and Goodwin, 1803), 6.

97. Dwight, *Address to the Emigrants from Connecticut*, 5.
98. Ibid.
99. Ibid., 17.
100. *Connecticut Evangelical Magazine* 3 (February 1803): 305.

2. Models of Piety: Protestant Missionaries on the Frontier

1. Thomas Robbins, *Diary of Thomas Robbins, D.D. 1796–1854*, ed. Increase N. Tarbox (Boston: Beacon Press; Thomas Todd, Printer, 1886), 1:203.

2. Thomas Robbins was ordained on May 20, 1803, in Norfolk, Connecticut. According to Robbins's diary, the participants include Rev. Abel Flint of Hartford, Connecticut; Rev, Nathan Strong of Hartford, Connecticut; Rev. Samuel J. Mills of Torringford, Connecticut; and Rev. Nathan Perkins of West Hartford, Connecticut. *Diary of Thomas Robbins, D.D.*, 1:200.

3. Joseph A. Conforti, "Jonathan Edwards's Most Popular Work: 'The Life of David Brainerd' and Nineteenth-Century Evangelical Culture," *Church History* 54 (June 1985): 188–201.

4. Jonathan Edwards, *The Life of David Brainerd*, ed. Norman Pettit, vol. 7 of *Jonathan Edwards, Works* (New Haven: Yale University Press, 1985). All citations of *Life of David Brainerd* are from this edition. The biographical information on Brainerd is found in Pettit's introduction and in Norman Pettit, "Prelude to Mission: David Brainerd's Expulsion from Yale," *New England Quarterly* 59 (1986): 28–50; Joseph A. Conforti, *Jonathan Edwards, Religious Tradition, and American Culture* (Chapel Hill: University of Chapel Hill Press, 1995).

5. Conforti, *Jonathan Edwards, Religious Tradition, and American Culture*, 72–74. Conforti notes that missionary students at Andover Seminary read Brainerd and often referred to him as a model missionary in their scholastic and personal writings. See also David L. Weddle, "The Melancholy Saint: Jonathan Edwards's Interpretation of David Brainerd as a Model of Evangelical Spirituality," *Harvard Theological Review* 81, no. 3 (1988): 297–318; David Morgan, *Visual Piety: A History and Theory of Popular Religious Images* (Berkeley: University of California Press, 1998), 78–81.

6. Conforti, *Jonathan Edwards, Religious Tradition, and American Culture*, 64–65.

7. Ibid., 78.

8. Edwards, *Life of David Brainerd*, 95. Taken from Edwards's preface to the edited diary.

9. David Brainerd died of tuberculosis at the age of twenty-nine in 1747.

10. Conforti, *Jonathan Edwards, Religious Tradition, and American Culture*, 74.

11. Eliphalet Austin to Connecticut Missionary Society Trustees, November 20, 1802, Incoming Correspondences, Connecticut Missionary Society Papers. The Correspondences, Board of Trustees' Minutes, Annual Reports, and Missionary Letters of the Connecticut Missionary Society are housed in the Connecticut Conference Archives, United Church of Christ, in Hartford, Connecticut. They are also available on microfilm.

12. I am interested in both the prescriptive message of the author, the editor, and the community that disseminates it (what constitutes a pious missionary), as well as individu-

2. Models of Piety: Protestant Missionaries on the Frontier

als' responses to that discursive construction. For a discussion of the relationship between representations of the self, discourse, and religious piety, see the introduction to Judith Perkin, *The Suffering Self: Pain and Narrative Representation in the Early Christian Era* (New York: Routledge, 1995), 1–14. For works on the relationship between texts and readers, see Roger Chartier, "Texts, Printing, Readings," in Lynn Hunt, ed., *The New Cultural History* (Berkeley: University of California Press, 1989), 154–75; Stanley Fish, *Is There a Text in This Class? The Authority of Interpretive Communities* (Cambridge: Harvard University Press, 1980).

13. Donald M. Scott, *From Office to Profession: The New England Ministry, 1750–1850* (Philadelphia: University of Pennsylvania Press, 1978), 53–56. Scott demonstrates that methods of clerical recruitment and training changed dramatically between the eighteenth and nineteenth centuries. Most clergy in the eighteenth century followed a father or grandfather into the sacred office, or were younger sons in an economically comfortable family, sons who displayed sincere piety and moral conduct and who would not benefit from the family estate. By the nineteenth century, pious men recruited for the ministry generally came from poorer families and relied on financial assistance to attend provincial colleges.

14. James R. Rohrer, *Keepers of the Covenant: Frontier Missions and the Decline of Congregationalism, 1774–1818* (New York: Oxford University Press, 1995), 118–21. Rohrer shows that of the 148 missionaries sent by the Connecticut Missionary Society between 1798 and 1818, only 35 graduated from Yale. He notes that many of the Connecticut Missionary Society missionaries received financial aid for college from a benefactor.

15. Scott, *From Office to Profession*, 62–63; James W. Fraser, *Schooling the Preachers: The Development of Protestant Theological Education in the United States, 1740–1875* (Lanham, Md.: University Press of America, 1988), 32; Henry K. Rowe, *History of Andover Theological Seminary* (Newton: Thomas Todd, 1933), 9.

16. Thomas Robbins to Abel Flint, February 24, 1804. Robbins wrote a similar comment a month later in a letter to Nathan Strong: "I find my work more laborious and toilsome than I had expected. I had been in new countries before, but never in one as new as this." Thomas Robbins to Nathan Strong, March 8, 1804, Robbins Family Papers. The Robbins Family papers are housed in the Connecticut Historical Society in Hartford.

17. Joseph Badger and Thomas Robbins also wrote memoirs that included their labors in the Western Reserve. Their memoirs follow the pattern of reporting religious events rather than documenting their own spiritual lives. Robbins, *Diary of Thomas Robbins, D.D.*; see vol. 1 for references to his Western Reserve mission. Joseph Badger, *A Memoir of Reverend Joseph Badger, Containing an Autobiography, and Selections from his Private Journal and Correspondence* (Hudson, Ohio: Sawyer, Ingersoll, 1851).

18. Thomas Robbins to his parents, November 29, 1803, Robbins Family Papers; Sarah Robbins to Thomas Robbins, January 21, 1804, Robbins Family Papers.

19. Connecticut Missionary Society Trustees, May 1801, Minutes, Connecticut Missionary Society Papers.

20. Abel Flint to Thomas Robbins, July 25, 1803, Robbins Family Papers.

21. Thomas Robbins to Connecticut Missionary Society Trustees, April 24, 1804, Thomas Robbins Letters, Connecticut Missionary Society Papers.

22. Joseph Badger, Letter, *Connecticut Evangelical Magazine* 2 (September 1801): 118.

This letter was written prior to Robbins's commission to serve as a Western Reserve missionary.

23. Ezekiel Chapman to Connecticut Missionary Society Trustees, July 9, 1802, Ezekiel Chapman Letters, Connecticut Missionary Society Papers.

24. Joseph Badger to Connecticut Missionary Society Trustees, August 19, 1804, Joseph Badger Letters, Connecticut Missionary Society Papers.

25. Joseph Badger to Connecticut Missionary Society Trustees, November 19, 1802, Joseph Badger Letters, Connecticut Missionary Society Papers.

26. The *Connecticut Evangelical Magazine* (Hartford: Hudson and Goodwin, 1800–1807) became the *Connecticut Evangelical Magazine and Religious Intelligencer* (Hartford: Lincoln and Gleason, 1808–1815). The journal was published monthly under the auspices of the Connecticut Missionary Society.

27. Thomas Robbins to Nathan Strong, March 8, 1804, Robbins Family Papers.

28. Thomas Robbins to Parents, November 29, 1803, Robbins Family Papers.

29. Ibid.

30. Peter Cartwright, *Autobiography of Peter Cartwright, the Backwoods Preacher*, ed. W. P. Strickland (Cincinnati: L. Swormstedt & A. Poe for the Methodist Episcopal Church, 1859), 359.

31. Ibid., 358.

32. Ibid.

33. Ezekiel Chapman to Connecticut Missionary Society Trustees, May 12, 1803, Ezekiel Chapman Letters, Connecticut Missionary Society Papers.

34. Joseph Badger to Connecticut Missionary Society Trustees, July 27, 1801, Joseph Badger Letters, Connecticut Missionary Society Papers.

35. Ibid., March 29, 1801.

36. Ibid.

37. Ibid., June 8, 1802.

38. Ibid., June 16, 1808.

39. Ibid.

40. Ibid.

41. Ibid.

42. Ibid., April 10, 1806.

43. Robbins attended Yale between 1792 and 1795. His father was a trustee of the new Williams College and arranged for Robbins to spend his senior year at Williams to show support for the fledgling school. As a result, Thomas Robbins graduated from both institutions in 1796. Robbins, *Diary of Thomas Robbins, D.D.*, 1:iv.

44. Joseph Badger to Connecticut Missionary Society Trustees, February 3, 1806, Joseph Badger Letters, Connecticut Missionary Society Papers.

45. Ammi Robbins to Thomas Robbins, October 10, 1804, Robbins Family Papers.

46. Ibid., November 22, 1804.

47. Ibid., October 10, 1804.

48. Samuel P. Robbins to Thomas Robbins, June 6, 1804, Robbins Family Papers.

49. Joseph Badger to Connecticut Missionary Society Trustees, February 3, 1806, Joseph Badger Letters, Connecticut Missionary Society Papers.

50. Ibid.

2. Models of Piety: Protestant Missionaries on the Frontier

51. The subtext of this criticism is that although the Connecticut Missionary Society asserted the homogeneity of New Connecticut settlers, Badger, perhaps unwittingly, provided evidence that many did not emigrate from Connecticut or even New England.

52. Joseph Badger to Connecticut Missionary Society Trustees, February 3, 1806, Joseph Badger Letters, Connecticut Missionary Society Papers.

53. Joseph Badger to Connecticut Missionary Society Trustees, March 4, 1805, Joseph Badger Letters, Connecticut Missionary Society Papers.

54. Ibid.

55. Joseph Badger to Abel Flint, March 19, 1803, Joseph Badger Letters, Connecticut Missionary Society Papers.

56. Ibid.,

57. Thomas Robbins to Nathan Strong, March 8, 1804, Robbins Family Papers.

58. Ibid.

59. Ibid.

60. Joseph Badger to Connecticut Missionary Society Trustees, March 19, 1803, Joseph Badger Letters, Connecticut Missionary Society Papers.

61. Joseph Badger to Abel Flint, March 19, 1803, Joseph Badger Letters, Connecticut Missionary Society Papers.

62. Thomas Robbins to Nathan Strong, March 8, 1804, Robbins Family Papers.

63. Joseph Badger to Connecticut Missionary Society Trustees, November 19, 1802, Joseph Badger Letters, Connecticut Missionary Society Papers.

64. Lyman Potter to Connecticut Missionary Society Trustees, January 16, 1806, Incoming Correspondences, Connecticut Missionary Society Papers.

65. Hosea Wilcox to Connecticut Missionary Society Trustees, June 5, 1805, Joseph Badger Letters, Connecticut Missionary Society Papers.

66. David Hudson to Connecticut Missionary Society Trustees, August 6, 1803, Incoming Correspondences, Connecticut Missionary Society Papers.

67. Thomas Robbins to Connecticut Missionary Society Trustees, June 8, 1805, Thomas Robbins Letters, Connecticut Missionary Society Papers.

68. Joseph Badger to Connecticut Missionary Society Trustees, April 10, 1806, Joseph Badger Letters, Connecticut Missionary Society Papers.

69. Badger's initial missionary contract paid him seven dollars per week; however, in 1803 the missionary society decreased all the missionaries' salaries to six dollars per week, a wage that he found insulting and ultimately untenable for supporting his family.

70. Calvin Chapin to Abel Flint, October 1, 1806, Calvin Chapin Letters, Connecticut Missionary Society Papers.

71. Ibid.

72. Robbins, *Diary of Thomas Robbins, D.D.*, 1:270.

73. Calvin Chapin to Abel Flint, October 1, 1806, Calvin Chapin Letters, Connecticut Missionary Society Papers.

74. Ibid.

75. Ibid.

76. Thomas Robbins to Connecticut Missionary Society Trustees, March 12, 1806, Thomas Robbins Letters, Connecticut Missionary Society Papers.

77. Thomas Robbins to Nathan Strong, March 8, 1804, Robbins Family Papers.

78. Calvin Chapin to Abel Flint, October 1, 1806, Calvin Chapin Letters.
79. Calvin Chapin to Abel Flint, July 21, 1806, Calvin Chapin Letters.
80. Calvin Chapin to Abel Flint, October 1, 1806, Calvin Chapin Letters.
81. Ibid.

3. The Moral Garden of the Western World: Bodies, Towns, and Families

1. Connecticut Missionary Society to Joseph Badger, January 16, 1805, Joseph Badger Letters, Connecticut Missionary Society Papers.
2. See, for example, Elizabeth Reis, *Damned Women: Sinners and Witches in Puritan New England* (Ithaca, N.Y.: Cornell University Press, 1997); Amy Schrager Lang, *Prophetic Women: Anne Hutchison and the Problem of Dissent in the Literature of New England* (Berkeley: University of California Press, 1987).
3. Charles Chauncy, "A Letter from a Gentleman in Boston, to Mr. George Wisehart, One of the Ministers of Edinburgh, Concerning the State of Religion in New England" (1742), in Richard Bushman, ed., *The Great Awakening: Documents on the Revival of Religion, 1740–1745* (Chapel Hill: University of North Carolina Press, 1989), 117.
4. Susan Juster, *Disorderly Women: Sexual Politics and Evangelicalism in Revolutionary New England* (Ithaca, N.Y.: Cornell University Press, 1994), 35–37.
5. Romans 16:16. Other scriptural mention of exchanging holy kisses is found in 1 Corinthians 16:20, 2 Corinthians 13:15, 1 Thessalonians 5:26, 1 Peter 5:14. For more on kissing as a Christian identity marker, see Jon F. Sensbach, *A Separate Canaan: The Making of an Afro-Moravian World in North Carolina, 1763–1840* (Chapel Hill: University of North Carolina Press, 1998), 114–15; Nicolas James Perella, *The Kiss Sacred and Profane: An Interpretive History of Kiss Symbolism and Related Religio-Erotic Themes* (Berkeley: University of California Press, 1969), 12–18.
6. B. Morse, J. Wright, R. Nettleton, S. Mills to Connecticut Missionary Society, March 2, 1805, Joseph Badger Letters, Connecticut Missionary Society Papers. We must keep in mind that at this point in time and space, the emotive behavior among members of the same sex remained within the bounds of propriety. While the attempt to keep the kissing and falling in a same-sex setting may have constituted the most appropriate response to the new religious behavior, mention of this seems in this instance to indicate that settlers did not consider, or were not concerned with, the homoerotic implications of the act.
7. Ibid.
8. Ibid.
9. Hosea Wilcox to Connecticut Missionary Society, June 5, 1805, Joseph Badger Letters, Connecticut Missionary Society Papers.
10. Michael Feher, ed., *Fragments for a History of the Human Body*, 3 vols. (New York: Zone Publishing, 1989); Thomas Laqueur, *Making Sex: Body and Gender from the Greeks to Freud* (Cambridge: Harvard University Press, 1990); Pierre Bourdieu, *Outline of a Theory of Practice*, trans. Richard Nice (Cambridge: Cambridge University Press, 1977), 18–19; Anthony Fletcher, *Gender, Sex, and Subordination in England, 1500–1800* (New Haven: Yale University Press, 1995).

3. The Moral Garden of the Western World: Bodies, Towns, and Families 201

11. Elizabeth Grosz, *Space, Time, and Perversion: Essays on the Politics of the Body* (New York: Routledge, 1995); Beatriz Colomina, ed., *Sexuality and Space*, Princeton Papers on Architecture (Princeton: Princeton Architectural Press, 1992); Gillian Rose, *Feminism and Geography: The Limits of Geographical Knowledge* (Minneapolis: University of Minnesota Press, 1993).

12. Susan R. Bordo, "The Body and the Reproduction of Femininity: A Feminist Approach to Foucault," in Alison M. Jagger and Susan R. Bordo, eds., *Gender/Body/Knowledge: Feminist Reconstructions of Being and Knowing* (New Brunswick: Rutgers University Press, 1989), 13–33; Michel Foucault, *Discipline and Punish: The Birth of the Prison*, trans. Alan Sheridan (New York: Vintage, 1979). Along with the physical body's cultural mutability, feminist theorists emphasize the complexity of the body and its interrelatedness to the mind. Rather than diminishing the importance of the body, or creating a binary opposition with the mind, their focus on the body revisits the problem of subjectivity. Simply put, our bodies position us both physically and mentally in our worlds.

13. For gender, the body, and religion, see Caroline Walker Bynum, *Fragmentation and Redemption: Essays on Gender and the Human Body in Medieval Religion* (New York: Zone Books, 1991), 181–238.

14. Thomas Robbins to Nathan Strong, March 8, 1804, Thomas Robbins Letters, Connecticut Missionary Society Papers.

15. Ezekiel Chapman to Connecticut Missionary Society, June 6, 1802, Ezekiel Chapman Letters, Connecticut Missionary Society Papers.

16. Abraham Scott to Connecticut Missionary Society, January 22, 1808, Abraham Scott Letters, Connecticut Missionary Society Papers.

17. Simeon Woodruff to Connecticut Missionary Society, March 15, 1814, Simeon Woodruff Letters, Connecticut Missionary Society Papers.

18. Ibid.

19. Juster, *Disorderly Women*, 24.

20. Board of Trustees of the Connecticut Missionary Society, *An Annual Report From the Trustees of the Missionary Society of Connecticut* (Hartford: Peter B. Gleason & Co., June 1, 1809).

21. Jonathan Lesslie to Connecticut Missionary Society, August 26, 1822, Jonathan Lesslie Letters, Connecticut Missionary Society Papers.

22. Timothy Dwight, *An Address to the Emigrants from Connecticut, and From New England Generally, in the New Settlements in the United States* (Hartford: Peter B. Gleason & Co., 1817), 17.

23. Ibid.

24. Ibid., 13–14.

25. Ibid., 9.

26. For an example of the merging of family and nation in contemporary Baptist literature, see Juster, *Disorderly Women*, 116–19.

27. Philip Doddridge, *A Plain and Serious Address to the Master of a Family on the Important Subject of Family Religion*. Reprinted for the Use of the Connecticut Missionary Society (Hartford: John Babcock, 1799), 10.

28. Ibid., 12. Emphasis on evil demons is printed in the text.

29. Connecticut Missionary Society, *A Summary of Christian Doctrine and Practice:*

Designed Especially, for the Use of the People in the New Settlements of the United States of America. By the Trustees of the Missionary Society of Connecticut (Hartford: Hudson and Goodwin, 1804), 54.

30. Jonathan Lesslie to Connecticut Missionary Society, November 11, 1808, Jonathan Lesslie Letters, Connecticut Missionary Society Papers.

31. Jonathan Lesslie to Connecticut Missionary Society, March 7, 1808, Jonathan Lesslie Letters, Connecticut Missionary Society Papers. See chapter 2 for an illustration of this letter.

32. Randolph Stone to Connecticut Missionary Society, March 28, 1822, Randolph Stone Letters, Connecticut Missionary Society Papers.

33. Simeon Woodruff to Connecticut Missionary Society, June 13, 1814, Simeon Woodruff Letters, Connecticut Missionary Society Papers.

34. Simeon Woodruff to Connecticut Missionary Society, September 24, 1819, Simeon Woodruff Letters, Connecticut Missionary Society Papers.

35. John F. Schermerhorn and Samuel J. Mills, *A Correct View of that Part of the United States Which Lies West of the Allegany Mountains, with Regard to Religion and Morals* (Hartford: Peter B. Gleason & Co., 1814), 17.

36. Connecticut Missionary Society, *Narrative of Missions* (1814).

37. Lumping threatening groups together resembles what historian David Brion Davis argues happened with the Masons, Catholics, and Mormons during the same period of American history. He believes that the three groups merged together in many Americans' minds as an internal threat to social order, since they were believed to embody antidemocratic ideals. David Brion Davis, "Some Themes of Countersubversion; An Analysis of Anti-Masonic, Anti-Catholic, and Anti-Mormon Literature," *Mississippi Valley Historical Review* 47 (1960): 205–24.

38. Giles Cowles to Connecticut Missionary Society, July 12, 1822, Giles Cowles Letters, Connecticut Missionary Society Papers.

39. John Seward to Connecticut Missionary Society, February 4, 1814, John Seward Letters, Connecticut Missionary Society Papers.

40. Connecticut Missionary Society, *Narrative of Missions* (1814), 7.

41. Connecticut Missionary Society, *Narrative of Missions* (1811), 14–15.

42. Connecticut Missionary Society, *Narrative of Missions* (1826), 10.

43. Simeon Woodruff to Connecticut Missionary Society, June 13, 1815, Simeon Woodruff Letters, Connecticut Missionary Society Papers.

44. William Hanford to Connecticut Missionary Society, July 1, 1814, William Hanford Letters, Connecticut Missionary Society Papers.

45. Abraham Scott to Connecticut Missionary Society, May 12, 1808, Abraham Scott Letters, Connecticut Missionary Society Papers.

46. Randolph Stone to Connecticut Missionary Society, April 26, 1824, Randolph Stone Letters, Connecticut Missionary Society Papers.

47. Ibid.

48. Simeon Woodruff to Connecticut Missionary Society, October 28, 1822, Simeon Woodruff Letters, Connecticut Missionary Society Papers.

49. John Seward to Connecticut Missionary Society, August 30, 1825, John Seward Letters, Connecticut Missionary Society Papers.

50. Luther Humphrey to Connecticut Missionary Society, April 26, 1817, Luther Humphrey Letters, Connecticut Missionary Society Papers.

51. Connecticut Missionary Society, *Narrative of Missions* (1825), 8.

52. A listing of the numbers of books sent to Western Reserve and other missionary sites is located at the end of each *Narrative of Missions*. In 1812, for example, the Connecticut Missionary Society sent 3,294 publications to new settlements. The books listed include Joseph Emerson's *Evangelical Primer*, Lyman Beecher's *Sermon on Divine Government*, *Summary of Christian Doctrine*, Isaac Watts's *Divine Songs*, *Connecticut Evangelical Magazine*, *Hartford Selected Hymns*, Benjamin Trumbull on *Divine Revelation*, *Poetical Address to a Deist*, *Panoplist*, Timothy Dwight's *Psalms and Hymns*, Nathanael Emmons on *Baptism*, and Bibles.

53. Ezekiel Chapman to Connecticut Missionary Society, January 29, 1803, Ezekiel Chapman Letters, Connecticut Missionary Society Papers.

54. Luther Humphrey to Connecticut Missionary Society, January 17, 1823, Luther Humphrey Letters, Connecticut Missionary Society Papers.

55. Randolph Stone to Connecticut Missionary Society, December 19, 1822, Randolph Stone Letters, Connecticut Missionary Society Papers.

56. Jonathan Lesslie to Connecticut Missionary Society, February 16, 1820, Jonathan Lesslie Letters, Connecticut Missionary Society Papers.

57. *Connecticut Evangelical Magazine* 4 (February 1804): 315.

58. James R. Rohrer, *Keepers of the Covenant: Frontier Missions and the Decline of Congregationalism, 1774–1818* (New York: Oxford University Press, 1995), 139.

59. Luther Humphrey to Connecticut Missionary Society, December 19, 1829, Luther Humphrey Letters, Connecticut Missionary Society Papers.

60. Simeon Woodruff to Connecticut Missionary Society, March 11, 1824, Simeon Woodruff Letters, Connecticut Missionary Society Papers.

61. Jonathan Lesslie to Connecticut Missionary Society, February 3, 1812, Jonathan Lesslie Letters, Connecticut Missionary Society Papers.

62. Randolph Stone to Connecticut Missionary Society, November 12, 1825, Randolph Stone Letters, Connecticut Missionary Society Papers.

63. William Hanford to Connecticut Missionary Society, December 6, 1814, William Hanford Letters, Connecticut Missionary Society Papers.

64. Randolph Stone to Connecticut Missionary Society, March 29, 1822, Randolph Stone Letters, Connecticut Missionary Society Papers.

65. John Seward to Connecticut Missionary Society, April 8, 1823, John Seward Letters, Connecticut Missionary Society Papers.

66. Simeon Woodruff to Connecticut Missionary Society, July 11, 1814, Simeon Woodruff Letters, Connecticut Missionary Society Papers.

67. Connecticut Missionary Society, *Narrative of Missions* (1822), 5.

68. Connecticut Missionary Society, *Narrative of Missions* (1823), 6.

69. David Hudson, "Some Accounts of the Religious Exercises of David Hudson," *Western Missionary Magazine* 1 (1803): 166.

70. Ibid., 170.

71. David Hudson, Journal, David Hudson Papers.

72. Philip R. Shriver, ed., *A Tour of New Connecticut in 1811: The Narrative of Henry*

204   3. The Moral Garden of the Western World: Bodies, Towns, and Families

Leavitt Ellsworth, Western Reserve History Studies Series, vol. 1 (Cleveland: Western Reserve Historical Society, 1985), 62–63. Emphasis on "painted" in the printed text.

73. First Congregational Church of Hudson, Records, March 9, 1819. The church was founded on September 4, 1802; the founding members included Stephen and Mary Thompson, David Hudson, Abraham and Susanna Hudson, Stephen and Abigail Thompson, George and Alamira Kilborne, Heman and Eunice Oviatt, Amos Lusk, and Hannah Lyndly.

74. Ibid., Article 7.

75. Ibid., March 30, 1804.

76. Ibid., January 5, 1809.

77. Ibid.

78. Giles Cowles to Connecticut Missionary Society, July 26, 1810, Giles Cowles Letters, Connecticut Missionary Society Papers.

79. Alexander T. Bobersky and David T. Stephens, "Early Towns in the Western Reserve: A Perspective From the Late Nineteenth Century," *Pioneer America Society Transactions* 9 (1986): 54.

80. Ibid., 55.

81. Ibid., 55.

82. Seth I. Ensign, *Volume of Survey Notes, 1806*, Seth I. Ensign Papers.

83. John Seward to Connecticut Missionary Society, August 10, 1812, John Seward Letters, Connecticut Missionary Society Papers. The churches were formed in the towns of Aurora, Hudson, Tallmadge, Springfield, Randolph, Rootstown, Charlestown, and Mantua.

84. Randolph Stone to Connecticut Missionary Society, August 14, 1822, Randolph Stone Letters, Connecticut Missionary Society Papers.

85. Erastus Ripley to Connecticut Missionary Society, December 19, 1817, Erastus Ripley Letters, Connecticut Missionary Society Papers.

86. William Hanford to Connecticut Missionary Society, July 1, 1814, William Hanford Letters, Connecticut Missionary Society Papers.

87. Randolph Stone to Connecticut Missionary Society, March 28, 1822, Randolph Stone Letters. Connecticut Missionary Society Papers.

88. Ibid.

89. Ibid.

90. Ibid.

91. Regional demographers have verified Stone's portrayal of the religious and regional diversity among settlers as well as the differing settlement patterns on the borders of the Western Reserve. They have found similarly higher incidents of delocalized town construction south of the Western Reserve. The majority of the settlers chose spots near natural resources rather than in close proximity to neighbors. Stone's assessment, while perhaps slightly alarmist, appears statistically accurate. David T. Stephens, Alexander T. Bobersky, and Joseph Cencia, "The Yankee Frontier in Northern Ohio: 1796–1850," *Pioneer America Society Transactions* 17 (1994): 4–7.

92. Randolph Stone to Connecticut Missionary Society, August 14, 1822, Randolph Stone Letters, Connecticut Missionary Society Papers.

93. All of the Plan of Union men supplied other churches and towns while attempting to build a strong home congregation.

3. The Moral Garden of the Western World: Bodies, Towns, and Families 205

94. Giles Cowles to Connecticut Missionary Society, October 24, 1817, Giles Cowles Letters, Connecticut Missionary Society Papers.

95. Ibid.

96. Ibid.

97. Luther Humphrey to Connecticut Missionary Society, April 17, 1818, Luther Humphrey Letters, Connecticut Missionary Society Papers.

98. Presbytery of Grand River, Records, August 20, 1816.

99. Four years later, in 1818, the Portage Presbytery separated from the Grand River Presbytery to oversee the churches in Portage County.

100. Autobiographical excerpt quoted in William S. Kennedy, *The Plan of Union; or, a History of the Presbyterian and Congregational Churches of the Western Reserve* (Hudson, Ohio: Pentagon Stream Press, 1856), 166.

101. Colleen McDannell, *Material Christianity: Religion and Popular Culture in America* (New Haven: Yale University Press, 1995), 4. McDannell argues that scholars of U.S. religion historically have been swayed by Calvinist interpretations that stress the salience of words over actions, and this has precluded them from considering material artifacts as historical evidence.

102. Asher Benjamin, *American Builder's Companion or, a System of Architecture Particularly Adapted to the Present Style of Building* (R.P.& C. Williams, 1827; reprint, 6th ed., New York: Diver Publications, 1969), 109.

103. Anthony N. B. Gravan, *Architecture and Town Planning in Colonial Connecticut* (New Haven: Yale University Press, 1951), 116–29.

104. I. T. Frary, *Ohio in Homespun and Calico* (Richmond, Va.: Garrett and Massie, 1942), 15.

105. Reverend Joseph Badger, *A Memoir of Reverend Joseph Badger, Containing an Autobiography, and Selections from his Private Journal and Correspondence* (Hudson, Ohio: Sawyer, Ingersoll, 1851), 39–40.

106. Christopher Gore Crary, "Frontier Living Conditions in Kirtland," in Harry F. Lupold and Gladys Haddad, eds., *Ohio's Western Reserve: A Regional Reader* (Kent, Ohio: Kent State University Press, 1988), 72.

107. For examples of New England architecture, see Russell F. Whitehead and Frank C. Brown, eds., *Early Homes of New England* (New York: Arno Press, 1977); Russell F. Whitehead and Frank Brown, eds., *Early Homes of Massachusetts* (New York: Arno Press, 1977); Norman B. Baker, *Early Homes of New England* (Rutland: Charles E. Tuttle, 1967). For a thorough analysis of eighteenth-century American home architecture and a comprehensive bibliography of recent and significant writings in that field, see Edward A. Chappell, "Housing a Nation: The Transformation of Living Standards in Early America," in Cary Carson, Ronald Hoffman, and Peter J. Albert, eds., *Of Consuming Interests*, 167–232 (Charlottesville: University of Virginia Press, 1994).

108. For a detailed example of how architecture reflects religious and social status, see Rhys Isaac, *The Transformation of Virginia, 1740–1790* (Chapel Hill: University of North Carolina Press, 1982), 30–42.

109. Barbara Welter, *Dimity Convictions: The American Woman in the Nineteenth Century* (Athens: Ohio University Press, 1976), 21–41. Michel Foucault noted that the desire to define white women as sexually pure emerged as traditional social distinctions based on

206   3. The Moral Garden of the Western World: Bodies, Towns, and Families

aristocratic lineage waned and sexual repression in the late eighteenth century became a mark of social status. Michel Foucault, *History of Sexuality*, vol. 1, *An Introduction*, trans. Robert Hurley (New York: Vintage, 1980), 122–27.

110. Bourdieu, *Outline of a Theory of Practice*, 89–91.

111. For an excellent example of "architecture's complicity in the exercise of patriarchal authority," see Mark Wigley's reading of Leon Battista Alberti's fifteenth-century work *On the Art of Building in Ten Books*. Mark Wigley, "Untitled: The Housing of Gender," in Beatriz Colomina, ed., *Sexuality and Space*, Princeton Architectural Papers (Princeton: Princeton Architectural Press, 1992), 327–65.

112. Henry Leavitt Ellsworth, *A Tour of New Connecticut in 1811: The Narrative of Henry Leavitt Ellsworth*, ed. Philip R. Shriver, Western Reserve History Studies Series, vol. 1 (Cleveland: Western Reserve Historical Studies Series, 1985), 8.

113. Ibid., 34.

114. Ibid., 69.

115. Ibid., 69.

116. Ibid., 71.

117. Dr. Zerah Hawley, *A Journal of a Tour Through Connecticut, Massachusetts, New York, the North Part of Pennsylvania and Ohio, Including a Years Residence in the Part of the State of Ohio, Styled, New Connecticut, or Western Reserve, in Which is Given, A Description of the Country, Climate, Soil, Productions, Animals, Buildings, Manners of People, State of Society, Population &c. From Actual and Careful Observation* (New Haven: Printed by S. Converse, 1822), 58.

118. Ibid., 43.

119. Ibid., 47.

120. Ibid., 58.

4. Geography Made Easy: Geographies and Travel Literature

1. Margaret Van Horn Dwight, *A Journey to Ohio in 1810*, ed. by Max Farrand, Yale Historical Manuscript Series, vol. 1 (New Haven: Yale University Press, 1912), 62.

2. George W. Knepper, "Early Migration to the Western Reserve," in Harry F. Lupold and Gladys Haddad, eds., *Ohio's Western Reserve: A Reader*, 33–34 (Kent, Ohio: Kent State University Press, 1988). Knepper states that there were two main routes to the Western Reserve from New England. A northern route went through New York to Buffalo. The southern route ran through Pennsylvania to Pittsburgh. Dwight writes concerning traveling with the Deacon: "I never will go to New Connecticut with a Deacon again, for we put up in every byeplace in the country to save expence—it is very grating to my pride to go into a tavern & furnish & cook my own provision—to ride in a waggon &c &c." Dwight, *A Journey*, 5.

3. Dwight, *A Journey*, 64.

4. Henry Leavitt Ellsworth, *A Tour of New Connecticut in 1811: The Narrative of Henry Leavitt Ellsworth*, ed. Philip R. Shriver, Western Reserve History Studies Series, vol. 1 (Cleveland: Western Reserve Historical Society, 1985), 57.

5. Robert A. Wheeler, ed., *Visions of the Western Reserve: Public and Private Documents of Northeastern Ohio, 1750–1860* (Columbus: Ohio State University Press, 2000), 130.

4. Geography Made Easy: Geographies and Travel Literature

6. Philip Shriver notes in his introduction to Ellsworth's journal that only about fifteen handwritten travel accounts by Connecticut travelers to the Western Reserve between 1796 and 1822 have survived. These include the journals of land surveyors Seth Pease of Suffield, Amzi Atwater of Cannan, John Milton Holley of Salisbury; land agent Turhand Kirtland of Wallingford; travelers and settlers David Hudson of Goshen, Jonathan Hale of Glastonbury, Rev. Giles Hooker Cowles of Bristol, Dr. Zerah Hawley of New Haven (?), Henry Newberry of Windsor, Margaret Van Horn Dwight of New Haven, William Eldredge of New London, Emery Goodwin of New Hartford, and Henry Leavitt Ellsworth of Windsor. Ellsworth, *A Tour of New Connecticut*, 5–6.

7. Promotional literature that included travel narratives, emigrant guides, and booster tracts blossomed during this time period. These texts, written for investors, migrants, settlers, and tourists, described the landscape by attention to utility, resources, potential, location, and comparison to similar regions. Malcolm G. Lewis, "Rhetoric of the Western Interior: Modes of Environmental Description in American Promotional Literature of the Nineteenth Century," in Denis E. Cosgrove and Stephen Daniels, eds., *The Iconography of Landscape: Essays on Symbolic Representation, Design, and Use of Past Environments*, 180–85 (Cambridge: Cambridge University Press, 1986).

8. For a description of the many forms of Ohio promotional literature, see Walter Havighurst, *Wilderness for Sale: The Story of the First Western Land Rush* (New York: Hastings House, Publishers, 1956), 164–83; Robert A. Wheeler, "The Literature of the Western Reserve," *Ohio History* 100 (1991): 101–28; Stewart H. Holbrook, *The Yankee Exodus: An Account of Migration from New England* (Seattle: University of Washington Press, 1968), 25–38.

9. Mary Louise Pratt, *Imperial Eyes: Travel Writing and Transculturation* (New York: Routledge, 1992), 29.

10. For an explanation of the role of precision in eighteenth-century cartographic memoirs and travelers' accounts, see Michael T. Bravo, "Precision and Curiosity in Scientific Travel: James Rennell and the Orientalist Geography of the New Imperial Age (1760–1830)," in Jaś Elsner and Joan-Pau Rubies, eds., *Voyages and Visions: Towards a Cultural History of Travel* (London: Reaktion Books, 1999), 162–83, esp. 163–65.

11. Richard J. Moss, *The Life of Jedidiah Morse* (Knoxville: University of Tennessee Press, 1995), ix. Morse was born in Woodstock, Connecticut, in 1776.

12. *Geography Made Easy* went through twenty-five editions. *The American Geography*, first published in 1789, was republished in 1792, 1794, 1795; and later as *The American Universal Geography* in 1793, 1796, 1805, 1812, 1819. He also published *Elements of Geography* in 1795, 1796, 1798, 1801, 1804, 1825. Another popular Morse text was *The American Gazetteer*, published in 1797, 1798, 1804, 1810; and published as *The American Universal Gazetteer* in 1802, 1805, 1819. For a detailed chronology of Jedidiah Morse's publications, see Ralph H. Brown, "The American Geographies of Jedidiah Morse," *Annals of the Association of American Geographers* 31 (1941): 145–217. See also Timothy Dillon, "Jedidiah Morse's Christian Republicanism: Reform and the Young Nation" (Ph.D. diss., University of Wisconsin–Madison, 1987), 125–26.

13. Moss, *The Life of Jedidiah Morse*, 44–47. Moss argues that Morse in his writing and preaching should be understood within the literary tradition of the Jeremiad. He views Morse's geographies as lamenting America's sins and calling citizens to remember America's purpose in sacred history.

14. Joseph W. Phillips, *Jedidiah Morse and New England Congregationalism* (New Brunswick, N.J.: Rutgers University Press, 1983), 18.

15. Morse relied heavily on geographers Thomas Hutchins, Lewis Evans, and Thomas Pownall, as well as Jeremy Belknap, Samuel Mitchell, and Noah Webster. See John C. Greene, *American Science in the Age of Jefferson* (Ames, Iowa: Iowa State University Press, 1984), 190.

16. Brown, "The American Geographies," 147.

17. Ibid., 162–64. Brown includes copies of three questionnaires sent out by Morse. The originals are housed at the Massachusetts Historical Society, the Boston Public Library, and the Beinecke Rare Book and Manuscript Library, Yale University.

18. Ibid., 146.

19. Phillips, *Jedidiah Morse and New England Congregationalism*, 33.

20. For a thorough account of the impact of Morse's geographies on the American reading public, see Dillon, "Jedidiah Morse's Christian Republicanism," 102–17. Also see Brown, "The American Geographies," 147.

21. Martin Brükner, "Lessons in Geography: Maps, Spellers, and Other Grammars of Nationalism in the Early Republic," *American Quarterly* 51, no. 2 (June 1999): 326.

22. Jedidiah Morse, *The American Geography; Or, A View of the Present Situation of the United States of America* (Elizabethtown: Shepard Kollock, 1789; reprint, New York: Arno Press, 1970), 145–48.

23. See, for example, Morse's description of North Carolina's population, character, manners, and customs. The inhabitants of that Southern state fare poorly when held against the New England ideal. Morse, *American Geography*, 417–18.

24. Ibid., 219.

25. Ibid.

26. Ibid., 221.

27. Ibid., 469.

28. Ibid.

29. Ibid., 68.

30. For an incisive interpretation of Morse's brand of Americanization, see Moss, *The Life of Jedidiah Morse*, 44–47.

31. One exception to his armchair approach to American geography was when he accompanied his friend Jeremy Belknap on a 1796 missionary tour of western New York to evaluate the Oneida and New Stockbridge missions. Here Morse personified the dual aims of mapping and missionizing. *Report on the Oneida, Stockbridge, and Brotherton Indians, 1796, by Jeremy Belknap and Jedidiah Morse* (Boston: Collection of the Massachusetts Historical Society, 1798, ser. 1, vol. 5, 12–32; reprint, New York: Museum of the American Indian, Heye Foundation, 1955).

32. Morse to his father, July 12, 1792, quoted in Brown, "The American Geographies," 170.

33. Morse, *American Universal Geography* (1812), 441.

34. For travel literature, see Pratt, *Imperial Eyes*; Mary B. Campbell, *The Witness and the Other World: Exotic European Travel Writing, 400–1600* (Ithaca: Cornell University Press, 1988); Georgia Frank, *The Memory of the Eyes: Pilgrims to Living Saints in Christian Late Antiquity* (Berkeley: University of California Press, 2000); Stephen Greenblatt, *Marvelous*

4. Geography Made Easy: Geographies and Travel Literature

Possessions: The Wonder of the New World (Chicago: University of Chicago Press, 1991); Peter Bishop, *The Myth of Shangri-La: Tibet Travel Writing and the Western Creation of Sacred Landscape* (Berkeley: University of California Press, 1989); Elsner and Robies, eds., *Voyages and Visions*; Dennis Porter, *Desire and Transgression in European Travel Writing* (Princeton: Princeton University Press, 1991); Philip Dodd, ed., *The Art of Travel: Essays on Travel Writing* (London: Frank Cass, 1982). For American travel literature, see Wayne Franklin, *Discoverers, Explorers, Settlers: The Diligent Writing of Early America* (Chicago: University of Chicago Press, 1979); Wayne Franklin, "Speaking and Touching: The Problem of Inexpressibility in American Travel Books," in Steven E. Kagle, ed., *America: Exploration and Travel*, 18–38 (Bowling Green, Ohio: Bowling Green State University Popular Press, 1979); Christopher Mulvey, *Anglo-American Landscapes: A Study of Nineteenth-Century Anglo-American Travel Literature* (Cambridge: Cambridge University Press, 1983); James Ronda, "Dreams and Discoveries: Exploring the American West, 1760–1850," *William and Mary Quarterly* 46 (January 1989): 145–62.

35. David Chidester, *Savage Systems: Colonialism and Comparative Religion in Southern Africa*, Studies in Religion and Culture (Charlottesville: University Press of Virginia, 1996), 6.

36. John [Jaś] Elsner, "From Pyramids to Pausanias and Piglet: Monuments, Travel and Writing," in Simon Goldhill and Robin Osborne, eds., *Art and Text in Ancient Greek Culture*, Cambridge Series in New Art History and Criticism (Cambridge: Cambridge University Press, 1994), 227.

37. Dwight, *A Journey*, 63.

38. Margaret Van Horn Dwight was raised by her grandmother Mary Edwards Dwight (daughter of Jonathan Edwards) in Northampton, Massachusetts. When her grandmother died in 1807, she moved to New Haven to live with her aunt Mary Edwards Dwight and her uncle William Walton Woolsey. Ibid., v.

39. Dr. Zerah Hawley, *A Journal of a Tour Through Connecticut, Massachusetts, New York, the North Part of Pennsylvania and Ohio, Including a Years Residence in the Part of the State of Ohio, Styled, New Connecticut, or Western Reserve, in Which is Given, A Description of the Country, Climate, Soil, Productions, Animals, Buildings, Manners of People, State of Society, Population &c. From Actual and Careful Observation* (New Haven: Printed by S. Converse, 1822), 59.

40. Edward Said, *Orientalism* (New York: Pantheon, 1978), 21. The form of writing resembled a fifteenth-century European tradition of "Instructions for Travelers," a genre that Joan-Pau Rubiés believes enabled the "intellectual elite to teach Europeans how to see the world." Joan-Pau Rubiés, "Instructions for Travelers: Teaching the Eye to See," *History and Anthropology* 9 (1996): 142.

41. Estwick Evans, *A Pedestrious Tour of Four Thousand Miles, through the Western States and Territories, during the Winter and Spring of 1818. Interspersed with Brief Reflections Upon a Great Variety of Topics: Religious, Moral, Political, Sentimental, &c., &c.* (Concord, N.H.: Joseph C. Spear, 1819).

42. Ibid., 102.

43. Ibid.

44. Here I obviously am indebted to the keen observations that Pratt made of many travel narratives in *Imperial Eyes*.

45. Evans, *A Pedestrious Tour*, 191.

46. Ibid.

47. Ibid.

48. Pratt, *Imperial Eyes*, 59.

49. John Melish, *Travels through the United States of America, in the Years 1806 & 1807 and 1809, 1810, & 1811; Including an Account of Passages Betwixt America and Britain, and travels through various parts of Britain, Ireland, & Canada. With corrections, and improvements, to 1815, and a set of new coloured maps* (Philadelphia: Thomas & George Palmer, 1815).

50. Melish's other published works include *A Geographical Description of the United States* (1816); *Information and Advice to Emigrants of the United States* (1819); *Travelers Directory through the United States* (1822).

51. Wheeler, *Visions of the Western Reserve*, 121.

52. Melish, *Travels in the United States of America*, 2:273.

53. As quoted in Wheeler, *Visions of the Western Reserve*, 120–122.

54. As quoted in ibid., 114.

55. Ibid., 115.

56. There are, of course, many geographical texts that focus on the West but are not travel narratives and do not embrace Morse's moral categories. See, for example, a geographical description of Connecticut's Western Reserve in Edmund Dana, *Geographical Sketches of the Western Country: Designed for Emigrants and Settlers* (Cincinnati: Looker, Reynolds and Co., 1819), 66, 70.

57. Numerous scholars write about the Garden of Eden metaphor and the American frontier. For example, see Leo Marx, *The Machine in the Garden: Technology and the Pastoral Ideal of America* (New York: Oxford University Press, 1964), 39–46; Roderick Nash, *Wilderness and the American Mind* (New Haven: Yale University Press, 1967), 15–43; Annette Kolodny, *The Land Before Her: Fantasy and Experience on the American Frontier, 1630–1860* (Chapel Hill: University of North Carolina Press, 1984), 9–13. For a specifically Puritan bifurcated vision of the frontier as "howling wilderness" or Garden of Eden, see Belden C. Lane, *Landscapes of the Sacred: Geography and Narrative in American Spirituality* (New York: Paulist Press, 1988), 114–23; Peter Carroll, *Puritanism in the Wilderness: The Intellectual Significance of the New England Frontier, 1629–1700* (New York: Columbia University Press, 1969); Alan Heimert, "Puritanism, the Wilderness, and the Frontier," *New England Quarterly* 26 (1953): 361–82; David R. Williams, *Wilderness Lost: The Religious Origins of the American Mind* (London and Toronto: Associated University Presses, 1987).

58. Henry Trumbull, *Western Emigration. Journal of Doctor Jeremiah Smipleton's* [sic] *Tour to Ohio. Containing An account of the numerous difficulties, Hair-breadth Escapes, Mortifications and Privations, which the Doctor and his family experienced on their Journey From Maine, to the "Land of Promise," and during a Residence of three years in that highly extolled country* (Boston: S. Sewall, 1819), 3.

59. There were many travel narratives, emigrant guides, and advice manuals aimed at Europeans hoping to settle in the West. For two illustrative examples, see John Noble, *Noble's Instructions to Emigrants. An Attempt to Give a Correct Account of the United States of America and Offer Some Information Which May be Useful to Those who Have a Wish to Emigrate to that Republic; and Particularly to those of the Poorer Class* (Boston: John Noble, 1819); John Melish, *Information and Advice to Emigrants to the United States*, reprinted in *Surveys for Travellers, Emigrants, and Others* (New York: Arno Press, 1976).

4. Geography Made Easy: Geographies and Travel Literature

60. John S. Wright, *Letters from the West; or a Caution to Emigrants: Being Facts and Observations Respecting the States of Ohio, Indiana, Illinois and Some Parts of New-York, Pennsylvania and Kentucky* (Salem, N.Y.: Dodd and Stevenson, 1819), v.
61. Ibid., vii.
62. Ibid., vi–vii.
63. Ibid., vii–viii.
64. Ibid., 21.
65. Ibid., 24.
66. Ibid., 52.
67. Ibid., 54.
68. Ibid., 23.
69. Ibid.
70. Ibid.,67.
71. Ibid., 67–68.
72. Hawley, *Journal of a Tour*.
73. Ibid., 4. Notice that Hawley's justification for publication mirrors Morse's in the introduction to *American Geography*.
74. Hawley, *Journal of a Tour*, 3.
75. Ibid., 46–47.
76. Ibid., 39.
77. Ibid., 38–40.
78. Ibid., 73.
79. Ibid.
80. Ibid., 27.
81. Ibid., 36.
82. Ibid., 37.
83. Ibid., 49–50.
84. Ibid., 56–57.
85. Ibid., 61.
86. Ibid., 35.
87. Ibid., 61.
88. Ibid., 58.
89. Ibid., 59.
90. Ibid., 71.
91. Ibid.
92. Ibid.
93. Ibid., 73, 71.
94. Ibid., 74.
95. Ibid., 40.
96. Trumbull, *Western Emigration*.
97. Ibid., 3.
98. Ibid., 6.
99. Ibid., 5.
100. Ibid., 19.
101. Ibid., 36.

102. Ibid., 27. Emphasis on truth in text.
103. As quoted in Wheeler, *Visions of the Western Reserve*, 196–97.
104. Ibid., 199.
105. Ibid.
106. David Griffiths, *Two Years' Residence in the New Settlements of Ohio, North America: With Directions to Emigrants* (London: Westley and Davis, J. Toller, 1835).
107. Griffiths, as quoted in Wheeler, *Visions of the Western Reserve*, 211.
108. Ibid.
109. John F. Schermerhorn and Samuel J. Mills, *A Correct View of that Part of the United States which Lies West of the Allegany Mountains: with Regard to Religion and Morals* (Hartford: Peter B. Gleason and Co., 1814). Their letters were excerpted and printed in the Massachusetts Missionary Society's journal the *Panoplist and Missionary Magazine* 9 (1813): 234; and the *Connecticut Evangelical Magazine* 6 (1813): 270.
110. Schermerhorn and Mills, *A Correct View*, 45.
111. Ibid., 2.
112. Ibid., 12.
113. Ibid., 11.
114. Ibid.
115. Ibid.
116. As quoted in Wheeler, *Visions of the Western Reserve*, 130.
117. Ibid., 129.

5. A Beacon in the Wildernes: Moral Inscriptions on the Landscape

1. Robert Samuel Fletcher, *A History of Oberlin College from Its Foundations to the Civil War* (Oberlin: Oberlin College, 1943), 1:71.
2. John Jay Shipherd to his parents, May 11, 1830, Fletcher Papers.
3. John Jay Shipherd to his father, April 6, 1831, Fletcher Papers.
4. John Jay Shipherd to his mother, September 3, 1832, John Jay Shipherd Letters.
5. John Jay Shipherd to his brother, March 14, 1831, Fletcher Papers.
6. Ibid.
7. Ibid.
8. The Oberlin Colony was named after Jean Frederic Oberlin (1740–1826), who was renowned for sacrificing worldly advantages to minister for sixty years in an impoverished area of Alsace. Oberlin came to Shipherd's attention by way of a biographical pamphlet published in 1830 by the American Sunday School Union, titled *The Life of John Frederic Oberlin, Pastor of Waldbach, in the Ban de la Roche.*
9. John Jay Shipherd to his parents, August 6, 1832, John Jay Shipherd Letters.
10. Ibid.
11. Covenant of the Oberlin Colony, Deeds and Other Legal and Historical Documents.
12. Ibid.
13. Ibid.
14. Philo P. Stewart to John Jay Shipherd, February 4, 1833, quoted in James H.

5. A Beacon in the Wilderness: Moral Inscriptions on the Landscape 213

Fairchild, *Oberlin: The Colony and the College* (Oberlin: E. J. Goodrich, 1883), 305–9. Stewart noted that "Mr. C," a Western Reserve College agent, was speaking out against the Oberlin Institute because he feared losing income to supporters of it.

15. Oberlin Colonists Meeting, August 18, 1837, Minutes, 154.

16. First Circular for the Oberlin Collegiate Institute, March 8, 1834, Fletcher Papers.

17. Philo P. Stewart to Fayette Shipherd, May 21, 1833, quoted in Fairchild, *Oberlin*, 311.

18. John Jay Shipherd to his parents, August 6, 1832, John Jay Shipherd Letters. Shipherd states in this letter that men will work four hours to defray all costs, and women working at the spinning wheels and looms will cover most of their expenses.

19. Fairchild, *Oberlin*, 43. James Fairchild was the president of Oberlin College from 1866 to 1889.

20. Arthur Tappan to John Jay Shipherd, June 15, 1835, Fletcher Papers.

21. Ibid.

22. Ibid.

23. T. S. Ingersoll to the Board of Trust for the Oberlin College Institute, March 9, 1836, Fletcher Papers.

24. Ibid.

25. Ibid.

26. Ibid.

27. Ibid. Ingersoll references Asher Benjamin. See note 102 in chapter 3.

28. In 1835 Charles G. Finney moved to Oberlin to set up the institute's Theological Department and to serve as pastor of the First Congregational Church (1836–1875). During his forty-year residence, he was professor of systematic theology (1835–1858) and professor of pastoral theology (1835–1875). In 1851 he succeeded Asa Mahan to become the college's second president, and he held that position until his resignation in 1865.

29. This was particularly appealing to New England young women who, from the college's inception, were granted admission.

30. Besides the Grand River Presbytery and the Portage Presbytery, the Huron Presbytery was organized in 1823. Grand River ministers included Joseph Badger, Harvey Coe, Giles Cowles, Nathan Derrow, Luther Humphrey, Jonathan Lesslie, and Randolph Stone. Portage ministers included William Hanford and John Seward. Huron ministers included Daniel Lathrop and Simeon Woodruff.

31. William Hanford to Connecticut Missionary Society, November 29, 1826, William Hanford Letters, Connecticut Missionary Society Papers.

32. Randolph Stone to Connecticut Missionary Society, January 7, 1825, Randolph Stone Letters, Connecticut Missionary Society Papers.

33. Colin B. Goodykoontz, *Home Missions on the American Frontier* (Caldwell, Idaho: Caxton Printers, 1939), 172–73.

34. John Seward to Connecticut Missionary Society, February 24, 1826, John Seward Letters, Connecticut Missionary Society Papers.

35. Giles Cowles to Connecticut Missionary Society, September 29, 1825, Giles Cowles Letters, Connecticut Missionary Society Papers.

36. John Seward to Connecticut Missionary Society, April 19, 1822, John Seward Letters, Connecticut Missionary Society Papers.

37. John Seward, "Report to Trustees of the College," quoted in William S. Kennedy,

The Plan of Union; or, a History of the Presbyterian and Congregational Churches of the Western Reserve (Hudson, Ohio: Pentagon Stream Press, 1856), 237.

38. Randolph Stone to Connecticut Missionary Society, November 12, 1825, Randolph Stone Letters, Connecticut Missionary Society Papers. "The materials are principally ready for erecting a college edifice. . . . The work is to be commenced early in the spring."

39. Simeon Woodruff to Connecticut Missionary Society, May 20, 1824, Simeon Woodruff Letters, Connecticut Missionary Society Letters.

40. Goodykoontz, *Home Missions*, 378.

41. William Hanford to Connecticut Missionary Society, November 19, 1827, William Hanford Letters, Connecticut Missionary Society Papers.

42. William Hanford to Connecticut Missionary Society, December 21, 1832, William Hanford Letters, Connecticut Missionary Society Papers.

43. Ibid.
44. Ibid.
45. Ibid.

46. William Hanford to Connecticut Missionary Society, January 29, 1833, William Hanford Letters, Connecticut Missionary Society Papers.

47. Ibid.
48. Ibid.

49. William Hanford to Horace Hooker, December 13, 1834, William Hanford Letters, Connecticut Missionary Society Papers.

50. Kennedy, *The Plan of Union*.
51. Ibid., 7.
52. Ibid., 11.
53. Ibid., 19.
54. Ibid., 63.
55. Ibid., 224.
56. Ibid., 244.
57. Ibid., 247.

58. John Keep, *Congregationalism, and Church-Action: With the Principles of Christian Union, etc.* (New York: S. W. Benedict & Co., 1845).

59. Ibid., 48.
60. Ibid., 76.
61. Ibid., 66.
62. Ibid., 68.
63. Ibid., 77.

64. Reverend Delavan L. Leonard, *A Century of Congregationalism in Ohio* (Oberlin: Pierce and Randolph, 1896), 35.

65. Ibid., 36.
66. Ibid., 37.
67. Ibid.
68. Ibid., 53.
69. Ibid.

70. Stewart H. Holbrook, *The Yankee Exodus: An Account of Migration from New England* (Seattle: University of Washington, 1968), 39.

71. Ibid.

Conclusion: Moral Geography

1. James A. Garfield, "Discovery and Ownership of the Northwest Territory and Settlement of the Western Reserve." An Address Delivered at Burton, before the Historical Society of Geauga County, O., September 16, 1873. Tract 20, *Western Reserve and Northern Ohio Historical Society Proceedings* (Cleveland: Western Reserve Historical Society, 1874).

Bibliography

Primary Sources

Manuscript Collections

WESTERN RESERVE HISTORICAL SOCIETY, CLEVELAND, OHIO

Missionaries

    Joseph Badger. Papers.
    John G. Heckewelder. Papers.
    John Seward. Papers.
    Randolph Stone. Papers.

Land Surveyors and Speculators

    Moses Cleaveland Papers.
    Connecticut Land Company. Records.
    Seth I. Ensign. Papers.
    John Milton Holley. Papers.
    Turhand Kirtland. Papers.
    William Law, Jr. Papers.
    Seth Pease. Papers.
    Abraham Skinner. Papers.
    Abraham Tappan. Papers.
    Elisha Whittlesey. Papers.

Settlers

    David Abbott Family. Papers.
    Quintus F. Atkins. Papers.
    William Eldredge. Papers.
    Jonathan Hale. Papers.
    David Hudson. Papers.
    Jonathan Law. Papers.
    James Newton. Papers.

Church Records

Presbytery of Grand River, Ohio.
Presbytery of Portage, Ohio.
First Congregational Church of Hudson.

Maps

Amos Spafford. Map of Cleveland (1796).
Seth Pease. "A Map of the Connecticut Western Reserve, from Actual Survey" (1797).
Western Reserve portion of the map of Ohio in John Melish, *Travels in the United States* (1812).
"Map of the Western Reserve, including the Firelands in Ohio" (1826).
Map of the County Seat, Huron.
Map of Chardon in the County of Geauga Ohio.
Heckewelder Map, 1796.

The Connecticut Conference Archives, United Church of Christ, Hartford, Connecticut

Connecticut Missionary Society Papers.

Incoming Correspondences.
Outgoing Correspondences.
Minutes.
Board of Trustees' Annual Reports.

Missionary Letters.

Joseph Badger
Thomas Barr
Calvin Chapin
Ezekiel Chapman
Giles Cowles
William Hanford
Luther Humphrey
Jonathan Lesslie
Thomas Robbins
Abraham Scott
John Seward
Randolph Stone
Simeon Woodruff

Connecticut Historical Society, Hartford, Connecticut.

The Robbins Family. Papers.

Bibliography

THE NEWBERRY LIBRARY, CHICAGO, ILLINOIS.

"An Exact Mapp of New England and New York."

OBERLIN COLLEGE ARCHIVES, OBERLIN, OHIO

Deeds and Other Legal and Historical Documents

John Jay Shipherd. Letters.
Robert S. Fletcher. Papers.
Charles Grandison Finney. Papers.
Oberlin Colonists' Meeting Minutes.

Map

"A Plan of Oberin Colony, 1835."

BEINECKE RARE BOOK AND MANUSCRIPT LIBRARY, YALE UNIVERSITY, NEW HAVEN, CONNECTICUT

Jonathan Edwards. Papers.

STERLING LIBRARY, MAP COLLECTION, NEW HAVEN, CONNECTICUT.

James Wadsworth. "A Plan of the Town of New Haven." 1748.

Maps Cited

de Champlain, Samuel. "Carte Geographique de la Novvelle Franse." 1613. An original is housed in the Collections Division, Library of Congress. A reproduction is printed in Seymour I. Schwartz and Ralph E. Ehrenberg, *The Mapping of America*. New York: Abrams, 1980.
Evans, Lewis. "General Map of the Middle British Colonies in North America." The original map was published in Philadelphia in 1755 in Evans's *Geographical, Historical, Political, Philosophical and Mechanical Essays*. It was republished a year later, with corrections, in Thomas Pownall, *A Topographical Description of Such Parts of North America as are Contained in the (Annexed) Map of the Middle British Colonies &c in North America*. London: Printed for J. Almon, 1776. An original is housed in the Newberry Library, Chicago.
Mitchell, John. "A Map of the British and French Dominions in America, with the Roads, Distances, Limits, and Extent of the Settlements." 1755. An original is housed in the Collections Division, Library of Congress.
Morden, Robert (?). "An Exact Mapp of New England and New York." An original is housed in the Ayer Collection, the Newberry Library, Chicago. A reproduction is

printed in William P. Cumming, *British Maps of Colonial America*. The Kenneth Nebenzahl, Jr., Lectures in the History of Cartography. Chicago: University of Chicago Press, 1974.

Rotz, Jean Nicolas. "Map of North America and West Indies." 1542. An original is housed in the Department of Manuscripts, British Library, London. A reproduction is printed in Seymour I. Schwartz and Ralph E. Ehrenberg, *The Mapping of America*. New York: Abrams, 1980.

Speed, John. *A Prospect for the Most Famous Parts of the World*. London: M. F. for William Humble, 1646. This text is located in the Beinecke Rare Book and Manuscript Library, Yale University, New Haven, Connecticut.

Vallard, Nicolas. "North America." 1547. An original is housed in the Henry Huntington Library and Art Gallery. A reproduction is printed in John A. Wolter and Ronald Grim, *Images of the World*. Washington, D.C.: Library of Congress, 1997.

Newspapers and Journals

Connecticut Courant (Hartford, Connecticut).
Connecticut Evangelical Magazine (Hartford, Connecticut), 1800–1807.
Connecticut Evangelical Magazine & Religious Intelligencer (Hartford, Connecticut), 1808–1815.
Panoplist and Missionary Magazine (Boston).
Western Missionary Magazine (Pittsburgh).

Published Reports, Sermons, and Addresses

Board of Trustees of the Connecticut Missionary Society. *An Annual Report From the Trustees of the Missionary Society of Connecticut*. Hartford: Peter B. Gleason and Co., June 1, 1809.

———. *Annual Report of the Missionary Society of Connecticut Trustees*. Hartford: Hudson and Goodwin, June 12, 1820.

Board of Trustees of the Missionary Society of Connecticut. *The Constitution of the Missionary Society of Connecticut: With an Address from the Board of Trustees, to the People of the State, and a Narrative on the Subject of Missions. To Which is Subjoined a Statement on the Funds of the Society*. Hartford: Hudson and Goodwin, 1800.

Dwight, Timothy. *An Address to the Emigrants from Connecticut, And From New England Generally, in the New Settlements in the United States*. Hartford: Peter B. Gleason & Co., 1817.

———. *A Second Address from the Trustees of the Missionary Society of Connecticut, to the People of the State, and a Narrative on the Subject of Missions. To Which is Subjoined a Statement of the Funds of the Society, to the End of the Year 1800*. Hartford: Hudson and Goodwin, 1801. The society published annual addresses for thirty years, with varying titles. All addresses hereafter referred to as *Narrative of Missions*, with the publication date.

———. *A Summary of Christian Doctrine and Practice: Designed Especially, for the Use of the*

People in the New Settlements of the United States of America. By the Trustees of the Missionary Society of Connecticut. Hartford: Hudson and Goodwin, 1804.
General Association. *An Address to the Inhabitants of New Settlements in the Northern and Western Parts of the United States.* New Haven: T & S Green, 1795.
General Association of Connecticut. *A Narrative of the Missions to the New Settlements, According to the Appointment of the General Association of the State of Connecticut; Together with an Account of the Receipts and Expenditures of the Money Contributed by the People of Connecticut in May 1793, for the Support of the Missionaries, According to an Act of the General Assembly of the State.* New Haven: T & S Green, 1794.
———. *A Continuation of the Narrative of the Missions to the New Settlements...* New Haven, 1795.
———. *A Continuation of the Narrative of the Missions to the New Settlements...* New Haven, 1797.
Strong, Reverend Cyprian. *A Sermon, Preached at Hartford, before the Board of Trustees, of the Missionary Society, in Connecticut. At the Ordination, of the Rev. Jedidiah Bushnell as a Missionary to the New Settlements; January 15th, A.D. 1800.* Hartford: Hudson and Goodwin, 1800.

Published Primary Sources

Badger, Reverend Joseph. *A Memoir of Reverend Joseph Badger, Containing an Autobiography, and Selections from his Private Journal and Correspondence.* Hudson, Ohio: Sawyer, Ingersoll, 1851.
Beecher, Lyman. *A Plea for the West.* Cincinnati: Truman and Smith, 1835.
Benjamin, Asher. *American Builder's Companion or, a System of Architecture Particularly Adapted to the Present Style of Building.* R.P.& C. Williams, 1827. Reprint, 6th ed., New York: Diver Publications, 1969.
Brunson, Alfred. "The History of Methodism on the Connecticut Western Reserve, Ohio." *Methodist Magazine and Quarterly Review* 14 (1832): 255–74.
Cartwright, Peter. *Autobiography of Peter Cartwright, the Backwoods Preacher.* Edited by W. P. Strickland. Cincinnati: L. Swormstedt and A. Poe for the Methodist Episcopal Church, 1859.
Cowles, Henry. *A Defence of Ohio Congregationalism and of Oberlin College in Reply to Kennedy's Plan of Union.* Oberlin: N.p., 1856.
Dana, Edmund. *Geographical Sketches of the Western Country: Designed for Emigrants and Settlers.* Cincinnati: Looker, Reynolds and Co., 1819.
Darlington, William M., ed. *Christopher Gist's Journals with Historical, Geographical and Ethnological Notes and Biographies of his Contemporaries.* Pittsburgh: J. R. Weldin & Co., 1893.
Doddridge, Philip. *A Plain and Serious Address to the Master of a Family on the Important Subject of Family Religion.* Reprinted for the Use of the trustees of the Missionary Society. Hartford: John Babcock, 1799.
Dwight, Margaret Van Horn. *A Journey to Ohio in 1810.* Edited by Max Farrand. Yale Historical Manuscript Series. Vol. 1. New Haven: Yale University Press, 1912.

Edwards, Jonathan. *The Life of David Brainerd*. Vol. 7 of *The Works of Jonathan Edwards, 1703–1758*. Edited by Norman Pettit. New Haven: Yale University Press, 1985.

Ellsworth, Henry Leavitt. *A Tour of New Connecticut in 1811: The Narrative of Henry Leavitt Ellsworth*. Edited by Philip R. Shriver. Western Reserve History Studies Series. Vol. 1. Cleveland: Western Reserve Historical Society, 1985.

Evans, Estwick. *A Pedestrious Tour of Four Thousand Miles, through the Western States and Territories, during the Winter and Spring of 1818. Interspersed with Brief Reflections Upon a Great Variety of Topics: Religious, Moral, Political, Sentimental, &c., &c.* Concord, N.H.: Joseph C. Spear, 1819.

Fairchild, James H. *Oberlin: The Colony and the College*. Oberlin: E. J. Goodrich, 1883.

Flint, Abel. *A System of Geometry and Trigonometry: Together With a Treatise on Surveying: Teaching Various Ways of Taking the Survey of a Field; Also to Protract the Same and Find the Area. Likewise, Rectangular Surveying; or, An Accurate Method of Calculating the Area of Any Field Arithmetically, Without the Necessity of Plotting it*. Hartford: Printed for Oliver D. Cooke, by Lincoln and Gleason, 1804.

Garfield, James A. "Discovery and Ownership of the Northwest Territory, and Settlement of the Western Reserve." An Address Delivered at Burton, before the Historical Society of Geauga County, O., September 16, 1873. *Western Reserve and Northern Ohio Historical Society Proceedings*. Tract 20. Cleveland: Western Reserve Historical Society, 1874.

Griffiths, D. *Two Years' Residence in the New Settlements of Ohio, North America: With Directions to Emigrants*. London: Westley and Davis, 1835.

Hawley, Dr. Zerah. *A Journal of a Tour Through Connecticut, Massachusetts, New York, the North Part of Pennsylvania and Ohio, Including a Years Residence in the Part of the State of Ohio, Styled, New Connecticut, or Western Reserve, in Which is Given, A Description of the Country, Climate, Soil, Productions, Animals, Buildings, Manners of People, State of Society, Population, &c. From Actual and Careful Observation*. New Haven: Printed by S. Converse, 1822.

Hudson, David. "Some Accounts of the Religious Exercises of David Hudson." *Western Missionary Magazine* 1 (1803): 166.

Keep, John. *Congregationalism, and Church-Action: with the Principles of Christian Union, etc*. New York: S. W. Benedict & Co., 1845.

Kennedy, William S. *The Plan of Union; or, a History of the Presbyterian and Congregational Churches of the Western Reserve*. Hudson, Ohio: Pentagon Stream Press, 1856.

Leonard, Delavan L. *A Century of Congregationalism in Ohio*. Oberlin: Pierce and Randolph, 1896.

Love, John. *Geodaesia: Or, The Art of Surveying and Measuring of Land Made Easy*. London: W. Innys and J. Richardson, 1753.

Mather, Cotton. *Magnalia Christi Americana; Or, The Ecclesiastical History of New England; From its First Planting, in the Year 1620, Unto the Year of Our Lord 1698: In Seven Books*. 1st American ed., from London ed. of 1702. Hartford: Silas Andrus, 1820. Reprint, New York, Russell and Russell, 1967.

Melish, John. *Information and Advice to Emigrants to the United States: and from the Eastern and Western States*. Philadelphia: John Melish, 1819. Reprinted in *Surveys for Travellers, Emigrants, and Others*. New York: Arno Press, 1976.

———. *Travels through the United States of America, in the Years 1806 & 1807 and 1809, 1810, & 1811; Including an Account of Passages Betwixt America and Britain, and travels* through various parts of Britain, Ireland, & Canada. With corrections, and improvements, to 1815, and a set of new coloured maps. 2 vols. Philadelphia: Thomas & George Palmer, 1812.

Mills, Samuel J., and Daniel Smith. *Report of a Missionary Tour Through that Part of the United States Which Lies West of the Allegany Mountains; Performed Under the Direction of the Massachusetts Missionary Society*. Andover: Flagg and Gould, 1815.

Morse, Jedidiah. *The American Geography; Or, A View of the Present Situation of the United States of America*. Elizabethtown: Shepard Kollock, 1789. Reprint, New York: Arno Press, 1970.

Noble, John. *Noble's Instructions to Emigrants. An Attempt to Give a Correct Account of the United States of America and Offer Some Information Which May be Useful to Those who Have a Wish to Emigrate to that Republic; and Particularly to those of the Poorer Class*. Boston: John Noble, 1819.

Norden, John. *The Surveyors Dialogue: Divided into Five Books: very profitable for all Men to Peruse, that have to do with the Revenues of land, or the manurance, use, or occupation thereof, both Lords and tenants: as also and especially for such as indevor to be seen in the faculty of Surveying all mannors, lands, tenements, &c*. London: Hugh Ally, 1607.

Robbins, Thomas. *Diary of Thomas Robbins, D.D. 1796–1854*. 2 vols. Edited by Increase N. Tarbox. Boston: Beacon, 1886.

Schermerhorn, John F., and Samuel J. Mills. *A Correct View of that Part of the United States Which Lies West of the Allegany Mountains, with Regard to Religion and Morals*. Hartford: Peter B. Gleason and Co., 1814.

Shriver, Philip R., ed. *A Tour of New Connecticut in 1811: The Narrative of Henry Leavitt Ellsworth*. Western Reserve History Studies Series. Vol. 1. Cleveland: Western Reserve Historical Society, 1985.

Speed, John. *A Prospect for the Most Famous Parts of the World*. London: M.F. for William Humble, 1646.

Trumbull, Henry. *Western Emigration. Journal of Doctor Jeremiah Smipleton's [sic] Tour to Ohio. Containing An account of the numerous difficulties, Hair-breadth Escapes, Mortifications and Privations, which the Doctor and his family experienced on their Journey From Maine, to the "Land of Promise," and during a Residence of three years in that highly extolled country*. Boston: S. Sewall, 1819.

Williston, Seth. *An Address to Parents, Upon the Importance of Religiously Educating Their Children*. Suffield, Conn.: Edward Gray, 1799.

Wright, John S. *Letters from the West; or a Caution to Emigrants: Being Facts and Observations Respecting the States of Ohio, Indiana, Illinois and Some Parts of New-York, Pennsylvania and Kentucky*. Salem, N.Y.: Dodd and Stevenson, 1819.

Secondary Sources

Albanese, Catherine L. *Nature Religion in America: From the Algonkian Indians to the New Age*. Chicago: University of Chicago Press, 1990.

Allen, David Grayson. *In English Ways: The Movement of Societies and the Transferral of English Local Law and Custom to Massachusetts Bay in the Seventeenth Century*. New York: Norton, 1982.

Anderson, Benedict R. O'G. *Imagined Communities: Reflections on the Origin and Spread of Nationalism.* Rev. ed. London: Verso, 1991.
Axtell, James. *The Invasion Within: The Contest of Cultures in Colonial North America.* New York: Oxford University Press, 1985.
Bachelard, Gaston. *The Poetics of Space.* Translated by Maria Jolas. New York: Orion, 1964.
Bagrow, Leo. *History of Cartography.* Chicago: Precedent Publishing, 1985.
Baker, Alan R., and Gideon Biger, eds. *Ideology and Landscape in Historical Perspective.* Cambridge: Cambridge University Press, 1992.
Baker, Norman B. *Early Homes of New England.* Rutland: Charles E. Tuttle, 1967.
Barton, Rev. W. B. "Early Ecclesiastical History of the Western Reserve." *Ohio Church History Society Papers.* Vol. 1. Oberlin: Oberlin College Press, 1899.
Basso, Keith H. "'Stalking with Stories': Names, Places, and Moral Narratives Among the Western Apache." In Daniel Halpern, ed., *On Nature: Nature, Landscape, and Natural History.* San Francisco: North Point, 1987.
Beasley, James R. "Emerging Republicanism and the Standing Order: The Appropriation Act Controversy in Connecticut, 1793 to 1795." *William and Mary Quarterly,* 3d ser., 29 (1972): 587–610.
Benes, Peter, ed. *New England Meeting House and Church: 1630–1850.* Boston: Boston University Press, 1979.
Berkhofer, Robert F. *Salvation and the Savage: An Analysis of Protestant Missions and the American Indian Response, 1787–1862.* Lexington: University of Kentucky Press, 1965.
———. *The White Man's Indian: Images of the American Indian from Columbus to the Present.* New York: Knopf, 1978.
Bercovitch, Sacvan. *The American Jeremiad.* Madison: University of Wisconsin Press, 1978.
Best, Sue. "Sexualizing Space." In Elizabeth Grosz and Elspeth Probyn, eds., *Sexy Bodies: The Strange Carnalities of Feminism.* New York: Routledge, 1995.
Bishop, Peter. *The Myth of Shangri-La: Tibet Travel Writing and the Western Creation of Sacred Landscape.* Berkeley: University of California Press, 1989.
Bobersky, Alexander T., and David T. Stephens. "Early Towns in the Western Reserve: A Perspective from the Late Nineteenth Century." *Pioneer America Society Transactions* 9 (1986): 53–56.
Bonin, Erin Lang. "Worlds of Their Own: Seventeenth-Century British Women Writers Envision Utopia." Ph.D. diss., University of North Carolina at Chapel Hill, 1998.
Bourdieu, Pierre. *Outline of a Theory of Practice.* Translated by Richard Nice. Cambridge: Cambridge University Press, 1977.
Bowden, Henry Warner. *American Indians and Christian Missions: Studies in Cultural Conflict.* Chicago: University of Chicago Press, 1981.
Braude, Ann. "Women's History Is American Religious History." In Thomas A. Tweed, ed., *Retelling U.S. Religious History.* Berkeley: University of California Press, 1997.
Brauer, Jerald C. "Regionalism and Religion in America." *Church History* 54 (1985): 366–78.
Brown, Ralph H. "The American Geographies of Jedidiah Morse." *Annals of the Association of American Geographers* 31 (1941): 145–217.
Brükner, Martin. "Lessons in Geography: Maps, Spellers, and Other Grammars of Nationalism in the Early Republic." *American Quarterly* 51, no. 2 (June 1999): 311–343.
Buisseret, David. *Rural Images: The Estate Plan in the Old and New Worlds.* Chicago: Newberry Library, 1988.

Buley, R. Carlyle. *The Old Northwest: Pioneer Period, 1825–1840*. Bloomington: Indiana University Press, 1962.
Bushman, Richard L. *The Refinement of America: Persons, Houses, Cities*. New York: Vintage, 1993.
—, ed. *The Great Awakening: Documents on the Revival of Religion, 1740–1745*. Chapel Hill: University of North Carolina Press, 1989.
Butler, Jon. *Awash in a Sea of Faith: Christianizing the American People*. Cambridge: Harvard University Press, 1990.
Bynum, Caroline Walker. *Fragmentation and Redemption: Essays on Gender and the Human Body in Medieval Religion*. New York: Zone Books, 1991.
Campbell, Mary B. *The Witness and the Other World: Exotic European Travel Writing, 400–1600*. Ithaca: Cornell University Press, 1988.
Candee, Richard M. "Land Surveys of William and John Godsoe of Kittery, Maine: 1689–1769." In Peter Benes, ed., *New England Prospect: Maps, Place Names, and the Historical Landscape*. The Annual Proceedings of the Dublin Seminar for New England Folklife. Vol. 5. Boston: Boston University Press, 1980.
Cardinal, Eric J. "New England and the Western Reserve in the Nineteenth Century: Some Suggestions." In Harry F. Lupold and Gladys Haddad, eds., *Ohio's Western Reserve: A Regional Reader*. Kent, Ohio: Kent State University Press, 1988.
Carroll, Peter. *Puritanism in the Wilderness: The Intellectual Significance of the New England Frontier, 1629–1700*. New York: Columbia University Press, 1969.
Cayton, Andrew R. L. *The Midwest and the Nation: Rethinking the History of an American Region*. Bloomington: Indiana University Press, 1990.
Chapman, Edmund H. *Cleveland: Village to Metropolis, A Case Study of the Problems of Urban Development in Nineteenth-Century America*. Cleveland: Western Reserve Historical Society, 1964.
Chappell, Edward A. "Housing a Nation: The Transformation of Living Standards in Early America." In Cary Carson, Robert Hoffman, and Peter J. Albert, eds., *Of Consuming Interests*. Charlottesville: University of Virginia Press, 1994.
Cherry, Peter P. *The Western Reserve and Early Ohio*. Akron: R. L. Fouse, 1921.
Chidester, David. *Salvation and Suicide: An Interpretation of Jim Jones, the Peoples Temple, and Jonestown*. Bloomington: Indiana University Press, 1991.
——. *Savage Systems: Colonialism and Comparative Religion in Southern Africa*. Studies in Religion and Culture. Charlottesville: University Press of Virginia, 1996.
Chidester, David, and Edward T. Linenthal, eds. *American Sacred Space*. Bloomington: Indiana University Press, 1995.
Clark, Joseph B. *Leavening the Nation: The Story of American Home Missionaries*. New York, 1903.
Colomina, Beatriz, ed. *Sexuality and Space*. Princeton Papers on Architecture. Princeton: Princeton Architectural Press, 1992.
Conforti, Joseph A. *Jonathan Edwards, Religious Tradition, and American Culture*. Chapel Hill: University of North Carolina Press, 1995.
——. "Jonathan Edwards's Most Popular Work: 'The Life of David Brainerd and Nineteenth-Century Evangelical Culture.'" *Church History* 54 (June 1985): 188–201.
Conlin, Mary Lou. *Simon Perkins of the Western Reserve*. Cleveland: Western Reserve Historical Society, 1968.

Cosgrove, Denis E. *Social Formations and Symbolic Landscapes.* London: Croom Helm, 1984.
Cosgrove, Denis E., and Stephen Daniels, eds. *The Iconography of Landscape: Essays on Symbolic Representation, Design, and Use of Past Environments.* Cambridge: Cambridge University Press, 1986.
Creel, Margaret Washington. *"A Peculiar People": Slave Religion and Community Culture Among the Gullahs.* New York: New York University Press, 1988.
Cronon, William. *Changes in the Land: Indians, Colonists, and the Ecology of New England.* New York: Hill and Wang, 1983.
Cumming, William P. *British Maps of Colonial America.* Chicago: University of Chicago Press, 1974.
Davis, David Brion. *The Fear of Conspiracy: Images of Un-American Subversion from the Revolution to the Present.* Ithaca: Cornell University Press, 1971.
———. "Some Themes of Countersubversion; An Analysis of Anti-Masonic, Anti-Catholic, and Anti-Mormon Literature." *Mississippi Valley Historical Review* 47 (1960): 205–24.
De Certeau, Michel. *The Practice of Everyday Life.* Translated by Steven Rendall. Berkeley: University of California Press, 1984.
———. *The Writing of History.* Translated by Tom Conley. New York: Columbia University Press, 1988.
Denzin, Norman K. *Symbolic Interactionism and Cultural Studies: The Politics of Interpretation.* Cambridge, Eng.: Blackwell, 1992.
Dillon, Timothy. "Jedidiah Morse's Christian Republicanism: Reform and the Young Nation." Ph.D. diss., University of Wisconsin–Madison, 1987.
Dodd, Philip, ed. *The Art of Travel: Essays on Travel Writing.* London: Frank Cass, 1982.
Douglas, Mary. *Purity and Danger: An Analysis of Concepts of Pollution and Taboo.* New York: Praeger, 1966.
Earle, Carville. *Geographical Inquiry and American Historical Problems.* Stanford, Calif.: Stanford University Press, 1992.
———. "Regional and Economic Development West of the Appalachians, 1815–1860." In Robert D. Mitchell and Paul A. Groves, eds., *North America: The Historical Geography of a Changing Continent.* Totowa: Rowman and Littlefield, 1987.
Edney, Matthew H. *Mapping an Empire: The Geographical Construction of British India, 1765–1843.* Chicago: University of Chicago Press, 1997.
Eliade. Mircea. *The Sacred and the Profane: The Nature of Religion.* Translated by Willard R. Trask. New York: Harcourt, Brace, Jovanovich, 1959.
Elsbree, Oliver Wendell. *The Rise of the Missionary Spirit in America, 1790–1815.* Williamsport, Pa., 1928.
Elsner, Jaś, and Joan-Pau Rubies, eds. *Voyages and Visions: Towards a Cultural History of Travel.* London: Reaktion, 1999.
Emlen, Robert P. *Shaker Village Views: Illustrated Maps and Landscape Drawings by Shaker Artists of the Nineteenth Century.* Hanover, N.H.: University Press of New England, 1987.
Etulain, Richard W., ed. *Writing Western History: Essays on Major Western Historians.* Albuquerque: University of New Mexico Press, 1991.
Fairbanks, Jonathan L., and Robert F. Trent, eds. *New England Begins: The Seventeenth Century.* Vol. 1. *Introduction/Migration and Settlement.* Boston: Museum of Fine Arts, 1982.

Feher, Michel, ed. *Fragments for a History of the Human Body*. 3 vols. New York: Zone Publishing, 1989.
Fish, Stanley. *Is There a Text in This Class? The Authority of Interpretive Communities*. Cambridge: Harvard University Press, 1980.
Fletcher, Anthony. *Gender, Sex, and Subordination in England, 1500–1800*. New Haven: Yale University Press, 1995.
Fletcher, Robert Samuel. *A History of Oberlin College from Its Foundation to the Civil War*. 2 vols. Oberlin: Oberlin College, 1943.
Foucault, Michel. *Discipline and Punish: The Birth of the Prison*. Translated by Alan Sheridan. New York: Vintage, 1979.
———. *History of Sexuality*. Vol. 1. *An Introduction*. Translated by Robert Hurley. New York: Vintage, 1980.
———. "Of Other Spaces." *Diacritics* 16 (Spring 1986): 22–27.
———. "Space, Knowledge, and Power." In Paul Rabinow, ed,. *The Foucault Reader*. New York: Pantheon, 1984.
Francaviglia, Richard V. *The Mormon Landscape: Existence, Creation, and Perception of a Unique Image in the American West*. New York: AMS Press, 1978.
Frank, Georgia. *The Memory of the Eyes: Pilgrims to Living Saints in Christian Late Antiquity*. Berkeley: University of California Press, 2000.
Franklin, Wayne. *Discoverers, Explorers, Settlers: The Diligent Writing of Early America*. Chicago: University of Chicago Press, 1979.
Frary, I. T. *Ohio in Homespun and Calico*. Richmond: Garrett and Massie, 1942.
Fraser, James W. *Schooling the Preachers: The Development of Protestant Theological Education in the United States, 1740–1875*. Lanham, Md.: University Press of America, 1988.
French, David. "Puritan Conservatism and the Frontier: The Elizur Wright Family on the Connecticut Western Reserve." *Old Northwest* 1 (1975): 85–95.
Gaustad, Edwin. *Historical Atlas of Religion in America*. New York: Harper and Row, 1962.
Geertz, Clifford. *The Interpretation of Cultures: Selected Essays*. New York: Basic Books, 1973.
Giedion, Sigfried. *Space, Time, and Architecture: The Growth of a New Tradition*. Cambridge: Harvard University Press, 1947.
Goldhill, Simon, and Robin Osborne, eds. *Art and Text in Ancient Greek Culture*. Cambridge Series in New Art History and Criticism. Cambridge: Cambridge University Press, 1994.
Goodykoontz, Colin B. *Home Missions on the American Frontier*. Caldwell, Idaho: Caxton Printers, 1939.
Gravan, Anthony N. B. *Architecture and Town Planning in Colonial Connecticut*. New Haven: Yale University Press, 1951.
Greenblatt, Stephen. *Marvelous Possessions: The Wonder of the New World*. Chicago: University of Chicago Press, 1991.
Greene, John C. *American Science in the Age of Jefferson*. Ames: Iowa State University Press, 1984.
Gregory, Derek. *Geographical Imaginations*. Cambridge: Cambridge University Press, 1994.
Gregory, Derek, and John Urry, eds. *Social Relations and Spatial Structures*. New York: St. Martin's, 1985.

Grosz, Elizabeth. *Space, Time, and Perversion: Essays on the Politics of the Body.* New York: Routledge, 1995.
Gutiérrez, Ramón. *When Jesus Came the Corn Mothers Went Away: Marriage, Sexuality, and Power in New Mexico, 1500–1846.* Stanford, Calif.: Stanford University Press, 1991.
Gutiérrez, Ramón, and Genevieve Fabre, eds. *Feasts and Celebrations in North American Ethnic Communities.* Albuquerque: University of New Mexico, 1995.
Habermas, Jürgen. *The Structural Transformation of the Public Sphere: An Inquiry Into the Category of Bourgeois Society.* Translated by Thomas Burger. Cambridge: MIT Press, 1989.
Hackett, David G. *The Rude Hand of Innovation: Religion and Social Order in Albany, New York, 1652–1836.* New York: Oxford University Press, 1991.
Hall, David D. *Worlds of Wonder, Days of Judgment: Popular Religious Belief in Early New England.* New York: Knopf, 1989.
Hall, David D., ed. *Lived Religion in America: Toward a History of Practice.* Princeton: Princeton University Press, 1997.
Harley, J. B. "Deconstructing the Map." *Cartographica* 26 (1989): 1–20.
Harris, Paul William. *Nothing but Christ: Rufus Anderson and the Ideology of Protestant Foreign Missions.* New York: Oxford University Press, 1999.
Harte, Brian. "Land in the Old Northwest: A Study of Speculation, Sales, and Settlement on the Connecticut Western Reserve." *Ohio History* 101 (1992): 114–39.
Harvey, David. *The Condition of Postmodernity: An Enquiry Into the Origins of Cultural Change.* Cambridge: Blackwell, 1990.
Hatcher, Harlan. *The Western Reserve: The Story of New Connecticut in Ohio.* Indianapolis: Bobbs-Merrill, 1949; rev. ed., Cleveland: World Publishing, 1966; reprint, Kent, Ohio: Kent State University Press, 1991.
Havighurst, Walter. *Wilderness for Sale: The Story of the First Western Land Rush.* New York: Hastings House, Publishers, 1956.
Heimert, Alan. "Puritanism, the Wilderness, and the Frontier." *New England Quarterly* 26 (1953): 361–82.
Hill, Patricia R. *The World Their Household: The American Woman's Foreign Mission Movement and Cultural Transformation, 1870–1920.* Ann Arbor: University of Michigan Press, 1985.
Hill, Samuel S. "Religion and Region in America." *Annals of the American Academy of Political Science* 480 (July 1985): 132–41.
Hine, Robert V. *Community on the American Frontier: Separate but Not Alone.* Norman: University of Oklahoma Press, 1980.
Holbrook, Stewart H. *The Yankee Exodus: An Account of Migration from New England.* Seattle: University of Washington Press, 1968.
Howe, Henry. *Historical Collections of Ohio.* Cincinnati: Kent State University Press, 1888.
Hunt, Lynn, ed. *The New Cultural History.* Berkeley: University of California Press, 1989.
Hunter, Jane. *The Gospel of Gentility: American Women Missionaries in Turn-of-the-Century China.* New Haven: Yale University Press, 1984.
Hurt, R. Douglas. *The Ohio Frontier: The Crucible of the Old Northwest, 1720–1830.* Bloomington: Indiana University Press, 1996.
Hutchison, William R. *Between the Times: The Travail of the Protestant Establishment in America, 1900–1960.* Cambridge: Cambridge University Press, 1989.

———. *Errand to the World: American Protestant Thought and Foreign Missions*. Chicago: University of Chicago Press, 1987.
Irigaray, Luce. *Speculum of the Other Woman*. Translated by Gillian C. Gill. Ithaca: Cornell University Press, 1985.
Isaac, Rhys. *The Transformation of Virginia, 1740–1790*. Chapel Hill: University of North Carolina Press, 1982.
Jackson, J. B. *Discovering the Vernacular Landscape*. New Haven: Yale University Press, 1984.
———. "The Order of a Landscape: Reason and Religion in Newtonian America." In D. W. Meinig, ed., *The Interpretation of Ordinary Landscapes: Geographical Essays*. New York: Oxford University Press, 1979.
Jagger, Alison M., and Susan R. Bordo, eds. *Gender/Body/Knowledge: Feminist Reconstructions of Being and Knowing*. New Brunswick: Rutgers University Press, 1989.
Jennings, Francis. *The Invasion of America: Indians, Colonialism, and the Cant of Conquest*. New York: Norton, 1975.
Joselit, Jenna Weisman. *The Wonders of America: Reinventing Jewish Culture, 1880–1950*. New York: Hill and Wang, 1994.
Juster, Susan. *Disorderly Women: Sexual Politics and Evangelicalism in Revolutionary New England*. Ithaca, N.Y.: Cornell University Press, 1994.
Kagle, Steven E., ed. *America: Exploration and Travel*. Bowling Green: Bowling Green State University Popular Press, 1979.
Kain, Roger J. P., and Elizabeth Baigent. *The Cadastral Map in the Service of the State*. Chicago: University of Chicago Press, 1992.
Keller, Catherine. *Apocalypse Now and Then: A Feminist Guide to the End of the World*. Boston: Beacon, 1996.
King, Geoff. *Mapping Reality: An Exploration of Cultural Cartographies*. New York: St. Martin's, 1996.
Kolodny, Annette. *The Land Before Her: Fantasy and Experience on the American Frontier, 1630–1860*. Chapel Hill: University of North Carolina Press, 1984.
———. *The Lay of the Land: Metaphor as Experience and History in America*. Chapel Hill: University of North Carolina Press, 1975.
Lane, Belden C. *Landscapes of the Sacred: Geography and Narrative in American Spirituality*. New York: Paulist Press, 1988.
Lang, Amy Schrager. *Prophetic Women: Anne Hutchison and the Problem of Dissent in the Literature of New England*. Berkeley: University of California Press, 1987.
Laqueur, Thomas. *Making Sex: Body and Gender from the Greeks to Freud*. Cambridge: Harvard University Press, 1990.
Lefebvre, Henri. *The Production of Space*. Translated by Donald Nicholson-Smith. Oxford: Blackwell, 1991.
Leyere, Blake. "Landscape as Cartography in Early Christian Pilgrimage Narratives." *Journal of the American Academy of Religion* 64 (1996): 163–84.
Livingstone, David N. *The Geographical Tradition: Episodes in the History of a Contested Enterprise*. Oxford: Blackwell, 1992.
Lottick, Kenneth V. "Cultural Transplantation in the Connecticut Reserve." *Historical and Philosophical Society of Ohio Bulletin* 17 (1959): 154–66.

———. "The Western Reserve and the Frontier Thesis." *Ohio Historical Quarterly* 70 (1961): 45–57.
Lowenthal, David, and Martyn J. Bowden, eds. *Geographies of the Mind: Essays on Historical Geography.* New York: Oxford University Press, 1976.
Lupold, Harry F., and Gladys Haddad, eds. *Ohio's Western Reserve: A Regional Reader.* Kent, Ohio: Kent State University Press, 1988.
Maffly-Kipp, Laurie F. *Religion and Society in Frontier California.* New Haven: Yale University Press, 1994.
Martin, Joel W. *Sacred Revolt: The Muskogees' Struggle for a New World.* Boston: Beacon, 1991.
Martin, John Frederick. *Profits in the Wilderness: Entrepreneurship and the Founding of New England Towns in the Seventeenth Century.* Chapel Hill: University of North Carolina Press, 1991.
Marx, Leo. *The Machine in the Garden: Technology and the Pastoral Ideal of America.* New York: Oxford University Press, 1964.
Massey, Doreen. *Space, Place, and Gender.* Minneapolis: University of Minnesota Press, 1994.
Mathews, Alfred. *Ohio and Her Western Reserve.* New York: Appleton, 1902.
Mathews, Donald G. *Religion in the Old South.* Chicago: University of Chicago Press, 1977.
———. "The Second Great Awakening as an Organizing Process, 1780–1830: An Hypothesis." *American Quarterly* 21 (1969): 23–43.
McDannell, Colleen. *The Christian Home in Victorian America, 1840–1900.* Bloomington: Indiana University Press, 1986.
———. "Interpreting Things: Material Culture Studies and American Religion." *Religion* 21 (1991): 371–87.
———. *Material Christianity: Religion and Popular Culture in America.* New Haven: Yale University Press, 1995.
McGiffert, Michael, ed. *Puritanism and the American Experience.* Reading: Addison-Wesley, 1969.
McTighe, Michael J. *A Measure of Success: Protestants and Public Culture in Antebellum Cleveland.* New York: State University of New York Press, 1994.
Mead, Sidney. *The Lively Experiment: The Shaping of Christianity in America.* New York: Harper and Row, 1963.
Meinig, D. W. "The Beholding Eye: Ten Versions of the Same Scene." In D. W. Meinig, ed., *The Interpretation of Ordinary Landscapes: Geographical Essays.* New York: Oxford University Press, 1979.
———. *The Shaping of America: A Geographical Perspective on 500 Years of History.* Vol. 1. *Atlantic America, 1492–1800.* New Haven: Yale University Press, 1986.
———. "Symbolic Landscapes: Models of American Community." In D. W. Meinig, ed., *The Interpretation of Ordinary Landscapes: Geographical Essays.* New York: Oxford University Press, 1979.
Middlekauff, Robert. *The Mathers: Three Generations of Puritan Intellectuals, 1596–1728.* New York: Oxford University Press, 1971.
Miller, Perry. *The New England Mind: From Colony to Province.* Cambridge: Harvard University Press, 1953; reprint, 1962.

Mills, William Stowell. *The Story of the Western Reserve of Connecticut.* New York: Brown and Wilson, 1900.
Miyakawa, T. Scott. *Protestants and Pioneers: Individualism and Conformity on the American Frontier.* Chicago: University of Chicago Press, 1964.
Monmonier, Mark. *How to Lie with Maps.* Chicago: University of Chicago Press, 1991.
Moore, R. Laurence. *Religious Outsiders and the Making of Americans.* New York: Oxford University Press, 1986.
Morgan, David. *Visual Piety: A History and Theory of Popular Religious Images.* Berkeley: University of California Press, 1998.
Morse, James King. *Jedidiah Morse.* New York: AMS Press, 1967.
Moss, Richard J. *The Life of Jedidiah Morse.* Knoxville: University of Tennessee Press, 1985.
Mulvey, Christopher. *Anglo-American Landscapes: A Study of Nineteenth-Century Anglo-American Travel Literature.* Cambridge: Cambridge University Press, 1983.
Mulvey, Laura. *Visual and Other Pleasures.* London: Macmillan, 1989.
Nash, Roderick. *Wilderness and the American Mind.* New Haven: Yale University Press, 1967.
Noricks, Ronald H. "Jealousies and Contentions: The Plan of Union and the Western Reserve, 1801–1837." *Journal of Presbyterian History* 60 (1982): 130–43.
Orsi, Robert. "The Center out There, in Here, and Everywhere Else: The Nature of Pilgrimage to the Shrine of Saint Jude, 1929–1965." *Journal of Social History* 25 (1991): 213–32.
Pankratz, John R. "The Written Word and the Errand Into Ohio, 1788–1830." Ph.D. diss., Cornell University, 1988.
Park, Chris C. *Sacred Worlds: An Introduction to Geography and Religion.* London: Routledge, 1994.
Parker, Edwin Pond. *Historical Discourse in Commemoration of the One Hundredth Anniversary of the Missionary Society of Connecticut.* Hartford: Case. Lockwood, and Brainerd, 1898.
Peacock, James L., and Ruel W. Tyson, Jr., eds. *Pilgrims of Paradox: Calvinism and Experience Among the Primitive Baptists of the Blue Ridge.* Washington: Smithsonian Institution Press, 1989.
Perella, Nicolas James. *The Kiss Sacred and Profane: An Interpretive History of Kiss Symbolism and Related Religio-Erotic Themes.* Berkeley: University of California Press, 1969.
Perkin, Judith. *The Suffering Self: Pain and Narrative Representation in the Early Christian Era.* New York: Routledge, 1995.
Peskowitz, Miriam. "Tropes of Travel." *Semeia* 75 (1996): 177–96.
Pettit, Norman. "Prelude to Mission: David Brainerd's Expulsion from Yale." *New England Quarterly* 59 (1986): 28–50.
Phillips, Joseph W. *Jedidiah Morse and New England Congregationalism.* New Brunswick, N.J.: Rutgers University Press, 1983.
Pointer, Richard W. "'Poor Indians' and the 'Poor in Spirit': The Indian Impact on David Brainerd." *New England Quarterly* 67 (1994): 403–26.
Porter, Dennis. *Desire and Transgression in European Travel Writing.* Princeton: Princeton University Press, 1991.
Porterfield, Amanda. *Mary Lyon and the Mount Holyoke Missionaries.* New York: Oxford University Press, 1997.

Power, Richard Lyle. "A Crusade to Extend Yankee Culture, 1820–1865." *New England Quarterly* 13, no. 4 (1940): 638–53.
Pratt, Mary Louise. *Imperial Eyes: Travel Writing and Transculturation*. London: Routledge, 1992.
Price, Edward T. *Dividing the Land: Early American Beginnings of Our Private Property Mosaic*. Chicago: University of Chicago Press, 1995.
Pritchard, Linda K. "The Spirit in the Flesh: Religion and Regional Economic Development." In Philip R. Vandermeer and Robert P. Swierenga, eds., *Belief and Behavior: Essays in the New Religious History*. New Brunswick, N.J.: Rutgers University Press, 1991.
Radway, Janice A. *Reading the Romance: Women, Patriarchy, and Popular Literature*. Chapel Hill: University of North Carolina Press, 1984.
Reis, Elizabeth. *Damned Women: Sinners and Witches in Puritan New England*. Ithaca, N.Y.: Cornell University Press, 1997.
Reps, John William. *Town Planning in Frontier America*. Columbia: University of Missouri Press, 1980.
Rice, Harvey. *Incidents of Pioneer Life in the Early Settlement of the Connecticut Western Reserve*. Cleveland: Cobb, Andrews, 1881.
Robinson, Arthur H., and Barbara Bartz Petchenik. *The Nature of Maps: Essays Toward Understanding Maps and Mapping*. Chicago: University of Chicago Press, 1976.
Robinson, Elmo Arnold. *The Universalist Church in Ohio*. Ohio Universalist Convention, 1923.
Rohrbough, Malcolm J. *The Trans-Appalachian Frontier: People, Societies, and Institutions, 1775–1850*. New York: Oxford University Press, 1978.
Rohrer, James R. *Keepers of the Covenant: Frontier Missions and the Decline of Congregationalism, 1774–1818*. New York: Oxford University Press, 1995.
Ronda, James. "Dreams and Discoveries: Exploring the American West, 1760–1850." *William and Mary Quarterly* 46 (January 1989): 145–62.
Rose, Gillian. *Feminism and Geography: The Limits of Geographical Knowledge*. Minneapolis: University of Minnesota Press, 1993.
Rubiés, Joan-Pau. "Instructions for Travelers: Teaching the Eye to See." *History and Anthropology* 9 (1996): 139–90.
Rowe, Henry K. *History of Andover Theological Seminary*. Newton, Mass.: Thomas Todd, 1933.
Ryan, Simon. *The Cartographic Eye: How Explorers Saw Australia*. Cambridge, Eng.: Cambridge University Press, 1996.
Ryden, Kent C. *Mapping the Invisible Landscape: Folklore, Writing, and the Sense of Place*. Iowa City: University of Iowa Press, 1993.
Said, Edward. *Orientalism*. New York: Pantheon, 1978.
Schama, Simon. *Landscape and Memory*. New York: Knopf, 1995.
Schlereth, Thomas J. "The New England Presence on the Midwest Landscape." *Old Northwest* 9 (1983): 125–42.
—, ed. *Material Culture: A Research Guide*. Lawrence: University Press of Kansas, 1985.
Schmidt, Leigh Eric. *Consumer Rites: The Buying and Selling of American Holidays*. Princeton: Princeton University Press, 1995.

Schneider, A. Gregory. *The Way of the Cross Leads Home: The Domestication of American Methodism.* Bloomington: Indiana University Press, 1993.
Scott, Donald M. *From Office to Profession: The New England Ministry, 1750–1850.* Philadelphia: University of Pennsylvania Press, 1978.
Scott, Joan Wallach. "Gender: A Useful Category in Historical Analysis." *American Historical Review* 91 (1986): 1053–75.
Sensbach, Jon F. *A Separate Canaan: The Making of an Afro-Moravian World in North Carolina, 1763–1840.* Chapel Hill: University of North Carolina Press, 1998.
Sheehan, Bernard W. *Savagism and Civility: Indians and Englishmen in Colonial Virginia.* Cambridge, Eng.: Cambridge University Press, 1980.
Shepard, Claude L. "The Connecticut Land Company: A Study in the Beginnings of Colonization of the Western Reserve." *Western Reserve Historical Society* Tract no. 96. Cleveland: Western Reserve Historical Society, 1916.
Smith, Jonathan Z. *Map Is Not Territory: Studies in the History of Religions.* Chicago: University of Chicago Press, 1993.
———. *To Take Place: Toward Theory in Ritual.* Chicago: University of Chicago Press, 1987.
Smith, Thomas H. *The Mapping of Ohio.* Kent: Kent State University Press, 1977.
––, ed. *An Ohio Reader: 1750 to the Civil War.* Grand Rapids: Eerdmans, 1975.
Sobel, Mechal. *The World They Made Together: Black and White Values in Eighteenth-Century Virginia.* Princeton: Princeton University Press, 1987.
Soja, Edward W. *Postmodern Geographies: The Reassertion of Space in Critical Social Theory.* London/New York: Verso, 1989.
Sopher, David E. *Geography of Religions.* Englewood Cliffs, N.J.: Prentice-Hall, 1967.
Stephens, David T., Alexander T. Bobersky, and Joseph Cencia. "The Yankee Frontier in Northern Ohio: 1796–1850." *Pioneer America Society Transactions* 17 (1994): 1–10.
Stilgoe, John R. *Common Landscape of America: 1580–1845.* New Haven: Yale University Press, 1982.
Sweet, William Warren. *The Congregationalists: A Collection of Source Materials.* Vol. 3 of *Religion on the American Frontier.* Chicago: University of Chicago Press, 1939.
———. *The Presbyterians, 1783–1840: A Collection of Source Materials.* Vol. 1 of *Religion on the American Frontier.* New York: Harper and Brothers, 1936.
———. *Religion in the Development of American Culture, 1765–1840.* New York: Scribner, 1952.
———. *Religion on the Frontier, 1783–1850.* New York: Cooper Square Press, 1964.
Tiffin, Chris, and Alan Lawson, eds. *De-Scribing Empire: Post-Colonialism and Textuality.* London: Routledge, 1994.
Tilly, Christopher, ed. *Reading Material Culture: Structuralism, Hermeneutics, and Post-Structuralism.* New York: Blackwell, 1990.
Tuan, Yi-Fu. "Sacred Space Explorations of an Idea." In Karl Butzer, ed., *Dimensions of Human Geography: Essays on Some Familiar and Neglected Themes.* Chicago: University of Chicago Press, 1978.
———. *Space and Place: The Perspective of Experience.* Minneapolis: University of Minnesota Press, 1977.
———. *Topophilia: A Study of Environmental Perception, Attitudes, and Values.* Englewood Cliffs, N.J.: Prentice-Hall, 1974.

Turner, Frederick Jackson. *The Significance of the Frontier in American History.* Madison: State Historical Society of Wisconsin, 1894.
Tweed, Thomas A. *Our Lady of the Exile: Diasporic Religion at a Cuban Catholic Shrine in Miami.* New York: Oxford University Press, 1997.
—, ed. *Retelling U.S. Religious History.* Berkeley: University of California Press, 1997.
Walsh, James P. "Holy Time and Sacred Space in Puritan New England." *American Quarterly* 32 (1980): 79–95.
Weddle, David L. "The Melancholy Saint: Jonathan Edwards's Interpretation of David Brainerd as a Model of Evangelical Spirituality." *Harvard Theological Review* 81, no. 3 (1988): 297–318.
Weigle, Marta. *Brothers of Light, Brothers of Blood: The Penitentes of the Southwest.* Santa Fe: Ancient City Press, 1976.
Welter, Barbara. *Dimity Convictions: The American Woman in the Nineteenth Century.* Athens: Ohio University Press, 1976.
Westphall, William. "Voices from the Attic." In Thomas A. Tweed, ed., *Retelling U.S. Religious History.* Berkeley: University of California Press, 1997.
Wheeler, Robert A. "Land and Community in Rural Nineteenth Century America: Claridon Township, 1810–1870." *Ohio History* 97 (1988): 101–21.
———. "The Literature of the Western Reserve." *Ohio History* 100 (1991): 101–28.
—, ed. *Visions of the Western Reserve: Public and Private Documents of Northeastern Ohio, 1750–1860.* Columbus: Ohio State University Press, 2000.
Whitehead, Russell F., and Frank C. Brown, eds. *Early Homes of Massachusetts.* New York: Arno Press, 1977.
———. *Early Homes of New England.* New York: Arno Press, 1977.
Williams, David R. *Wilderness Lost: The Religious Origins of the American Mind.* London and Toronto: Associated University Presses, 1987.
Wood, Denis. *The Power of Maps.* New York: Guilford Press, 1992.
Wood, Joseph S. "Elaboration of a Settlement System: The New England Village in the Federal Period." *Journal of Historical Geography* 10, no. 4 (1984): 331–56.
———. *The New England Village: Creating the North American Landscape.* Baltimore: Johns Hopkins University Press, 1997.
———. "Village and Community in Colonial New England." *Journal of Historical Geography* 8, no. 4 (October 1982): 333–46.
Wright, Louis B. *Culture on the Moving Frontier.* Bloomington: Indiana University Press, 1955.
Zelinsky, Wilbur. "An Approach to the Religious Geography of the United States: Patterns of Church Membership in 1952." *Annals of the Association of American Geographers* 51 (June 1961): 139–67.

Index

Address to the Emigrants from Connecticut, 58–59, 97–100
Address to the Inhabitants of the New Settlements, 47, 58
advertising, 13, 22
Allen, David Grayson, 41–42, 193n48
Allen, Silas, 15–16
American Bible Society, 167
American Builder's Companion (Benjamin), 121
American Geography, The; Or, a View of the Present Situation of the United States of America (Morse), 132
American Home Missionary Society, 157, 167–68, 172, 178
American Sacred Space (Chidester, Linenthal), 8
American Tract Society, 167
American Universal Geography, The (Morse), 29, 112, 132, 135
architecture, 41–42; frontier, 122–23; New England, 120–21; Oberlin, 162–63; privacy and, 122–23; Puritan, 193n48
Arminianism, 157
Austin, Eliphalet, 65, 82

Bacon, David, 34, 62
Badger, Joseph: on Brainerd, 67; Chapin and, 84–87; on effective missionaries, 82, 83–84; engraving of, 69; family of, 74–77; home of, 122; kiss of charity and, 90–93; letters of, 51, 71–72; memoirs of, 197n17; on missionary character, 86–87; Robbins and, 78–81, 86; struggles of, 62; success of, 175; tales of, 73; and Wyandot tribe, 34
baptisms, registers of, 70
Baptists, 96–98; religious rivalry and, 103–11; Schermerhorn on, 154
Barr, Thomas, 119–20
Beecher, Lyman, 106
benevolent societies, interdenominational, 36–37
Benjamin, Asher, 121
biblical images of frontier, 17, 53–58; Eden, 17, 53–55, 128–29, 136–37, 142; in Nash, 155–56; Native Americans in, 33–34; wilderness, 2, 53, 55–58; Zion, 17, 53–54, 136–37, 158
Biddle, Owen, 121
Bishop, Samuel, 113
Bobersky, Alexander T., 115
body, the, 125–26, 201n12; charity kisses and, 90–93; cultural understandings of, 93–101; home/family and, 120–26; religious practice and, 5, 90–95; religious rivals and, 90–95, 107–8; Sabbath and, 95–96; Shipherd on, 160
boundaries, 7; biblical imagery and, 55; Native Americans and, 34–35; Oberlin and, 160–61; town, 115–17
Bourdieu, Pierre, 122–23
Brace, Jonathan, 39
Bradley, Abraham, 29–30
Brainerd, David, 37; Badger and, 74–77; as model, 63–65
Brown, Ralph, 132
Brückner, Martin, 132

Builder's Assistant (Haviland), 121
Bunyan, John, 72

Calvinists: Hopkins, 39; Morse and, 133; Puritan influence on, 3
Cartwright, Peter, 73–74
Catholic Church, 134
Champion, Henry, 45
Chapin, Calvin, 84–89, 168
Chapman, Ezekiel J., 59; compared with Brainerd, 65; criticism of, 81; ineffectiveness of, 81–82, 88; letters of, 71; on revivals, 107; on the Sabbath, 96; on settlers, 74; struggles of, 62
Chardon, Ohio, 114
charity kisses, 90–93, 125–26
Chauncy, Charles, 91
Chidester, David, 8, 135, 182
Chippewa tribe, 34
circuit riders, 168–69. *See also* Methodists
Clapp, Thomas, 42
Cleaveland, Moses, 22–24; Allen and, 15–16; as Land Company partner, 22
Cleveland, Ohio, 22–24, 190n8; Native Americans and, 33
Coe, Harvey, 52, 106
commons, town, 114–15, 116–17
community: individual vs., 7; land sales and, 45–47; order and, 55; Puritan ideal and, 39–40
Conforti, Joseph, 64
Congregationalism, and Church-Action (Keep), 176–77
Congregationalists: on frontier moral dangers, 1–3; Keep on, 176–77; Oberlin and, 172–73; religious rivalry and, 103–11. *See also* Connecticut Missionary Society
Connecticut Courant, 22
Connecticut Evangelical Magazine, 47, 48–52, 73, 103
Connecticut Land Company, 21–32; advertising, 13, 22; grid plan of, 9–10; lot sales, 16–17; missionary societies and, 40; purchases by, 190n8; vision of, 17–21

Connecticut Missionary Society, 35–40; American Home Missionary Society and, 168, 178; Chapin report to, 84–89; conflict in, 52; established, 1–3; financial base of, 40; formation of, 36; fundraising by, 52–53; homogeneity emphasized by, 41–44; missionary management by, 168–69; missionary tours increased by, 117–20; motivations of, 37–38; *Narrative of Missions*, 20; New Divinity men in, 39–40; New England promoted by, 5; publications, 47–60; self-definition of, 18–19; vision of, 17–21. *See also* Plan of Union
Connecticut's Western Reserve, 3, 185–86n5; British claims to, 28–29; conflicting views of, 7–8; publications about, 19–20; routes to, 206n2. *See also* New Connecticut
conversion, religious, 6, 38–39. *See also* salvation
Correct View of that Part of the United States which Lies West of the Allegany Mountains, A (Schermerhorn, Mills), 154–55
Country Builder's Assistant (Benjamin), 121
Cowles, Giles, 97, 113; clergy position of, 117; missionary tours and, 117–18; on missionary work, 169; on religious rivals, 103
Croghan, George, 28
Cronin, William, 44–45
cultural geography, 17
cultural practices, 6–7
culture, 188–89n21; homogeneity vs. diversity of, 41–42; material, 8–9; space and, 8–9
Cuyahoga tribe, 16

Davenport, Jonathan, 39
Davis, David Brion, 202n37
Dedham Half-Way Covenant (1662), 28
Diary of Thomas Robbins, D.D. 1796–1825, 68

Index

disinterested benevolence, 39, 173
diversity, 181–82; as danger, 97–100; downplayed by mission society, 41–44; homogeneity vs., 18, 41–42; religious, 11–12, 40; of settlers, 116–117, 204n91; social order and, 52–53
documentation, 19–20
Doddridge, Philip, 100
Dwight, Margaret, 127–28, 136
Dwight, Timothy, 1; on moral habits, 3; *Travels in New England and New York*, 41

Eden, frontier as, 17, 53–55; travel narratives and, 128–29, 136–37, 142
Edwards, Jonathan, 38–39, 64
Eliade, Mircea, 8
Eliot, John, 37
Ellsworth, Henry Leavitt, 112, 124, 127
Elsner, Jaś, 135
Emerson, Joseph, 106
Ensign, Seth I., 115
Erie tribe, 16
Euclid, Ohio, 24, 115–16
Evangelical Primer (Emerson), 106
Evans, Estwick, 138–40
Evans, Lewis, 29
expectations, 10; in environment description, 17; in maps, 30, 32; of missionaries, 20; of surveyors, 20

Fairchild, James H., 162
family: changes in, 93–101; frontier, 120–26; missionaries', 74–77, 118; religious rivalry and, 109–10; salvation and, 98, 100
farms, 143–45
Finney, Charles G., 157, 162, 164, 173, 177–78; at Oberlin, 213n28
Flint, Abel, 19, 67, 70
frontier life, physical challenges of, 10, 35, 71–74
future, 58

Garfield, James A., 181–82

General Association of Connecticut (Congregational), 35–36
"General Map of the Middle British Colonies in North America" (Evans), 29
geography: books on, 130–35; New England towns and, 44. *See also* landscape
Geography Made Easy (Morse), 130–31
Gist, Christopher, 28
Grand River Presbytery, 119–20
Gravan, Anthony N. B., 193n54
grid system, 21–22; problems with, 24, 25, 113–14
Griffiths, David, Jr., 153

habits, 5; moral, 56; New England, 98, 100–101
Hanford, William, 97, 167; clergy position of, 117; on compensation, 171–72; Kennedy on, 175; on religious rivals, 105, 109–10; on settlers, 116
Harley, J. B., 28, 30, 189–90n2
Haviland, John, 121
Hawley, Zerah, 124–25, 136–37, 143, 145–49
Heckewelder, John, 30, 31
Holbrook, Stewart, 178
holiness, 173
Holley, John Milton, 24
home, 20–21, 187n15; in morality, 120–26
homogeneity, 18; mission society portrayal of, 41–44; in Oberlin, 163–64
Hopkins, Samuel, 39
Hudson, David, 83, 128, 170; town planning and, 111–12
Hudson, Ohio, 112–13
Hughes, Thomas E., 87; on Lesslie, 100–101
Humphrey, Luther, 106, 109; clergy position of, 117; Kennedy on, 175; missionary tours and, 118–19; on religious rivals, 107
Huron, Ohio, 45, 46
Hutchins, Thomas, 29

identity, religious, 11–12, 183

imagining the unknown, 15–19; biblical comparisons in, 17; nostalgia in, 16–17
individuality, 7, 186n9
Ingersoll, Jared, 42
Ingersoll, T. S., 163
Iroqouis people, 16
Isaac, Rhys, 44
Israel, frontier compared with, 1, 2. *See also* Zion, frontier as
itinerant preachers, promiscuity among, 91

Jackson, J. B., 41
Journal of a Tour Through Connecticut, Massachusetts, New York, the North Part of Pennsylvania and Ohio (Hawley), 145–49
Juster, Susan, 91

Keep, John, 176–77
Kelly, Thomas, 152–53
Kennedy, William S., 174–76
King, Geoff, 32–33
kiss of charity, 90–93

Land Ordinance (1785), 16, 21, 28, 34; town planning and, 44–45
land practices, 44–45
land sales, 16–17; appropriation of funds from, 194n73; community and, 45–47; rate of, 59
landscape: in missionary letters, 72–73; morality articulated through, 10; as reflection of soul, 6; renaming to remove Native Americans, 33; travel narratives and, 137–38
Landscape and Memory (Schama), 4
landscape imagery, 4
laziness, 148
Lea, Philip, 26
Leonard, Delavan, 177–78
Lesslie, Jonathan, 50, 97; Eden imagery in, 55; on good habits, 55; on Hughes, 100–101; map by, 102; on order, 108; on religious rivals, 105, 109
letters: missionary, 47–52, 66–74, 171–72;

missionary society guidelines on, 70–71; physical difficulties in, 71–74; purpose of missionary, 66; settler, to missionary society, 82–83; spiritual progress in, 71–74; success and need balanced in, 70–71; travel narratives, 127–56
Letters from the West; or a Caution to Emigrants (Wright), 143–45
Life of Brainerd, 64
Linenthal, Edward T., 8
Lyon, Widow, 42, 44
Lyon, William, 42

Maffly-Kipp, Laurie, 45, 186n9, 193n52
Magnalia Christi Americana (Mather), 24, 26–28
Mahan, Asa, 163
manners, settler, 138
mapmakers, status of, 33
Map of North America and the West Indies (Rotz), 32
"Map of the British and French Dominions in America . . . , A" (Mitchell), 28
"Map of the Connecticut Western Reserve, from Actual Survey, A" (Pease), 25
"Map of the Northern Parts of the United States" (Bradley), 29–30
mapping: Connecticut Land Company, 21–32; definition of, 4–5, 186n7; moral values in, 24, 26–28; politics in, 28–30
maps: Heckewelder's, 30, 31; Mather, 24, 26–28; by missionaries, 30; objectivity/interests in, 30, 32; pre–Land Ordinance, 28–30; status and, 33
Massachusetts Missionary Society, 36
material culture, 8–9
Mather, Cotton, 24, 26–28
Mayhew, Experience, 37
Melish, John, 140–42
Methodists, 96–98; efficiency of, 40; religious rivalry and, 103–11; Schermerhorn on, 154; success of, 71

Index

Mills, Samuel J., 103, 134, 154–55
missionaries: in American Protestantism, 11–12; changing goals of, 167–68; commonalities among, 66–67; compensation of, 171–72; conflict among, 100–101; denominational rivalry among, 101–11; education of, 77–78, 160, 166–73, 169–70, 197n13; employer expectations and, 20; families of, 74–77; finding competent, 35, 36; landscape shaping by, 5; land surveyors compared with, 10; letters of, 47–52, 66–74; maps by, 30; to Native Americans, 34–35; Oberlin and, 160, 163–66; physical challenges of, 10, 35; Plan of Union, 60–89; publications of, 47–60; real life of, 60–89; recruitment of, 197n13; resistance to, 50, 52; rivalry among, 52; self-governing among, 81–84; social status among, 77–81; success of, 84; tours of increased, 117–20; western-born, 86–88, 97. *See also individual missionary names*
missions, interdenominational, 36–37
Mitchell, John, 28
morality: family in, 120–26; Finney on, 173; maps reflecting, 24, 26–28; missionary letters on, 50, 52–53; missionary view on, 89; in Morse's geography, 130–35; spatial order and, 1–3, 53–54; travel narratives and, 137–38
Morden, Robert, 24
Morse, Jedidiah, 11, 130–35; *The American Universal Geography*, 29, 112; geography by, 19, 129
mother imagery, 57
Muscouten tribe, 16
Muskingum River, 29

Narrative of Missions, 20, 47, 53; on religious rivals, 103, 105
Narrative on the Subject of Missions with a Statement of Funds, 47
Nash, Emily, 155–56
Native Americans, 16; as barbarians, 7; Brainerd and, 63–65; cartography of, 192n33; Estwick on, 139–40; European encounters with, 32–33, 44–45; ignored by grid system, 21–22; land claims of, 22; missions to, 36, 37; portrayal/removal of, 32–35
nature, 188–89n21
Newberry, Roger, 39
New Connecticut, 3. *See also* Connecticut's Western Reserve
New Divinity men, 39–40; Morse and, 133
New England: dominance of in Western Reserve, 9; frontier towns portrayed as, 41–46; Land Company and, 21–32; Mather's map of, 24, 26–28; migration from, 40, 84; as model, 5; Morse on, 133; nostalgia for, 17; travel narratives and, 128–29, 136–37
New Haven, Connecticut, 42, 43, 193n54
New Lights, 39
"New Map" (Hutchins), 29
New York Missionary Society, 36
Northwest Ordinance (1787), 16
nostalgia, 16–17, 20, 45–47, 183; connection to the East and, 59; New England in, 41–46

Oberlin, Jean Frederick, 212n8
Oberlin Colony and Institute, 11, 156–66, 178–79; attitudes toward, 163–66; education in, 161–62, 164, 166; Finney at, 213n28; Holbrook on, 178; Keep on, 176–77; layout of, 162–63; Leonard on, 177–78; Plan of Union and, 172–73, 174
objectivity, 30, 32
Ojibwe tribe, 34
Old Lights, 39
order, 5; as morality, 95; religious fervor and, 90–93; religious rivalry and, 109–10; revivals and, 90–93; settlers' lack of, 52
spatial and moral, 53–54; town planning as, 111–20
other, portrayal of, 135–36, 188n16

Pease, Seth, 22; map by, 25; towns named by, 33
Pedestrious Tour of Four Thousand Miles, A (Estwick), 138–40
perfectionism, 178
Peskowitz, Miriam, 20
piety, models of, 63–65; Badger and, 74–77; missionary questioning of, 64–65, 67, 70, 74
pilgrimage, 188n18
Pilgrim's Progress, The (Bunyan), 72
Plain and Serious Address to the Master of the Family on the Important Subject of Family Religion (Doddridge), 100
"Plan of the Town of New Haven, A" (Wadsworth), 42, 43
Plan of Union, 37; arguments over collapse of, 174–78; biblical imagery and, 53–54; breakup of, 166–73; denominational rivalry and, 85–86, 103–11; Grand River Presbytery and, 119–20; Oberlin and, 166, 173–74; presbyteries in, 166–67; Schermerhorn on, 154–55
Plan of Union, The (Kennedy), 174–76
Plymouth Colony, 26, 28
political stability, 98, 100
Potter, Lyman, 82–83
Pratt, Mary Louise, 129, 139
preaching: moral behavior and, 55; physical challenges of, 73
"Presbygational" churches, 37
Presbyterians: Badger and, 85; Kennedy on, 174–76; Plan of Union and, 37; religious rivalry and, 103–11
privacy, 122–23
promiscuity, 90–93. *See also* sexuality
Prospect of the Most Famous Parts of the World, A (Speed), 32, 191n31
publications, 19–20; debunking, 142–52; missionary, 47–60; promotional, 207n7; religious rivalry and, 105–6
Puritans: Cleveland modeled on, 23; Connecticut Missionary Society and, 35–40; English towns and, 193n48; importance of space to, 3; landscape under, 2–3; Mather's map and, 26, 28; New Divinity men on, 39; nostalgia for, 17; Oberlin and, 159–83; on piety, 185n4; town planning by, 41–44

Quasioto Mountains, 29

ranges, 21
religion: competition among, 96–98; dissenters, 110–11; frontier diversity in, 11–12; identity and, 11–12; rivalry among, 101–11
religious awakenings, 36
religious revivals, 38–39; charity kisses and, 90–93; denominational competition and, 96–98; intermixing of sexes in, 94–95; landscape affected by, 44; Oberlin and, 164–65; Plan of Union missionaries and, 107–8; promiscuity and, 90–93; Shipherd and, 158–59
Richmond, Ohio, 117
Ripley, Erastus, 116
ritual practices, 8–9
Robbins, Samuel P., 79
Robbins, Thomas, 61–62; on Badger, 73; Badger and, 78–81, 86; on Brainerd, 67; Chapin on, 85–87; on effective missionaries, 82, 83–84; engraving of, 68; letters of, 67, 70–71, 78–79; memoirs of, 197n17; on missionary character, 86–87; on preaching, 73; qualifications questioned, 82–83; on revivals, 94–95, 108; social status of, 78–80; struggles of, 62
Rohrer, James, 109
Rotz, Jean, 32

Sabbath, 55, 95–96
sacred space, 8–9
Salem, Ohio, 116
salvation, 6; America in, 37–38; family/political stability and, 98, 100; land use and, 55; Oberlin and, 159–83; religious rivals and, 106–8
Savage Systems (Chidester), 182

Index

Schama, Simon, 4, 188–89n21
Schermerhorn, John, 103, 134, 154–55
School Fund Act (1795), 194n73
school maintenance, 21
Scott, Abraham, 50, 56, 105–6
Scott, Donald M., 197n13
Sermon on Divine Government (Beecher), 106
settlers, 89–126; diversity of, 116–17, 204n91; families of, 120–26; frustrations of, 128; Hawley on, 146–48; homes of, 121–26; isolation of, 56–57, 150, 152; manners of, 138; on missionaries, 82–84; missionaries as, 97; religious diversity of, 11–12; resistance of, 50, 52, 64–65; settlement patterns of, 113, 115–17; travel narratives on, 138, 140, 142, 146–48; views of missionaries among, 72–73, 74
Seward, John, 54, 97; clergy position of, 117; Eden imagery in, 55; on missionary work vs. pastorates, 168–69; on religious rivals, 104, 106, 110; on western born missionaries, 169–70
sexuality, 200n6; industrialization and, 122–23; segregation of sexes and, 122–23, 148
Shipherd, John J., 11, 156–83
Shriver, Philip, 207n6
"Sinners in the Hands of an Angry God" (Edwards), 38
Skinner, Abraham, 45
Smith, Jonathan Z., 8
Smith, Thomas H., 28
social class: architecture and, 122–25; home architecture and, 121–123; missionaries and, 77–81, 100–101; in New England towns, 42, 44; Oberlin and, 159–66
social stability, 50, 52–53
Some Thoughts Concerning the Present Revival of Religion in New England (Edwards), 38–39
space, 101; morality and, 1–3; religion and, 4–7; sacred, 8–9
Spafford, Amos, 22, 23

Speed, John, 32, 191n31
squatters, 21–22
Stephens, David T., 115
Stewart, Philo Penfield, 159, 160–61
stewardship, 54–55
Stiles, Ezra, 132
Stone, Randolph, 97, 204n91; clergy position of, 117; on Euclid, 115–16; optimism of, 167; on religious rivals, 106, 107–8, 109; on sectarian feelings, 101; on settlers, 116–17
subliminal geography, 28
Summary of Christian Doctrine and Practice, A, 47
surveyors: difficulties encountered by, 22, 24; employer expectations and, 20; grid plan and, 113–14; missionaries compared with, 10. *See also* Connecticut Land Company
surveys, Land Ordinance on, 16
Swift, Hemen, 39

Tallmadge, Ohio, 115
Tappan, Arthur, 162–63
Thompson, Steven, 113
Thornton, John, 24
town planning, 3, 111–20; boundaries in, 115–17; changes in, 93–101; clergy position in, 117–20; English, 42; Hawley on, 146; New England nostalgia in, 41–46; Oberlin and, 162–63; order in, 9–10; religious rivalry and, 109–10; settlement patterns and, 113, 115–17; surveys and, 113
townships, 21
transplantation metaphor, 9
travel narratives, 10–11, 127–56; debunking in, 142–52; Estwick, 138–40; on farms, 143–45; Hawley, 145–49; Melish, 140–42; Nash, 155–56; perspectives in, 142; post-1820s, 152–56; Schermerhorn, 154–55; Trumbull, 149–52; Wright, 142–45
Travels in New England and New York (Dwight), 41

Travels in the United States (Melish), 140–42
Treadwell, Jonathan, 39
Treaty of Greenville (1795), 30
Trumbull, Henry, 143, 149–52
Tweed, Thomas A, 186n7
Two Years' Residence in the New Settlements of Ohio, North America (Griffiths), 153

Universalists, 96, 103–11

Vitruvius, 193n54

Wadsworth, James, 42, 43
Wayne, Anthony, 30
weather, 146–47
Western Emigration. Journal of Doctor Jeremiah Smipleton's Tour to Ohio (Trumbull), 149–52
Western Missionary Journal (Hudson), 111
Western Reserve. *See* Connecticut's Western Reserve

Western Reserve College, 161, 164, 169–71
Western Reserve Synod, 166–67, 172, 174
Wheeler, Robert, 140, 142
Wheelock, Eleazor, 37
White Woman's Town, 29, 191n22
Wick, William, 174–75
Wilcox, Hosea, 83, 92
wilderness metaphor, 2, 53, 55–58
Williams, Ezekiel, 124
Woodruff, Simeon, 96, 97; clergy position of, 117; on missionary education, 170; on religious rivals, 105, 109, 110; on sectarian feelings, 101, 103
Woolsey, Elizabeth, 127
Wright, Elizur, 170
Wright, John Stillman, 142–45

Yankee Exodus, The (Holbrook), 178
Young Carpenter's Assistant, The (Biddle), 121

Zion, frontier as, 17, 53–54; Oberlin and, 157–83; travel narratives and, 136–37

GPSR Authorized Representative: Easy Access System Europe, Mustamäe tee 50, 10621 Tallinn, Estonia, gpsr.requests@easproject.com

www.ingramcontent.com/pod-product-compliance
Lightning Source LLC
Chambersburg PA
CBHW072140290426
44111CB00012B/1932